BRITISH MILITARY UNIFORMS
From Contemporary Pictures

PLATE 1: Parade of the Scots Fusilier Guards at Buckingham Palace (before Her Majesty the Queen and His Royal Highness the Prince) on the morning of their departure for the Seat of War, March 2nd, 1854.

BRITISH MILITARY UNIFORMS

From Contemporary Pictures

Henry VII to the present day

W. Y. Carman F. S. A., F. R. Hist. S.

Arco Publishing Co., Inc.

New York

By the same author

A History of Firearms

Published by Arco Publishing Company, Inc.
219 Park Avenue South, New York, N. Y. 10003

© Copyright W. Y. Carman 1957

Library of Congress Number 62-14983
Arco Catalog Number 953

Printed in Czechoslovakia by Tisk, Brno
T 1867

FOREWORD

by

FIELD-MARSHAL SIR GERALD TEMPLER

G.C.B., G.C.M.G., K.B.E., D.S.O.

I AM an unrepentant believer in the traditions and customs that are still preserved in the uniforms of the British Army. This does not mean that I and those who think like me wish to see the soldier train or fight dressed in anything other than the most practicable garments and accoutrements that the scientists and tailors can devise.

Through the years there have been far too many changes in the soldiers' dress. These have often cost the country (and the individual officer) much money, and they have irritated both those who are misguided enough to think that such things do not matter, as well as those who know most assuredly that they do.

Thank goodness it is common knowledge in the Army that the fur is likely to fly whenever that august body, the Army Council, has some small matter of dress distinction on its agenda. If ever the day should come when time-honoured Regimental distinctions can be abolished by departmental action without comment, then the British Army will have lost something of itself that is unique.

The customs and traditions of every Regiment are guarded jealously by the officers and men who value them so richly. That is why soldiers are always averse to any far-reaching reform of uniform or head-dress, for they know that some element of Regimental tradition is liable to disappear with it. And if it does they will not rest until it can be restored to them, because they do not wish to deprive posterity of its rightful heritage.

In November 1956 Her Majesty The Queen did honour to the Army by dining in the Great Hall at Chelsea Hospital. Every Corps and Regiment was represented by its Colonel Commandant or Colonel, nearly all of whom wore the distinctive and colourful mess dress peculiar to his own Corps or Regiment.

The many different uniforms, worn so proudly on that unique occasion, were a symbol of the greatness of the long military history of our country. Few of the many, who witnessed that historic spectacle on television, can have failed to have been moved by what they saw. And indeed, I am sure that there were some who were prompted to wish for a little more colour in our present-day military uniforms.

So long as our soldiers appreciate the importance of safeguarding the cherished elements of our past finery, then the British Army will retain something of the intangible character that such things foster and of which other nations are so justly envious.

This book is a careful study of the evolution of British uniform from medieval days to the present time. 'Plus ça change, plus c'est la même chose.' Taking the Army as a whole, too little authoritative literature has appeared on this subject.

The book contains much that will add to the knowledge of those who are already fascinated by this absorbing subject. It should also stimulate the layman's interest, for it is attractively written and tells something of England's greatness through the history of the fighting man's apparel.

ACKNOWLEDGEMENTS

Such a work as this could only be completed with the aid and co-operation of many personages, departments and firms, and thus it is necessary to record gratitude to as many as possible.

It will be noted that many plates are reproduced by the gracious permission of Her Majesty the Queen and foremost to help in the selection has been Sir Owen Morshead, K.C.V.O., the Librarian at Windsor Castle.

Field-Marshal Sir General Templer, G.C.B., G.C.M.G., K.B.E., D.S.O., has not only been kind enough to write the Foreword but also gave much help in other directions. The Public Relations section of the War Office and especially the Scottish branch, went to considerable trouble to find suitable pictures of modern dress.

Several departments of the British Museum helped provide material illustrated later, and the National Portrait Gallery also permitted reproduction.

Three sets of blocks from the old *Cavalry Journal* (now the *R.A.C. Journal*) were lent through the kindness of Captain D. Anderson, now unfortunately deceased. The Grenadier Guards have also kindly lent blocks of examples recently seen in their successful Tercentenary Exhibition at St James's Palace. Thanks are given to the Society for Army Historical Research for lending a block.

The unstinting co-operation of the Parker Gallery, 2 Albemarle Street, London, W.1., is to be noted in the numerous rare pictures reproduced herewith; and special thanks are due to Captain R. G. Hollies-Smith for his patience and care in filling troublesome gaps in the series. Messrs Pawsey and Payne of Bury Street, London, S.W.1., kindly lent a print.

Thanks are also given to Sir Danvers Osborn, Colonel Lloyd Owen, D.S.O., O.B.E., M.C., Colonel Peter Young, D.S.O., M.C., L. R. Bradley Esq., C.B.E.

W. Y. CARMAN

CONTENTS

LIST OF ILLUSTRATIONS

LIST OF ILLUSTRATIONS

INTRODUCTION

FULL dress, levee dress and stable dress. These are but a few of the facets of army uniform that conjure up colourful pictures of the bygone days; yet they have not receded too far into the past for there are still persons alive who have worn and loved these uniforms. But it is sad to think that these glamorous garments are obsolescent. Today we can see but few of the vestiges of this raiment which was well known and respected in all parts of the world when British history and traditions were being made. Another hundred years could see all traces of the traditional dress lost and only the vaguest conceptions remaining. Will the historians of the future have but a few rags and pieces of metal on which to build their knowledge; or will sufficient records be available? In the past the putting on record of such facts has been the effort of few enthusiasts and no apology is needed for an endeavour to add more. But as much as one desires it is not possible to cover so vast a field in one volume and thus one can but develop a theme and illustrate only certain parts. This book endeavours to give a general outline of the uniforms of cavalry and infantry, but by no means attempts to describe all changes and distinctions.

It may be well to examine the source material available. Actual garments and head-dresses give an admirable idea but these are scarce, especially before 1800. Even these items cannot always be relied upon completely, for restoration and adaptation for theatrical purposes often creates false clues. Also there are many unique items which are no more than trial patterns and were never adopted.

The next obvious source is the official document or regulation: these too have their pitfalls—being scarce or even lacking for the earlier periods and not explicit or comprehensive for later times. Also an authorising date is not necessarily evidence for the introduction of articles—frequently it followed and regularized an existing custom. Diaries and private documents frequently yielded clues, but often little more than that.

The last rich field which springs to mind is that of illustration and pictures, but with the emphasis on the contemporary example. A nineteenth-century version of an eighteenth-century costume can be less reliable than a twentieth-century picture of earlier times so antiquity need not give verisimilitude. True, a contemporary picture may not be accurate in detail, but at least it will have 'the feel of the period', showing the fullness of the skirts, the style of the cuff or some other aspect. Modern interpretations might tend to show the cuff of the Victorian reign rather than say the very full cuff of William III's time. Apart from militant details the cut and style followed the civilian trends. The pressure of continental ideas as to what the best soldier should wear might or might not appear at once.

Although the contemporary picture should give the truest evidence there are reasons why it cannot be trusted implicitly. The most competent artist might prefer to sacrifice detail for the broader artistic presentation. Also he may be tempted to emphasize certain parts even to the point of caricature, as in making a head-dress much larger and imposing than it was in real life. A foreign artist when portraying a British soldier might 'see' details and a style which he knew well in his own country. Another trap is the depicting of uniform which although in the main is of the actual date, contains new items of dress recently introduced. The picture by Daniel Maclise in the House of Lords of 'Wellington Meeting Blucher' is an example of very mixed dress which at the time was thought to be a fine example of the military art. The tendency to glamorize war also led to full dress rather than true campaign dress being shown.

Portraits from life suffer from their own defects. The suppression of detail to emphasize the character, the painting-in of the uniform after the sitter has departed, the alteration of the original to give most recent decorations or even promotion with the passing years and modern 'restoration', can all play havoc with a contemporary work.

But in the main the result is not so bad as might be suggested and intelligent estimation of a picture at other than its face value can give valuable information if one is prepared to make allowances for reasons which urged or limited the artist.

A classic example of the limitation put on the recording of evidence is the famous Bayeux tapestry. This unique work was made years after the event—thus the knowledge of the details may have been blurred. It was made by ladies—who must have had their own ideas about the armour and battle behaviour. It was also made in *appliqué*, a method which imposed stiffness and a lack of reality. Also the contemporary convention for armour and other materials was such that even now the expert is not clear as to what is meant. Yet in its day it must have been considered a minor wonder of art without obvious shortcomings.

It will be noted that the actual material for making records has changed with the years, as have also the reasons for recording the subject matter. Technical progress and the rise of democracy have taken military art through many diverse paths. The common soldier was not deemed worthy of being painted in the early days, and it was the rich man who was put down on board or canvas for futurity. The lords and captains could afford to have themselves reproduced in either picture or stone, but the humble soldier was hardly considered at all as a subject. Henry VIII was an enlightened man and his interest in the military arts went deeper than artillery and warfare: contemporary pictures exist of his tent system and of his army. The loss of the fine wall paintings at Cowdray took away much evidence, but prints and water-colours help to reconstruct the times.

The fulsome reign of Queen Elizabeth I contains many incidents of sea and land warfare by many famous men but is disappointingly lacking in military pictures. Apart from an occasional portrait, and even then only in armour, little remains to be found apart from funerals and an Irish work to give us an idea of the common soldier. This is striking because the period is a long one with many changes; perhaps the Royal parsimony which touched so many fields also affected the artistic one.

The Thirty Years War and the religious conflicts on the Continent brought into being many prints, but Great Britain seemed to be content to republish already accepted military works. The visits to these shores by European painters only brought further portraits of noble figures and no English 'Wouvermans' recorded the many engagements between the Royalists and the Parliamentarians.

With the restoration of Charles II a certain return to richness of outlook is observable, although the tight purse strings held by the government and the patent unpopularity of the standing army kept martial ebullience at a low level. Prints record the ceremonial use of troops and the portraits of military commanders occasionally give details of battles in the background.

By the time of William III the battle scene was in full popularity, for the Dutch engravers had produced much in this line. The episode of Tangier gave an opportunity to record this fleeting British possession in pictures by W. Hollar and D. Stoop, but always with the common soldier so overwhelmed by the general settings so as to give few regimental details.

Marlborough saw that the wars of Queen Anne's reign were well recorded. His own tapestries, specially made for Blenheim Palace, and the murals in Marlborough House, Pall Mall, record the battles on a grand scale where the presence of certain regiments can be recognized.

One would have thought that the coming of the Hanoverian Kings would have brought a great increase in the military paintings but the period of George I is almost devoid. It is not until 1742 that the coloured print of the common soldier begins to be generally available and to give the details so desired. *The Duke of Cumberland's Book*, that magnificent set of hand-coloured engravings, is the first major work recording pictorially and individually the British forces, although certain earlier manuals of exercise give other illustrations of the uniform of the time. The presence in this country of David Morier, a Swiss, did much to record the army of the next few years. Apart from the fine series of oil-paintings at Windsor Castle about the date of 1751, there are other groups in noble homes, usually where a member of the family was a commander of a regiment. Wootton also contributes his share in the oil-paintings of the era. Prints and caricatures also appear in London, frequently mocking the auxiliary forces and showing the seamy side of army life. Many officers of rich families now had pictures made of themselves in military dress. Ramsey, Gainsborough and Beechey are but a few of the famous to record these details.

Service in warm Mediterranean stations gave the leisure moments to adopt exotic dresses, mainly for undress and for grenadiers. But strangely enough the American War of Independence produced little in the manner of personal details but rather on the scale of heroic and stylized combats, where unfortunately commercialism was beginning to rear its head and greater cash produced a more conspicuous place in the battle picture, non-payers being frequently ignored and lost to posterity. Certain officers also appeared in borrowed clothing so that one must examine these works carefully to ascertain the truth.

In 1792—3 the beautifully finished coloured plates by E. Dayes showed the dress of the Foot Guards and the first nine regiments of foot. The careful water-colour work is said to have been that of Turner when serving as an apprentice. The *British Military Library*, produced in monthly parts from 1799 to 1801, contained many coloured plates showing many cavalry and several infantry regiments as large individual figures. Charles Hamilton Smith, when in the West Indies, passed his enforced exile by drawing almost everything and noting all manners of military dress in notebooks which are still preserved. This industry served him in good stead when he produced in 1812 a work of some sixty plates of regulation uniform, now in the Adjutant-General's Office.

The Napoleonic Wars brought a great spate of coloured prints ranging from the small, carefully finished plates of Goddard and Booth, to the French caricatures. The Dighton family not only produced prints with popular appeal, but Royal patronage took Denis Dighton under its wing and many fine examples of his work are still preserved at Windsor. Departing officers due for long periods of service overseas left mementoes behind them in the form of miniatures of their loved ones, thus providing another rich field for research.

After Waterloo, such publishers as Heath and Maclean recorded the more striking forms of uniforms but the most beautiful group of pictures is that of Denis Dighton. Now the prints pour forth in almost untraceable numbers: Hull, Spooner, Mansion and Eschauzier are all names of this time, famous in the world of coloured prints. Another branch in the field of oil-painting is the series of nearly a hundred pictures made by Dubois Drahonet of British uniforms, also preserved in the military collection at Windsor.

Photography came into being early in Queen Victoria's reign, thus affording yet another medium to record information. Fenton is famous for his Crimean photographs but Scottish and French photographers also did their share. The competition between the old art and the new invention led to many posed photographs being carefully over-painted and coloured by artists to give the utmost information. Carte-de-visite photographs became numerous, comparatively cheap and much easier to leave behind, than the costly miniature on ivory or bone. Retiring officers and others were frequently given elaborately bound presentation albums containing photographs of their brother-officers.

Photographs gradually grew larger in size and took on a studio aspect—of course they still remain popular as may be seen in many Bond Street display cases. Another encouragement to the photograph was the improvement in the reproduction methods employed by periodicals. The quality of the half-tone blocks, and the surfaced paper used at the end of Queen Victoria's reign was employed to good effect in reproducing the more homely and everyday aspects of the soldier's life. The fine pictures by the various photographers which appeared in the *Navy and Army Illustrated* can hardly be bettered even by modern methods and materials.

Prints had now lost their aesthetic appeal and the expensive products of the earlier part of the century were no longer to be seen. Such publications as the *Army and Navy Gazette*, *The Graphic* and *Boy's Own Paper* could afford to give large coloured plates. The very long series by Richard Simkin issued by the first-named *Gazette* was only a part of this artist's output, for he also illustrated many other children's books and other popular works which showed in colour the might of the British Empire.

Uniforms had now reached a peak—the last full dress period. The outbreak of the First World War was the death knell of the red coat. The Indian Mutiny, the many colonial wars, the South African War all saw khaki as a fighting dress but the red coat held its own in the peaceful interludes. It took the long years from 1914 to 1919 to bring a change of ideas and a poverty which precluded the general re-issue of full dress.

Thus although the modern methods of recording uniform are many and comprehensive, there is little incentive to make much effort in the popular press. True, the Household Brigade and the old uniforms which appear at Tournaments and tattoos are recorded from time to time, but the dull No. I Dress, too reminiscent of other public servants, offers little in the way of glamour, although more exciting colour parties and those die-hards of tradition, the Scottish regiments, still gain a place in the public eye.

Away from the United Kingdom the red coat does have a certain vogue. Canada has many of her troops in full dress, sparing no expense. The Netherlands gave the Princess Irene Regiment a scarlet dress in honour of (and in memory of?) the English red coat. The Danes have red coats and even some of the troops on the Indian peninsula can sport a red coat. Field-Marshal Sir Gerald Templer in his foreword has spoken of the historic dinner honoured by Her Majesty the Queen where many scarlet mess jackets appeared. As a private wish, it is pleasant to think that perhaps an increase of finance, of patriotism or the invention of new dyes, might be responsible for the re-introduction of the red coat, that garment which was a symbol throughout the world of a force which achieved great deeds and carved an empire based on justice and recognition of rights which still serves as an example to other countries.

CHAPTER I

TUDORS—HENRY VII TO ELIZABETH I

1485—1603

THE creation of uniforms as we know them today has been a slow development and has reached the present result by a variety of reasons. One of the main factors would appear to be economy, because if a body of men are to be clothed it is obviously much simpler to produce several garments all of one pattern rather than many of differing styles and materials. Pride also plays a strong part in the development, for what better method is there for showing possession than for a proprietary leader to demonstrate his claim that the followers are his alone by having them clad in his livery or colours? Thus we can find a beginning.

The Assyrians and the Ancient Egyptians made attempts at uniformity in equipment, but it is the Middle Ages which sees the widespread development of the idea. When a lord or chieftain was permitted by the laws of Heraldry to wear his coat of arms in his dress, then the retainers also showed their connexion by wearing a sign derived from the coat of arms or a family badge. The Black Prince had his retainers dressed in black with the badge of a white feather on the chest, a device which he had acquired from his mother, Phillipa of Hainault. Richard Neville, Earl of Warwick, had a levy of 600 men for the Garrison of Calais all dressed in red jackets embroidered with the Beauchamp badges of the ragged staves which were placed before and behind. These men accompanied him when he made his attendance at the Great Council of Westminster in January 1458.

Powlett, Marquis of Winchester, had his gentlemen and yeomen wear a livery of 'Reading tawny' which took three yards of broadcloth for each person. Thomas Lord Cromwell, Earl of Essex, 'kept the like or greater number in a livery of grey marble, the gentlemen guarded with velvet, the yeomen with the same cloth' yet 'their skirts large enough for their friends to sit upon them'. The gentlemen of the late Earl of Oxford were eighty in number in a livery of Reading tawny, and with chains of gold about their necks and a hundred tall yeomen in a like livery, to follow without chains, but all having his cognizance of the blue boar embroidered on the left shoulder.

Besides retainers of a lord, levies were also made on towns and districts. Thus they had no precedent for dress and might choose anything from colours chosen in compliment to a high-ranking person, or a particular colour because it was readily available from the mills or weavers. A contingent from Rye in 1461 which went to join the army of Warwick, was dressed in red coats, which colour was already becoming the distinction of an Englishman abroad. It was again seen in 1470 when a levy of men from Canterbury went to join the Garrison of Calais. On this occasion they were supplied with 'jakettes' of red cloth costing three shillings a yard and having on them roses of white 'karsey' as badges. William

I

Stanley in 1485 had his men clad in red coats with harts' heads as badges, the animals' heads being part of his coat of arms. Other colours apart from red were also used.

However, a power was rising which was destined to make an impression on the established system, and this power was Henry VII. With so many powerful factions in England, this King did much to establish his strength and he took steps to curb the power not only of the church but of his noblemen, who had large bands of personal retainers. He passed a law, the Statute of Liveries, by which he limited retainers and endeavoured to dissolve these military households. Such a drastic step was not a hundred per cent effective, and there is an old story of a visit which Henry VII made to the Earl of Oxford. In 1496 the King paid a visit to Hedingham, the home of this ardent supporter of the Lancastrian cause. Here he was welcomed by a specially raised guard, all well dressed. The King commented on the fine array and asked if these gentlemen were only servants; upon the Earl of Oxford's admission that they were retainers, Henry VII responded by fining the Earl 15,000 marks.

The King of France had established a Standing Army and Henry VII was not long in establishing his own personal bodyguard: this, the oldest British military force, is still in existence. There was a bodyguard around Henry on that eventful day on Bosworth Field when he became King, and men from this fighting force served in the *valecti garde domini regis*—the 'Yeomen of the Guard of our Lord the King', which was established almost as soon as he became King. There had always been retainers of the Crown and Household. An ordinance of 1478 permitted the King's Watch of Edward IV clothing for the 'wynter and Sumer' as well as watching clothes, but these men had not been established as a regular body. The many duties of the Royal Household brought into being various categories of servants some of which were almost indistinguishable from soldiers. Besides the Yeomen of the Guard, there were the Yeomen of the Door and the King's Chamber, the Yeomen of the Robes and so on. These men all wore the King's livery and must have appeared alike. The armament of the Guard, however, distinguished them from the more menial servants. At the Coronation there were fifty of the yeomen equipped as archers and another fifty were armed with halberds. At Henry's funeral there were 126 men of the King's Guard clothed in a special mourning dress of black cloth. Normally russet cloth was issued every year to be made into new clothes. It must be noted that only the gown or doublet was 'uniform', the leg-wear, caps and other items of clothing were varied in pattern and found by the wearers. In fact many years later, the only uniform item of clothing was the uniform coat. The russet coat appears to have been worn mainly for watching or night duties.

For the troops fighting on the Continent, the usual distinction was the red cross. We know that men serving in the artillery wore these red crosses on their white coats, and when Sir Edward Wydeville sailed from the Isle of Wight with 400 men to assist the Bretons to fight against the French, the red cross was used as the national sign. At the disastrous battle of St Aubin in 1488, the many thousand Bretons who fought as allies under the Duke of Orleans wore the white coats and red crosses of the English. The old coat based on a personal coat of arms was not used and national influences were predominant.

Accounts for 1497 show that the Yeomen of the Crown had jackets of white and green with guards of green and white, no doubt parti-coloured with trimmings of opposite colours on the skirts and sleeves. The Guard also had one hundred riding jackets of green

PLATE 2. Cavalry at the
time of Henry VIII.

By kind permission of the Lieutenant-Colonel commanding the Grenadier Guards

PLATE 3. The First Foot Guards at the Battle of Blenheim, 1704.

PLATE 4. Grenadiers of the First
Foot Guards.

From the Exercise *by Bernard Lens, 1735.*
Original book in the Victoria & Albert Museum

PLATE 5. Drummer and private of Coldstream Guards, 1792, after print by E. Dayes and T. Kirk.

and white cloth with crimson velvet for bordering and guarding the same. When Arthur, Prince of Wales, married Catherine of Spain, in 1501, the Yeomen of his Guard were clad in large jackets of damask, white and green, with a red rose embroidered in gold on their backs. These three hundred men were also armed with bright halberds.

HENRY VIII 1509—1547

The Lord Chamberlain's record for the Coronation of Henry VIII noted that each Yeoman was to have 4½ yards of red cloth worth 6s. a yard; this indicates that yet a third type of doublet was in use. It is possible that the gilt spangles and fine gold embroidery mentioned in records were used on these state garments. The wreaths and letters (meaning the Royal initials) also quoted in these early records could be worn on these garments. Riding jackets for a hundred Guards in 1510 were to be green and white with crimson velvet as mentioned before. In the same year Henry VIII held a tournament in honour of Queen Catherine of Aragon on the occasion of the birth of their son, Prince Henry. The attendants and henchmen were all equipped with the same parti-coloured livery of green and white, red hose and black caps. Slightly later illustrations show the jacket striped green and white, with yellow and red hats, and red or white hose.

Henry also had a liking for plain white clothing and this colour—or absence of colour— occurs frequently during his reign. On May Day of 1510 there were great festivities and the King clothed 'all his knyghtes, squiers and gentelmen in whyte satyn, and all his Garde and Yomen of the Croune in whyte sarcenet and so went every man with his bowe and arrowes shotying to the wood, and so repaired again to the courte, every man with a grene boughe in his cappe'.

The Expedition to France in 1513 was a well-equipped venture to strike a blow for English causes and was an occasion on which personal badges were displayed, but mainly in the standards of the Captains and Petty Captains, as the lords were called. The garments still displayed nationalist tendencies and the Tudor colours of white and green were much in evidence. At the siege of Terouenne Henry had 600 archers of his Guard clothed in white 'gabberdines and cappes'. The Earl of Northumberland's guards, a hundred strong, were dressed in Almain rivetts, a type of splinted armour; they also wore coats of white cloth 'garded with grene embroudert, which were ensigned with red crosses, roses and silver crescents.' Yellow bonnets with white feathers topped the elaborate dress. Nicolo di Favri, a chronicler, states that Henry VIII had 12,000 men armed with a weapon never seen till now, one which was surmounted by a ball with six steel spikes. It was in this reign that the battle of Guinegate 1513 took place, an occasion which remains as a battle honour, a most ancient one, and to be seen on the standard of the Gentlemen-at-Arms.

Henry VIII also used his visits to France to further his social aims and the meeting with the French King, Francois Ier, near Guynes, was so gorgeous an occasion that the historians called it the meeting of the Field of the Cloth of Gold. Needless to say this was an opportunity to clothe the retainers of both sides in splendid dresses, and luckily oil-paintings and bas-reliefs as well as contemporary descriptions, do much to preserve for us the elegance of the meeting. The Yeomen of the Guard were prominent in the processions and gatherings: not only were they on foot but in many instances they were mounted. A bas-relief at the Hotel de Bougtheroulde in Rouen shows the Yeomen mounted and armed with bows and javelins. The tight-waisted jacket or coat had a large rose on the chest. The large oil-painting at Hampton Court was painted a few years after the event. Here Henry is to be seen mounted on a white horse proceeding in the midst of many dismounted Yeomen of the Guard. Their scarlet jackets are uniform in style but the hose and nether wear are white, yellow, red or black. The linings of the doublet sleeves differ but the body of the doublet has the rose and crown in gold in all cases, and the guards on the heavy puffed sleeves and bases follow a pattern.

The full dress cap appears to be red with an edging of white ostrich feathers, but the oil-painting of the embarkation of Henry VIII, also to be seen at Hampton Court, shows undress caps of black. A slightly later painting shows Henry meeting the Emperor Maximilian in 1513, and here are men in full armour carrying halberds and wearing red caps. For use when travelling, jackets were made of grey broadcloth.

At the Field of the Cloth of Gold, Queen Catherine had her own guard of soldiers equipped distinctively. They had Flanders halberds and they wore coats of russet cloth and green velvet stripes. Their badge worn on the chest was a large rose on a sheaf of arrows: these arrows were the sign of Granada, and the rose, of course, represented England. Among the bills which are still preserved is the item of $112\frac{1}{4}$ yards of white kersey to make hose for these men.

Although an initial on a treaty of 1527 shows a servitor in a green and white coat, from this time onwards the scarlet or red coat was more generally worn and seems to have become the full dress garb of the Yeomen of the Guard. The full dress coat had guards of black velvet on the sleeves and bases. The undress coat was similar but without the guards on the sleeves.

At a time when mercenary troops were no disgrace and it was convenient to lend troops without actually taking open opposition to another nation, there was nothing unusual in Henry VIII lending English troops to Margaret, Duchess of Savoy and daughter of the Emperor Maximilian. When their purpose was served this lady returned the men to England, clad in new clothes. At first reading of the description, their woollen coats of red, yellow, white and green might appear better fitted for harlequins rather than sober fighting men; but the garments resolve themselves into logical parti-coloured dresses: the white and green make the well-known Tudor colours while the red and yellow may indicate the Duchess, though one would expect red and white to indicate Savoy. The left side of the garment could be one main colour guarded with the secondary one, while the right side could be the other main colour guarded or trimmed with its appropriate colour.

Henry VIII did much to organize the fighting forces of England and had a great Muster of the troops of London which took place on 8 May, 1539. The result was a great event which was spoken about many years later and one which was noted by chroniclers at the time. Only able-bodied persons were to take part and white was to be the dominant hue of the clothing. The more sumptuous the dress was, the higher was the rank of the wearer. 'Every man of substance provided himself with a coat of silk and garnished their bassinetts with turbes of silk, etc. Some had their harness and poleaxes gilt, and breast-plates covered with silver bullion; the meaner sort had coats of white cotton, with the arms of the City before and behind. The Wyffelers and Minstrels were all in white, and so were the Standard-bearers, who were the tallest men in every ward, and carried thirty new standards, with the arms of the City thereon. Every Alderman inspected the men of his ward to see that they all had swords and daggers.'

After this '... all the citizens of London mustered in their harnes afore the Kinge; they gathered and assembled together at Myles End and Stepney, and so there were sett in array in three battells, and so went in arayin at Algate and through Cornehill and Cheape to Westminster and round about the Kinge's park at St James, and soe over the feildes to Holborne and in at Newegate and there brake everyman to his house.

'The battalles were thus ordered: fyrst gonners and four great gonnes drawne amongst them in cartes; then morris pykes; the bowe men; then bill men; all the cheife house-holders of the City havinge coats of white damaske and white satten on their harness richly besene, the constables in journets of white satten, and the aldermen ryding in coates of blacke velvet for the crosse and sworde for the City on their coates over theyre harnes, and their deputyes ryding after them in coates of white damaske, every alderman having his standard borne before him by one of the tallest householders in his warde, the mayor ryding in the middest of the battell in a coate of blacke velvet on his harnes, and his two hensmen following him in coates of cloth of gold and blacke velvet, the officers going about him in harnes, and the shirives following the end of the middle battell with their officers, every alderman having foure footemen with bylles and jerkins of white satten, and all the rest of the city in coates of white cotton, which was a goodly sight to behold.

'My Lord Cromwell had amonge them gunners, morris pykes and bowemen, goeing in jerkins after the socheners fashion, and his gentlemen goeing by, to sett them in aray, in jerkins of buffe leather, dublets and hose of white satten and taffeta sarsenet, which he did for the honour of the cityе; and Mr. Gregory Crumwell, with Sir Christopher Norris, Master of the Ordinance, and others of the Kinge's servauntes, followed the ende of the last battell, ryding on goodly horses and well apparayled.

'The Kinge's Grace stoode in the gatehouse of his pallace of Westminster to see them as they passed by, with the lordes and familey of his household; and the Lord Chancellor, Duke of Norfolke, Duke of Suffolke, and other lordes of the Kinge's household, stoode at the Duke of Suffolke's place by Charinge Crosse to see them as they passed by. They were numbered by My Lord Chauncellor to the number of sixteen thousand and a halfe and more, howbeit a man would have thought they had bene above 30 thousand, they were so longe passing by;—they went five men of every weapon on a front together, and began to enter the cityе in aray at Aldgate at 9 of the clocke, and by 12 they beganne to come before the Kinge, and yt was past 4 of the clocke ere the ende passed before the Kinge; and ere the last battell was entered Cornehill, the first battell was breaking home at Newegate.

'There was never a goodlyer sight in London, nor the citizens better besene, than this muster was, which was a great rejoycing to the Kinge's Majestie, and a great honour to the cityе.'

The City forces made other appearances, notably on Midsummer's Eve when the 'Marching Watch' took part in the night march which was combined with pageants and dancers. 'The Marching Watch contained in number about two thousand men, part of them old soldiers of skill, to be captains, lieutenants, sergeants, corporals etc., wifflers, drummers and fifers, standard and ensign bearers, sword players, trumpeters on horse-back, demi lances on great horses, gunners with hand-guns or half-hakes, archers in coats of white fustian ensigned on the breast and back with the arms of the city, their bows bent in their hands with sheaves of arrows by their sides, pikemen in bright corselets, burgonets, etc., halberds, the like billmen in almain rivets and aprons of mail in great number.'

A uniform frequently quoted in modern writings is that ordered by the Duke of Norfolk in 1544. The contemporary account which was in the College of Arms runs:

'Furst, every man sowdyer to have a cote of blew clothe, after suche fashion as all foot-mens cotes be made here in London to serve his majestie in this jorney, and that the same be garded with red clothe, after such sorts as others be made here. And the best sene to be trymmed after such sort as shall please the captayne to devise.

'Provided alwayes that noe gentleman nor other wear any manner of silk uppon the garde of his coate, save only upon his lefte sleeve, and that no yeoman wear any manner of silke upon his saide coate; nor noe gentleman, nor yeoman to wear any manner of badge.

'Item, every man to provide a payer of hose for every of his men, the right hose to be all red and the lefte to be blew, with oone stripe of three fingers brode of red upon the outside of his legg from the stocke downwards.

'Item, every man have an arming doublette of fustian or canvas.

'Item, every man to have a cap to be made to put his sculle or sallete in, after such fashion as I have devised, which William Taylor, capper within Ludgate doth make for me, where you may have as many of them as ye lyst for eight pence the pece.'

The last comment seems to show commercial preference but the interesting point is that a badge was not to be worn. Whereas heraldic devices are taboo unless authorized by the College of Arms, badges are often tolerated by the fact that they are not true heraldry. But at this time even the badge was forbidden as the proclamation tells us. 'My lord lieutenant doth farther straytley charge and command, that no man of this armye, not any resortinge to the same, be he soldier, victualler or other do presume after this pro-clamation to come withing the circuit or presynckt of this campe, oneles he have a red crosse sew'd upon his uppermost garment, upon payne of 15 dayes imprisonment ——'.

There is no doubt that the national cross would be the best known device and the greatest safeguard to the straggler. Another order emphasized this point saying that the cross should be sufficient and large, but as a concession said that a soldier should bear 'no cognessance but the kinge's and his captaine's.'

'The statutes and ordinances for the warre' printed in London 1544 further stated that no man who came 'unto the kynges obeysance' should be harmed if he wore a cross of St George. In the siege of Boulogne there were two main armies, one of which had horse-men and infantry clothed alike in blue jackets with red guards. The main body at Boulogne were under the Duke of Suffolk and they wore red jackets with yellow trimming, as did the rear guard under the Duke of Norfolk. The Duke of Norfolk had a red field to his coat of arms and there was also a yellow escutcheon included but these colours may only be co-incidental. Twenty men to serve in France as archers and billmen came from Cambridge. The Duke of Norfolk was Steward of Cambridge, and bills show that twenty-four shillings was paid for the yellow cloth of these 'sogyer's cotes'.

In Cowdray House, Sussex, were contemporary wall paintings on stucco which had been painted under the direction of Sir Anthony Browne, who carried the King's standard during the siege of Boulogne and was Captain of the Yeomen of the Guard. Unfortunately the house and contents were destroyed by fire in 1793. However, good engravings had been made by the Society of Antiquaries and thus valuable information has been preserved. The red crosses on the fronts and backs of the jackets of the soldiers are shown very clearly. Other accounts of this occasion are not so reliable. Montluc, the French historian, writing in his 'Camisade of Boulogne', says that the English wore cassocks of red and white, of green and white and black and yellow, but an early writer says that had Montluc been present he would have seen different colours.

There are fine contemporary water-colours preserved in the British Museum MSS Room in a folio known as Augustus III. These show not only the tents and camps of the period but typical battle scenes and, what is more to our purpose, large pictures of soldiers of varying types, infantry and horsemen. The garments they wore are most unusual to our eyes: one leg is clothed differently from the other, overtunics go over one arm but not the other; the skirts are fluted and the patterns are geometrical, but always the red cross is prominent, sometimes large on the chest and also as a row of decoration in various parts of the clothing. These costumes strike one as being theatrical and fantastic, but knowing the times and the willingness to try new ideas, one can understand.

EDWARD VI 1547—1553

The Yeoman of the Guard of this reign were dressed in scarlet doublets and caps, but the coloured engravings of the Coronation procession show the trunk-hose of different colours. The Yeomen were now losing their more militant functions and were becoming more of a ceremonial guard. Little information is available for the fighting men of this short reign, and when we do discover their dress we find that it is that unsuitable battle hue of white. At the Battle of Pinkie, 1547, the Lowland infantry had doublets of white fustian or leather and 'jackes' covered with white leather. White hose was also common wear at that time. Other colours may have been worn for we get a reference to an occasion in 1551 when eleven companies assembled bearing standards and with the men clad in the family colours, although precise details are lacking.

The infantry at this period consisted of various types of soldiery, archers, billmen, harquebusiers and pikemen who had recently been added to the fighting forces, no doubt because of their popular work on the Continent. The units were divided into companies of a hundred men, each with its own captain, lieutenant, ensign and sergeant, but regiments as we now know them had not evolved.

A review of 1552 in Greenwich Park, held before the King, included the Gentlemen Pensioners (now the Gentlemen-at-Arms) and other bands of men parading under banners carrying heraldic badges and devices. The hundred and fifty men of the Earl of Pembroke had black coats bordered with white and they used the Green Dragon as their device. The Earl of Huntingdon had but fifty men dressed in blue and they carried the Black Bull's head of the Hastings' family as their distinction.

QUEEN MARY 1553—1558

When Queen Mary came riding into London, her new capital, she was accompanied by her Guard. These men were armed with bows and javelins. They wore scarlet habits bordered with black velvet and embroidered with a crowned rose and the Royal initials. There were also other more menial troops who were dressed in green and white, some in red and white and others in blue and green. The Royal or Tudor colours will be noted and also the National colours as seen in the flag of St George.

White was still a favourite colour with the Queen, no doubt because her father had also favoured it. Thus when Wyatt led his rebels into London they were dressed in white coats, as were the common soldiery of the Queen. But the rebels' long march enforced by the closure of London Bridge took them through Southwark, Kingston and Brentford and made their garments in a sorry state. When they did come in contact with the Queen's troops, the cry was 'Down with the daggle-tails!'

Levies of troops were also made in this reign and in 1556 the city of Reading sent forty billmen for the service of King Philip and Queen Mary. These men were dressed in blue coats with red crosses which cost six shillings and fourpence per man.

It was in 1557 that Calais, a hard won English foothold on the Continent and called at that time the 'Chief Jewell of the Realm', was lost by our forces and reverted to French control. The deed having taken place, the English made great military preparations to regain the town. The first day after the sad news was received, the City of London raised a force of a thousand men and made for them white coats with red crosses. An account also tells us that these white coats were welted with green. The Venetian Ambassador who occupied himself extensively with intelligence work, reported to his home that the English troops had only light sallats for head-dress, more like skull caps than morions. They did have a poor sort of breastplate and also shirts of mail, but in the main relied more on the canvas doublet which was quilted in many layers and being up to two inches thick stood up to the shock of arms and was lighter than metal.

QUEEN ELIZABETH 1558—1603

White was still a popular colour at the beginning of Elizabeth's reign and when she visited Sandwich there 'stood three hundred persons or thereabouts appareled in whyte doblets with blacke and whyte rybon in the sleves, black gascayne hose and whyte garters, euery of them having a muryon and a calyver or a musket, having thre dromes, thre ensignes and thre capitans'. In the Scottish campaign when the English suffered casualties, Pitscottie the chronicler was quick to note that a hundred of the English white cloaks were slain.

But the Yeoman of the Guard were different and having attained a ceremonial dress, kept it. Thus when the Guard accompanied the Queen to Whitehall in 1561 they wore their scarlet coats guarded with black velvet and embroidered with a gold Tudor Rose.

Although white might be considered an honourable colour for fighting on the Continent or even in Scotland, it was not deemed satisfactory for the troubles in Ireland. Whether the poor weather or the sombreness of the situation affected the issue is not clear, but dull and uninteresting shades were usually chosen for the dress. Thus two hundred men sent to

Portsmouth in 1563 were clad in coats of blue guarded with yellow. The records of the dress of Lancashire archers specify cassocks of blue cloth with two small guards of white cloth, a scull in a red cap, a jerkin of stag or buckskin, etc. These cassocks were a type of loose coat which went over the upper part of the body; the length was variable, being both short or long. These garments were necessary in Ireland to combat the bad weather.

Derbyshire and Midland contingents of the time wore similar dresses—cassocks of watchet blue, but men from Stafford who joined the same rendezvous wore red. Watchet was the word used in Elizabethan times to indicate a cloth of a light blue colour, made popular by seamen and named after the Somerset sea-town of Watchet. Another account of 1567 requests that the cassock be of blue watchet but the cloth is to be Yorkshire, 'guarded with two small guards, stitched with two stitches of blue apiece'. A red cap and a buckskin jerkin were also to be part of the dress of these particular bowmen who also carried a sheaf of arrows, a sword and a dagger—to say nothing of 13s. 4d. in their purse.

In 1569 ten arquebusiers were raised in Salisbury for service with the Queen and they had red caps and blue coats. A few years later another firearm became popular—the caliver. This was a lighter version of the musket and was distinguished by being made with barrels or calibres all of one size instead of the odd sizes previously in use, which called for many different bullets. Men carrying firearms often wore steel or iron head-pieces such as morions or burgonets. Swords and daggers were additional weapons. There were also billmen or halbardier men who acted as a guard to the colours or flags. They were equipped with a staffed weapon, wore a 'coat of plate', a sallette for headpiece and carried the usual sword and dagger.

About 1574 a new distinction of dress was making its appearance and we read of soldiers having coats of 'gasconie fashion, colour bleu'. This was no doubt another example of a well-tried continental fashion being taken into use. Gally-gascoines or gally-gashins were loose breeches which were tied with points of lace. The new style coats were apparently tied after the same fashion with laces or points. A levy of labourers, artificers and soldiers had red coats 'gasconie fashion' 'tyed under the arme with whitte incle (tape)' with further equipment of dagger, sword and girdle. The next year, 1576, saw another levy of artisans and labourers for Ireland from Lancashire, and these were in coats of white cloth made in the fashion of a cassock and guarded with worsted laces, one red and the other green.

The Canterbury troops sent against Sir Thomas Wyatt were dressed in yellow, an unusual colour, which the city changed to red after 1590.

Lancashire had another levy of soldiers in 1577. Their pale blue coats were made of Yorkshire broadcloth bordered with two guards of yellow or red cloth. The doublets were of white Holmes fustian—showing that white was not yet completely out of favour. The pale blue Venetian trousers had red or yellow cloth two fingers broad down the side seams. 'Venetians' was the name given to the newly introduced breeches which came down to the knee and although named after the place of origin, were made in England. The old style of long stockings or trunk hose had given away to a new fashion when cannons or canions were introduced; these were of cloth or material and came from the base of the trunk hose to part way down the thigh. They would have been worn by officers, but the Venetians were common garments and worn by all. To return to the levy, they also had white kersey stockings and shoes with large ties. The pikeman of this body of men wore 'a corselet furnished', a gorget and headpiece. The archers had the same dress but with a coat of plate instead of the corselet or cuirass and skulls of iron worn under a Scottish cap: being archers they were also equipped with shooting gloves, bracelets and strings. The pioneers had doublets and breeches of white, but the doublet was of a poorer material than broadcloth and the sole armour was a small scull or cap of iron. Swords and daggers were the sidearms for all.

The gentlemen of this period had a peculiar upper garment known as a Mandelion or Mandeville which was something like a Herald's tabard. The side seams of the body and the inner seams of the arms were not sewn up, so that the front and back hung loosely on the body. The coat 'in gasconie fashion' appears to be a poor man's version of this garment but tied under the arms to keep it in place. All the pikemen of the Essex levy of 1585 had mandelions of blue cloth.

It may have been noticed that little reference has been made to cavalry. It had been the function of the knights, and later the gentlemen, to find their own horses and be an élite part of the army. But democracy was causing alterations even in this field and towards the end of Queen Elizabeth's reign the cavalry were being recruited from yeomen and commoners. The nearest approach to the old-fashioned knight in full armour were the 'lances', who wore cuirasses and were relatively heavy cavalry. Next down the scale came the 'demilance', who was mounted on a lighter horse and also lighter armed. Details in the Surrey Musters tell us that 'A demylaunce must be furnished with a sufficient stoned horse or large geldinge, a stronge leather harnis, a steell sadle or strong large bolstred sadle with the furniture thereunto: and for the man a Demylaunce harnis furnyshed. A Demylaunce staffe, a sword and a dagger, a cassock of redde clothe garded with twoe gardes of white clothe one ynche broade.'

The light horseman was a somewhat similar cavalryman and the same Musters detail the needs of such a man as being 'a sufficient geldinge with a strong sadle and lether harnis furnyshed, the man to be furnyshed with a coate of plate or brygandyne or the Curate of a corslett, sleves with Chaines of mayle, a northern staffe, a Case of pistolls, sword and dagger, a Cassock of redde clothe with twoe gardes of white clothe one ynch broade.' It will be noticed that the cavalry now carry firearms and the term 'shot on horseback' became popular. Petronels somewhat like carbines were carried, but the infantry man was still the soldier to turn the tide of battle.

When five light horsemen were levied from the Wapentakes of Yorkshire for service in Ireland in 1575, the authorities demanded a good plate coat and a scull or sallet. The head piece was to have a blue covering, which colour was also chosen for the coat. Doublet, hose and a pair of boots were also requested. A sword and dagger were the usual sidearms but when on service in Ireland a spear was to be carried. A short while later the Bishop of Chester was called upon to provide light horsemen for service in Ireland. The order stated that 'for their apparell yt shal be convenient that you see them furnished of redd clokes, lined, without sleeves and of length to the knees, dubletts, hose, hatts, boots and all other necessaire apparell for their bodies'.

Such items as weapons and armour were regulated not only by Royal decree but by the needs of the various companies and associations of manufacturers who sought to protect their own craft. Thus a proclamation of 1580 repeated an order of 1566 which forbade swords to be longer than one and a quarter yards or daggers more than twelve inches.

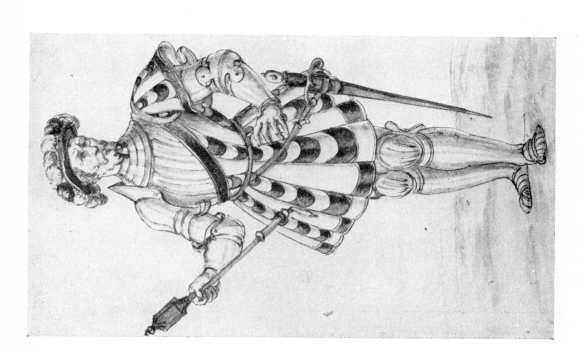

British Museum. From Augustus IIIa Manuscript Room

PLATE 6. Officer (*left*) and soldier at the time of Henry VIII.

PLATE 7. Yeomen of the Guard escorting Henry VIII on the Field of the Cloth of Gold. From the oil painting at Hampton Court.

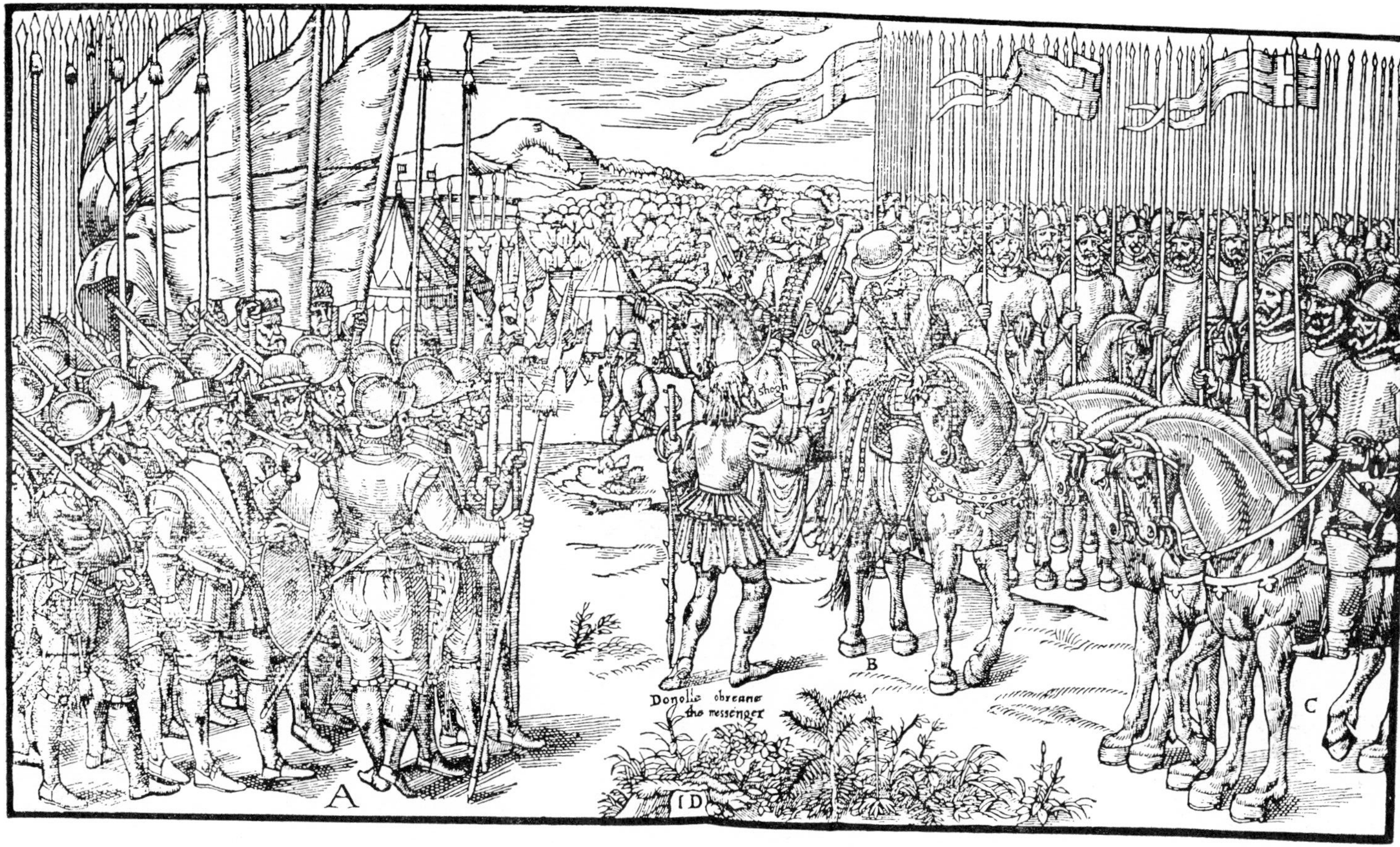

British Museum

PLATE 8. The messenger and the English army, 1581. From *Image of Ireland* by J. Derricke.

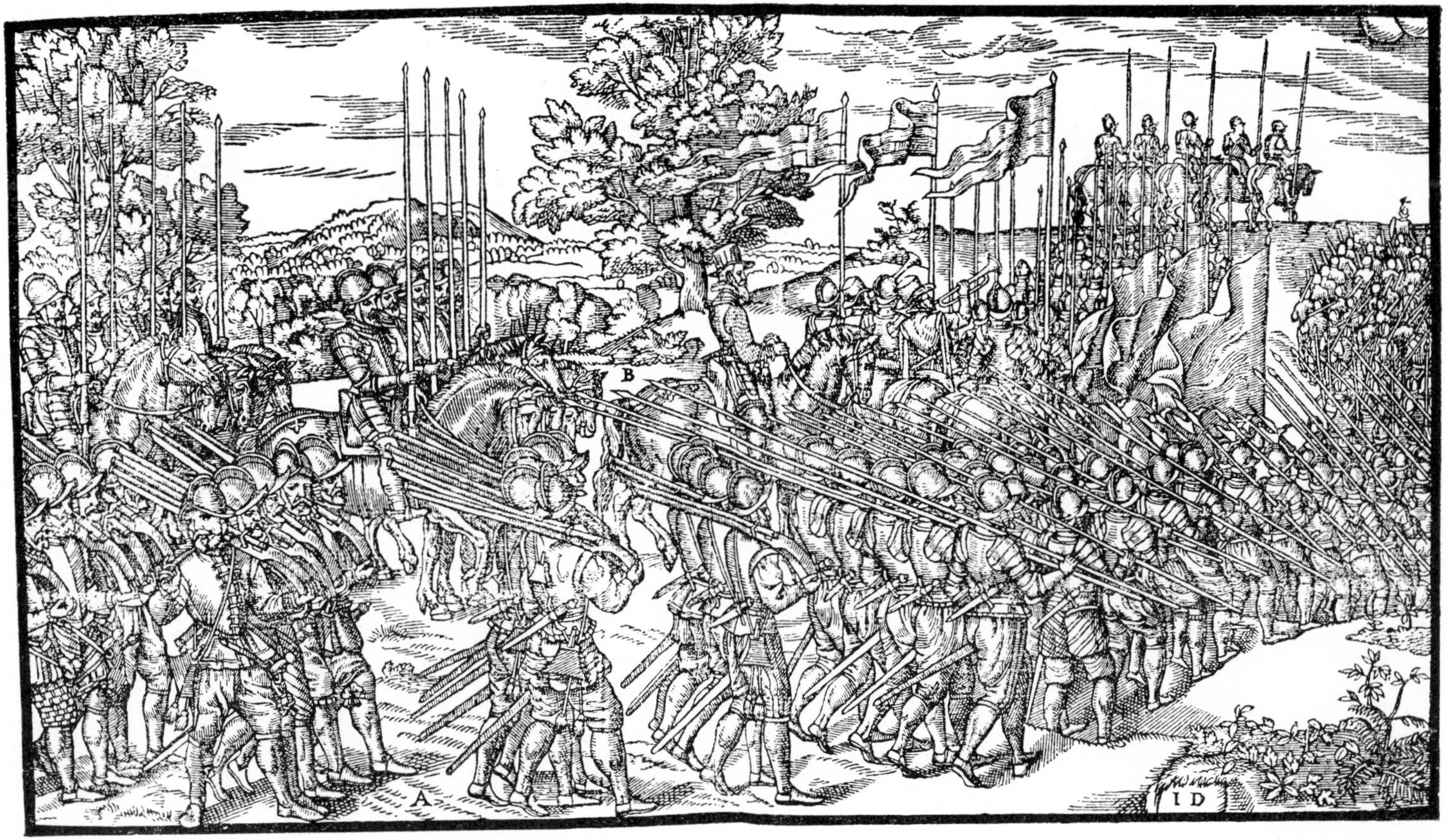

British Museum

PLATE 9. English army on the march, 1581. From *Image of Ireland* by J. Derricke.

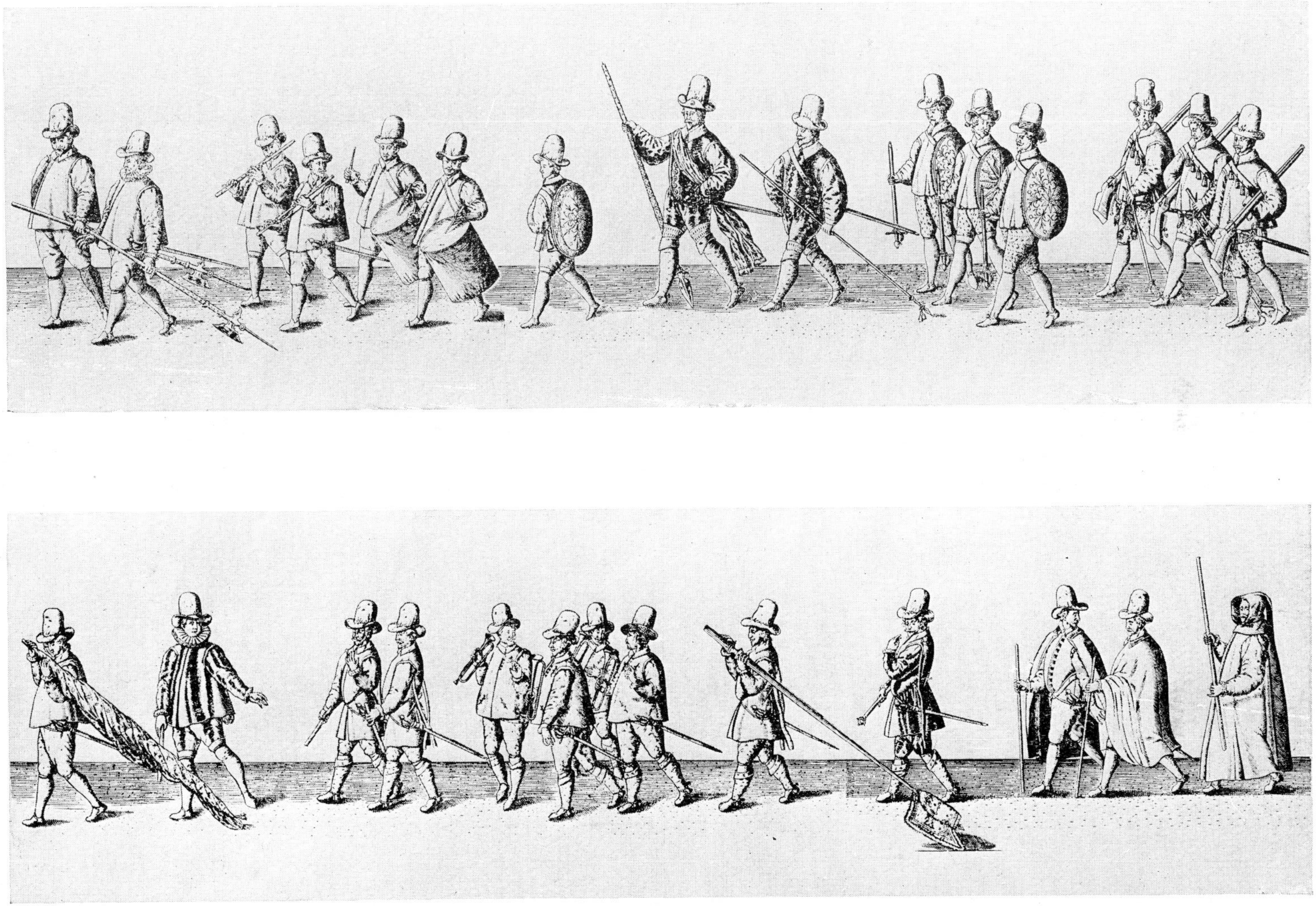

Manuscript Room British Museum

Plate 10. The funeral of Sir Philip Sidney, 1587.

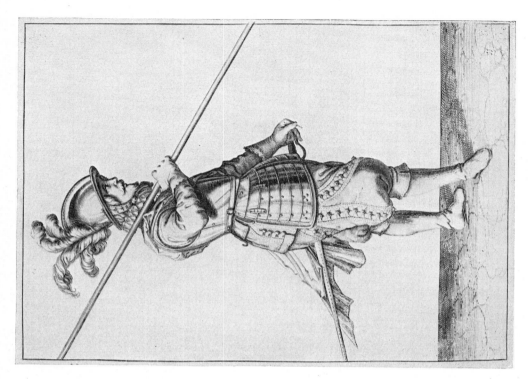

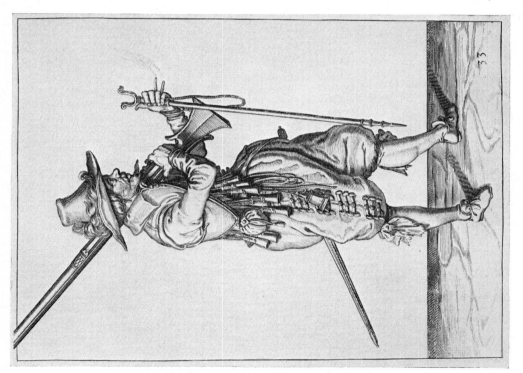

PLATE 11. Musketeer and pikeman. From *Maniement d'Armes* by Jacob de Gheyn, 1608.

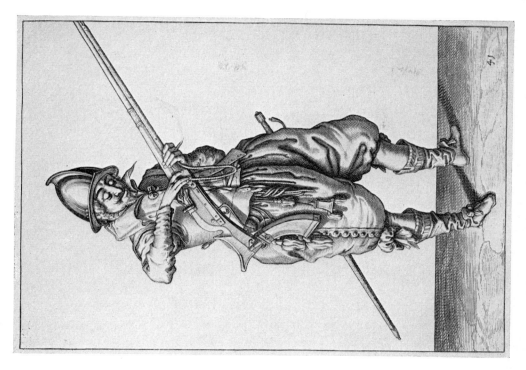

PLATE 12. Two harquebusiers. From *Maniement d'Armes* by Jacob de Gheyn, 1608.

PLATE 13. Scottish mercenaries, 1630.

PLATE 14. Charles I and Sir E. Walker.

PLATE 15. Parliamentarian musketeer, pikeman, fifer and drummer. From statuettes on staircase in Highgate House.

PLATE 16. Charles II leaving Holland, 1660. From the oil painting at Hampton Court.

(*a*)

(*b*)

PLATE 17. (*a*) The Duke of York's Troop at the Coronation of Charles II, 1661. (*b*) Musicians from 'Funeral of the Duke of Albemarle', 1670.

The Kettledrums.

S Trumpets.

British Museum

PLATE 18. State musicians at the Coronation of James II, 1686.

Reproduced by gracious permission of Her Majesty the Queen

PLATE 19. The landing of William III at Brixham. From the oil painting at Hampton Court.

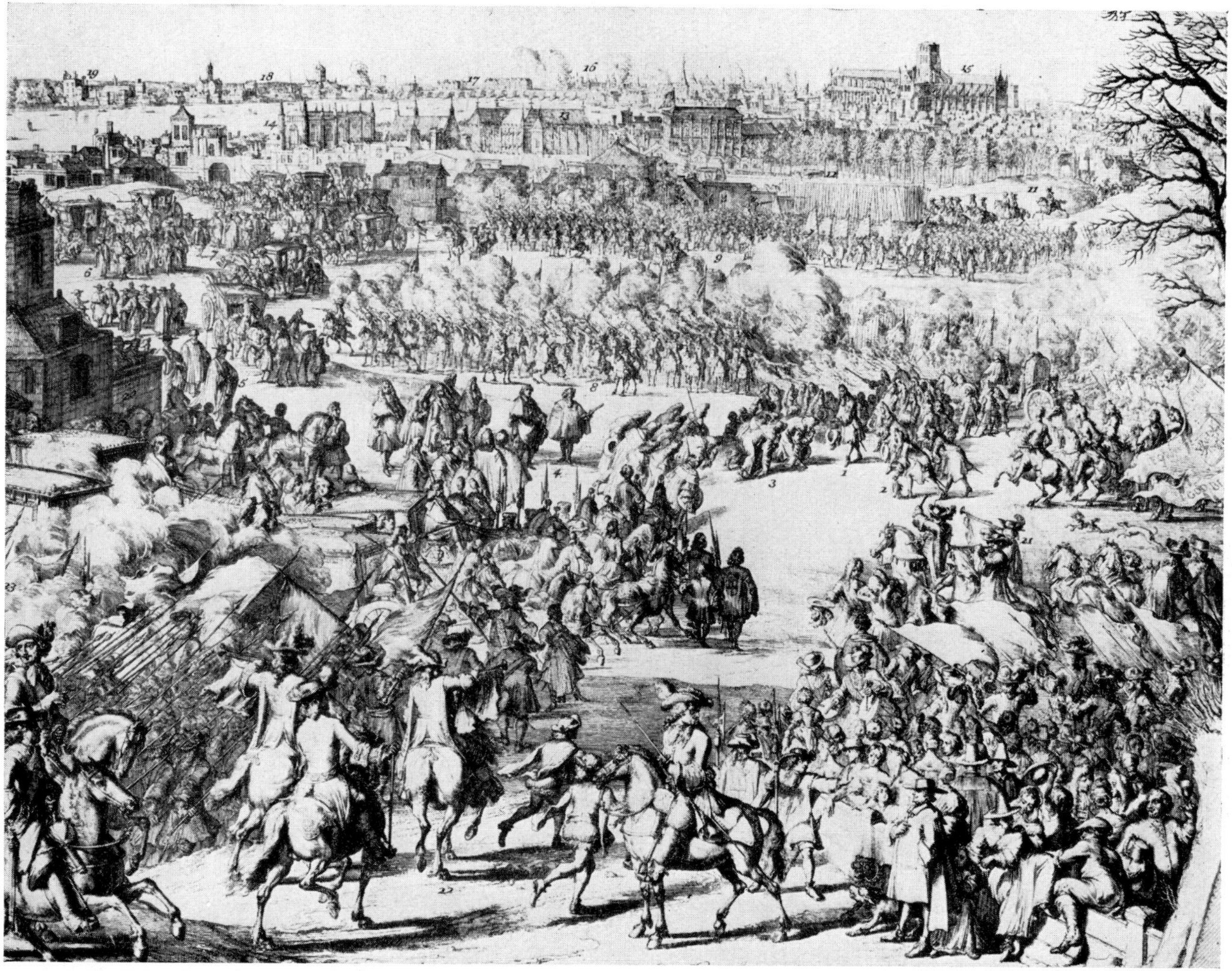

Print Room British Museum

PLATE 20. Reception of the Prince (of Orange) in London, 1688.

PLATE 21. Battle of the Boyne, 1690.

PLATE 22. Cavalry and infantry from the 'Funeral of Queen Mary', 1694.

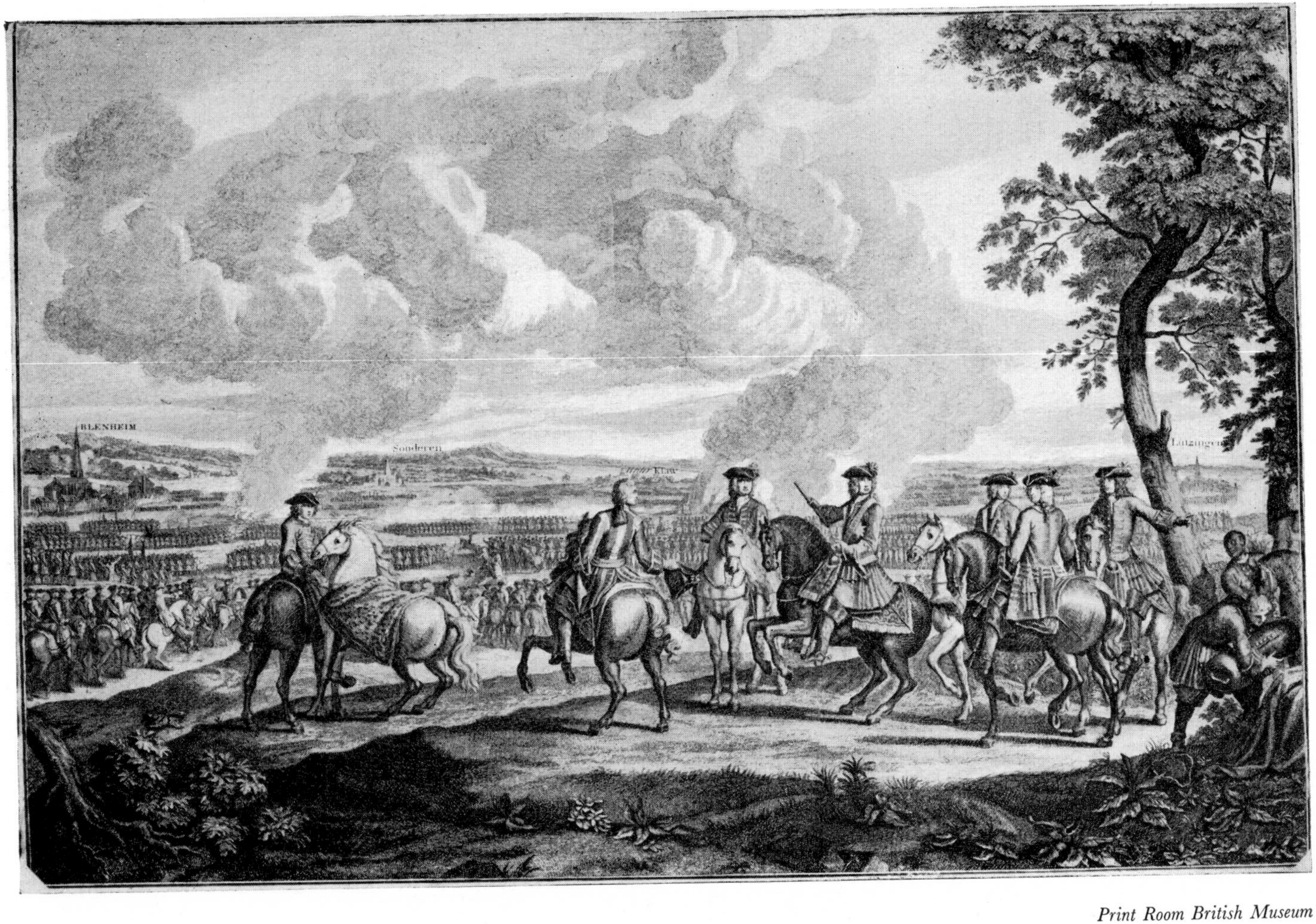

Print Room British Museum

PLATE 23. The Battle of Blenheim, 1704.

Malplaquet

PLATE 24. The Battle of Malplaquet, 1709.

PLATE 25. Picture-board figures of Grenadiers, The Queen's Regiment of Foot, *circa* 1727.

Even bucklers or small shields were not to have a point above two inches. These regulations seem to have been framed, not with a view to fighting abroad but rather to cause the minimum trouble in local frays and quarrels. Stow, in his *Chronicles,* tells us that the bucklers were made a foot across and had a spike four or five inches long; the size was then increased to about nineteen inches across with sharp spikes about ten or twelve inches long. These bucklers were fashionable items of dress and rich men had small boys to walk behind carrying them. They were said to have been sold in every haberdasher's shop and the young braves carried them on their arms when out for a stroll. Jostlings and duelling were steps which often followed, and the term 'swashbuckler' refers to the showy and troublesome bucks of the period. Some bucklers were made entirely of steel and these defences, besides being part of a duellist's equipment, were the signs of officers in the battlefield. Small boys who attended the captains carried the bucklers until the moment of conflict when the officers took them over.

Leicestershire men levied by the Earl of Rutland and due to be sent to the Netherlands were given cassocks and hose of red cloth—a colour becoming more popular and typical of the English soldier. Red was also the colour of troops levied at the expense of the City of London in 1585, also due to fight in the Low Countries. But blue was chosen for pikemen sent from Colchester, and a larger body from Yorkshire in 1586 had cassocks and breeches of blue guarded with yellow.

The troops raised for service in Ireland, 1584, were to have 'convenient dubletts and hose, and also a cassocke of the same motley, or other sadd greene colour or russet'. Another order to the Justices of Berkshire also suggested that men for Ireland should have coats 'of some dark or sadd colour, as russett or suchlike and not so light a colour as blew and redd which heretofore hath commonly been used.' A little later Ireland-bound troops were ordered cassocks of motley, sea-green or russett, and even at the end of the century the colours were still 'dark and sad'. These dull colours show the trials of the Irish weather as do requests for heavy lined coats. It was also suggested that the local plaids instead of cassocks might offer better protection against the rain. There was considerable objection to this proposal mainly on the reason of finance, a peculiar point—that English money might be re-employed to fight against the soldiers. Stockings of Irish frieze and brogues were also rejected for the same reason but eventually the Earl of Essex prevailed in his counsels, and in 1600 the introduction of brogues and plaids or long cassocks was permitted.

A picturesque adjunct to a fighting body was the music which varied according to the arm. The infantry usually had two drummers appointed for each company, but on the evidence of old pictures it will be noted that they are frequently employed as drummer and fifer. These musicians were considered something apart from the common fighting man. They were often part of the captain's personal retinue and as such were given a dress to distinguish them. On the Continent, they wore the livery of famous families and great expense produced elaborate garments covered with gold and silver thread. In England, riches were not the order of the day. In the Norwich accounts of 1587—8 is the information that a drummer's coat was made of 'grene carsey (kersey)' embellished with eleven yards of lace and 'VI yards of poynting'. Other drummers had had white 'yncle' or linen tape to put on their coats. When the fighting men wore helmets the drummers frequently wore caps or soft head-dresses.

There were other musicians like those which the Queen had to beguile her at a meal. On this occasion there were twelve trumpets and two kettle-drums which made the hall ring for half-an-hour; but these were more Royal musicians rather than military men, although trumpeters were part of cavalry troops. Trumpeters frequently appeared on state occasions and at tournaments where they served a definite purpose in the proceedings. These Royal musicians also accompanied ambassadors and representatives of the State on their various functions and visits. The coat cut after the fashion of the time had hanging sleeves and in the elaborate knot and patterning could be seen the Royal initials.

The cavalry men as shown by Derricke carry lances and charge with them. The lances are shown in a few cases with pennons having the St George's cross. A helmet with a combed ridge is general wear for the horsemen and the long coat of chain-mail that they all wear reaches to the knees. There are high boots coming up to the knee so that nether-wear is not very discernible. For defence they carry round shields about eighteen inches across, once again with St George's cross on its surface. The infantry march five abreast and although the standard-bearer is without armour, the pikemen had helmet, cuirass with long tasses and shoulder-pieces. The bill-men and caliver men also wear helmets or morions. Officers when not on the battlefield appear in the height of civilian fashion.

The equipment of pikemen in 1585 included a corselet, a burgonett, a pike, a sword and a dagger. Thomas Styward in 1581 tells us that 'corseletes furnished' comprised 'good curates for their bodies, taces for the thighes, paldrones and vambraces for the shoulders and arms.' The back and front pieces of a cuirass were always popular as were the taces or tassets, but the shoulder and arm pieces were not always worn. Pikemen are often referred to in *Musters* as 'corselets', their armour being sufficient to distinguish them.

The 'shot' carried calivers, powder flasks, touch boxes, morions, bullet moulds, swords and daggers. Another striking item of equipment comprised the six charges covered with leather, which later developed into the complicated bandolier.

The use of wood blocks as a medium of expression was a cheap one and the increase of this medium brought illustrations of many subjects and events. Derricke's 'Image of Ireland' has already been quoted. Another fine work which displayed the common soldier was the 'Funeral Roll of Sir Philip Sidney': herein details can be seen of troops of 1587 who marched at the funeral with their arms reversed. The puffed and bombastic lower wear is not for these men and they all wear knee-length breeches. The long netherstocks are replaced by stockings either below or above the breeches. The padded peascod doublet is out of fashion and the short loose coat is worn. The head-dress is the most striking change: gone is the flat cap. Even the poked up bonnet is not shown and a hat with a high domed crown somewhat like an elongated bowler is worn; officers have one side of the brim turned up and held in place by a jewel; around the base of the hat is a narrow twisted turban; scarves of cypress with fringed ends are worn in the hat bands.

The naval combats with Spain and that nation's great efforts at the attempted attack with the Armada, brought an equal reaction in the Elizabethan land forces, for at that time there was not much difference between the navy and the army. The officers were expected to perform their duties as ably on land as sea. Although it was an age for the seamen, the land troops did their duty fully, and no doubt would have performed great deeds had an invasion taken place. The great assembly of the army at Tilbury was a military occasion for the visit of the Queen. The occasion was well recorded in print, and doggerel verse of the period speaks of the Yeomen of the Guard in coats of scarlet and still armed with bows and arrows. Unfortunately, factual details of the various troops are few, and we must look to other days for information. In the same year the Chancellor presented to the Queen, when she was being entertained at his house, a company of retainers very well accoutred in red and yellow.

Such were the conditions of the time that the spy of King Philip of Spain was able to write to his master on the details of a review held in August 1588. Here he saw a company of sixty musketeers, sixty harquebusiers on horseback and two hundred light horsemen clad in orange-coloured cloth with facings of white silk. Orange may have been chosen because the Earl of Essex was responsible for the review and orange was a family colour. Several of the Light Horsemen had velvet surcoats also orange in colour but trimmed with silver. It is interesting to note that twenty-five light horsemen raised in Essex by Sir Anthony Cooke in 1599, had hoods and coats of orange tawny cloth lined with white baize and trimmed with white lace. Reverting to the earlier Light Horse, an odd note was that of the veil of gold placed at the top of the standard, which the spy deemed a lady's favour, possibly that of the Queen. The practice of carrying a lady's favour was still kept up, for the Earl of Cumberland was given a glove by Queen Elizabeth and thereafter he wore it as an ornament in the upturned brim of his hat, as may be seen in his military portrait by Nicholas Hilliard.

Three light horse companies raised in Essex, 1590, were well equipped with a coat of plate, a scull and the usual weapons, including a case of pistols. The livery cassock of broadcloth, Friar's grey in colour, was made to close before and be open on every side. It was decorated with two guards of cloth, one blue and the other yellow.

It has been mentioned that the hat and hat-cap were replacing the bonnet. The hat-cap was probably made of pieces of cloth sewn together like a brimmed hat and coming to a point at the top. The true hat made with a wide brim and a flat top was more an article of the end of the century.

The references to red as an English dress increase. A London levy of 1585 to the Netherlands all wore red. In 1591 at the siege of Rouen, we hear of a Frenchman donning the red coat of a dead English soldier in order to come close enough to kill one of the Earl of Essex's captains. Troops of Norfolk in 1596 were to have coats of 'strong cloth and coloured red guarded with white'. Russett, a colour akin to red, was abroad in 1599 when four specially raised Essex companies went to the Low Countries. The cloth hose of these men was the same colour and the stockings were knitted instead of cloth. At the siege of Ostend 1601, were 1,500 soldiers from England all in red cassocks. A thousand of these were Londoners and were said to be the ancestors of the Third Regiment of Foot, the Buffs.

Although uniformity of colour may have been an ideal, a realistic attitude was taken, for an order of 1594 said that coats were 'to be of such colours as you can best provide'.

Linings to garments are noted as necessary because of the cold in the winter season. At the end of the century clothing was issued for the troops in the Netherlands twice yearly, both for officers and common soldiers. The garments are much the same as those worn previously. The officer is noted as having silk lace on his cassock which cost 27s. 7d. His canvas doublet had silk buttons and his shirts had bands, normally meaning a turn-down collar. His trousers were still 'Venetians' of Kentish cloth and with their silver lace cost 15s. 4d. The hat issued in summer was of felt and had a band. The common soldier had a coloured hat-cap and his clothing was trimmed with buttons and loops.

A reference to the issue of basket-hilted Turkey swords to a levy of two thousand soldiers in 1601 shows that the fashion in weapons was changing.

CHAPTER II

STUARTS (PART 1)—JAMES I TO JAMES II

1603—1688

JAMES I 1603—1625

WHEN James VI of Scotland became James I of England he brought with him a certain influence on the fashions. His outlook on life somewhat tempered the flamboyant inclination of the continental trends.

In the first year of his reign the King was accompanied on one occasion by the Sheriff of Essex and several hundred followers who were distinguished by hats which had red and yellow bands and feathers in them. Red and yellow velvet was the clothing of the King's guard of three hundred sent to Spain in 1605, according to the *Somerset Herald* of that day. Red and yellow feathers were borne by the Gentlemen Pensioners (now the Gentlemen-at-Arms) when the Danish King—the Queen's father—was entertained in the City of London in 1606; they also wore very large scarves ornamented at each end with gold lace. The men of the City were dressed in yellow fustian, wore red scarves and had red bands to the ash-coloured hats. It will be remembered that the Scottish coat of arms is a red lion on a gold field—thus the preference for yellow and red.

Apart from the troops which James I directly employed at home, there were many Britishers who distinguished themselves on the Continent during the course of the Thirty Years War which was raging at the time. According to the History of the Royal Scots, Gustavus Adolphus, King of Sweden, had two Scottish regiments in his service as early as 1612 and other Scots followed later. Elizabeth, the daughter of James I, had married Frederick the Elector Palatine and so support had to be given to the latter's cause. In 1620, a long official statement gave details of an army of 25,000 foot, 5,000 horse and 20 pieces of ordnance and artillery to be raised for the recovery and protection of the Palatinate. This ambitious scheme dwindled away and only one regiment was sent to the seat of war. Sir Horace Vere was placed in command with such captains as the Earl of Essex, the Earl of Oxford and other high-sounding names.

Portraits of the Lord Vere and other military men of this period show little distinguishable in the way of uniform, but rather the height of civilian fashion.

The Brigades of Swedish forces were known by colours, like the Blue Brigade, the Green Brigade and so on; these distinguishing colours appeared in the hat plumes, and the ribbons worn on the shoulders, knees and shoes. Regimental colours also of the basic hues were said to have been carried.

The main distinction of opposing forces at this era was the sash or scarf. On the Continent scarves of the colours of certain coats of arms were favoured. The troops from

Saxony had yellow and black scarves, the main colours in the arms of the Elector Jean-Georges; the Swedish troops took the blue and gold from the Swedish arms, the troops of Bavaria had silver and blue scarves after the blue and white diamond field of Wittelsbach. In the National Portrait Gallery is a painting of Lord Vere wearing a blue scarf worn crosswise over a black cuirass. A life-size portrait of Robert de Vere who was also in these campaigns, shows a blue scarf across the body, and the helmet had white and blue plumes. A continental writer suggests that the English officers had scarves of blue and gold based on the colours of the Order of the Garter. James I's Scottish descent may have been another reason for choosing the colours of the national flag, but blue also seems to have been chosen because they were aiding the Swedish cause.

A careful engraver of the early seventeenth century was Jacob de Gheyn; he limned a series of engravings called 'The Management of Arms' which showed step by step how soldiers were to perform exercises with their weapons. The work was dedicated to Prince Maurice of Nassau and depicts the evolutions of a musketeer, a caliverman and a pikeman. Each picture shows some slight difference in dress or equipment and emphasizes the fact that uniformity was an ideal of the future.

Although the date of the prints—1607—shows the costume to be that of the continental Thirty Years War, the work serves as a good guide for the dress of James's reign. The loose and ornamental trousers are more typical of the continental dress and they show how the individuality (or purse) of the wearer influenced military dress. The stockings hanging around the ankles are the pair issued 'for rowling' and could be pulled up for extra warmth of left loose as an indication of ornamentation or nonchalance.

On the right hip of the caliver man can be seen a dagger of a shape which would fit conveniently into the muzzle of a musket and be the precursor of the bayonet. The caliver being a lighter weapon than a musket did not need a rest. The rest of the musketeer was an awkward item to hold, especially when going through the complicated actions of loading and firing a musket. The loop or thong under the U-shaped head permitted the rest to hang from the wrist leaving the hands free, but even then the long stick got in the way. The burning match can be observed held between the fingers and when the moment came for firing, one end was screwed in the jaws of the cock. The spare charges are in the little bottles on the bandolier, known as the 'Twelve Apostles' and a priming flask hangs down the right leg.

The armour of the pikeman consisted of a combe-helmet with plumes of feathers and a cuirass with tassets; at the back of the cuirass can be observed a hook: this is said to have carried the helmet on the march when the pikeman adopted the broad-brimmed hat worn by other soldiers. The destinctive pikeman's scarf is worn over the right shoulder and ties on the left hip. The wired ruff of the collar is the remains of an old-fashioned custom and in general had given way to the soft falling collar.

The Scottish mercenaries employed in great numbers during the Thirty Years War were depicted in contemporary prints which gives us a good idea of the native dress. Blue bonnets and loosely wound plaids were distinctive features of the costume, trousers and lower leg coverings are shown on one soldier. This tartan material was not cut on the bias as were the later trews, but shows the weave placed horizontally to make full netherwear instead of the tight fit of the biased trews. It will be noted that the kilt and shoulder plaid were made of one piece, wrapping around the body and kept in place by a waistbelt.

16

The material on the upper part of the body could be worn in a variety of ways to leave the arms free for action or entirely covered for bad weather. The common musket was carried but these men also had their distinctive bows and long knives. The German writers confused the Irish mercenaries with the Scots because their language was similar and because they did serve together. A German account says that their dress and caps were altogether barbarous, being 'almost entirely black because as it is well known all the sheep in their whole country are black.'

But whether the Scottish dress was worn when actually fighting or only up to the time of joining 'The Lion of the North' is not clear. In the Krigarkivarie, Sweden, are many documents relating to the Scots in Swedish service. Despite the extensive research undertaken by Dr Birger Steckzen, the Director, nothing on the point of dress has been found. The evidence seems to point to the fact that the Scottish dress was despised. In 1627 the Chief of the MacNaughtons raised a hundred bowmen for overseas service. It was at Falmouth that MacNaughton wrote to the Earl of Morton saying that 'our bagpipes and marlit plaids served us to guid wise in pursuit ane man of war' but he entreated his Lordship to prepare 'clothes for the corps, for your lordship knows that though they be men of personages, they cannot muster before your lordship in their plaids and blue caps.' In the same year the Earl of Sutherland had a letter from his uncle, Sir Robert Gordon, in which he was advised to 'take away the reliques of the Irish barbarity which as yet remain in your country, to wit the Irish language and the habit; purge your country piece by piece from that uncivil kind of clothes, such as plaids, mantles, trues and blew bonnets; make severe acts against those that shall wear them.' Thus it would appear that poor Scots would wear their national dress until they were re-clothed and equipped by the power with which they were to serve and then they would assume the normal European dress. This would be the reason for producing the well-known Köler print which recorded an unusual happening.

The suggestion that these troops wore green tartan because they were part of the Green Brigade is not valid. The various colours of the Brigades referred rather to ribbons, flags, etc., as mentioned previously. It is interesting to note that the Royal Scots trace their ancestry back to some of these early Scots mercenaries. Another point of distinction is, that although the Royal Scots are definitely a Lowland regiment, their ancestors wore the dress of Highlanders.

The officers of these men appear in portraits but they show little trace of a uniform. Silver buttons and gold chains worn around the neck were claimed as distinctions and many wore miniatures showing the head of Gustavus Adolphus, but this custom was not confined to the Scots.

CHARLES I 1625—1649

Back in the United Kingdom, the battle experience gained by these veterans was employed in the King's expedition to Scotland in 1639, but thankfully little bloodshed occurred.

The troops were specially raised and organized for this occasion. As the regimental colours were of simple hues it may be that there was little in the way of clothing distinctions. We do know of efforts towards uniformity, for the troop of horse raised by Sir John

Suckling, the well-known poet, were very distinct. This troop of a hundred men under Lord Holland were all 'very handsome proper young men—clad in white doubletts and scarlet breeches and with coloured feathers in their bonnets.'

A letter of 1638 said that 'it would be good if your Lordship's men had red breeches to their buff coats, because otherwise being country fellows they will not be so neatly habited as the other Lords' men.' Thus red breeches were the sign of a soldier.

Head-dress was also inclined to the red colour for the military. In 1639 Thomas Fairfax raised a troop of 160 dragoons which were to fight in Scotland. These men were known as the Yorkshire Redcaps which seems to indicate an early use of dragoon caps instead of the normal hats. Caps were commonly used by dragoons on the Continent, frequently with the turn-up of fur.

Netherwear was various and generally speaking of normal civilian character. Grey, white and black were the common colours but red and blue were favoured, no doubt because of their military flavour. William Salisbury, the Governor of Denbigh, was called a stout cavalier 'in his true-blue stockings'.

Late in September 1642, just before the Civil War broke out, Oxford was the scene of faction fights. Lord Saye, later a Roundhead leader, had his own Oxfordshire regiment dressed in blue coats and it is noted that when they marched out of the town towards Woodstocke, their rivals, the 'russett coates' stayed behind, the captains fearing to have them parading together at the same time. However, a day or so later the russett or red coats departed from Oxford and that city had peace for a short while.

When the Civil War did break out the King took an active part in the actual fighting. Although there were two long-established bodyguards, the Gentlemen-at-Arms and the Yeomen of the Guard, they were not employed as combatant bodies. The Gentlemen Pensioners as they were then known, were rather old in years and it was found better to employ them as captains to newly raised levies. In 1641 we read of the Gentlemen accompanying the King on his return from Scotland to London; on this occasion they were mounted, bore 'pole-axes' and had pistols at their saddles. A Gentleman of the Guard claimed that he preserved the King's life at the Battle of Edgehill.

The service of the Yeomen of the Guard in the Civil War is not well recorded. We read that they attended the King in the field, that they took the Queen abroad in 1642 and accompanied her back the following year when the Court returned to Oxford. The duties would appear to have been more in the nature of ceremonial or personal guards and not for service on the battlefield. There are records of the reign of Charles I in which their clothing is described as brown velvet coats long to their hocks (knees) and bound with bands of black velvet and His Majesty's Arms wrought in raised and embossed work of silver and gold upon the breast and back. A print of the visit of Marie de Medici to London shows the Yeomen on foot in Carolian hats, their coats of a shortened variety with roses embroidered on the front.

The dress of high ranking officers is shown very well in the portrait group with King Charles dictating to Sir Edward Walker. The costume is in the main simple but sufficiently embellished as to make it luxurious and striking. The King wears a simple cuirass without inlay or embossing, thus being eminently practical. A helmet with a spray of white ostrich feathers is placed behind him but one wonders if it is included only for effect, as mentions are made of the King's hat being used in warfare. Under his cuirass is a buff coat, the

PLATE 26. 1st Troop of Horse Grenadier Guards, *circa* 1760; said to be by Parrocel.

PLATE 27. Carabiniers, 1742. From the *Representation of Cloathing*.

PLATE 28. 10th Dragoons, 1742. From the *Representation of Cloathing*.

PLATE 29. The Duke of Cumberland's Dragoons, *circa* 1747, by David Morier.

skirts of which are ornamented with gold lace: the sleeves are made of a soft grey material which would permit freedom of movement denied by leather sleeves. The same grey material makes the breeches and gold embroidery enriches them. The soft leather boots are not fully pulled up and the white inner lining is revealed: the left boot has the top lowered to show the Order of the Garter at the knee. The pale blue sash of the Order is over the left shoulder and the absence of the elaborate gilt and enamel pendant seems to indicate active service. The laced collar and cuffs are snug-fitting and do not present any awkward portions which might prove disastrous in a hand-to-hand encounter. A gilt-hilted sword shows the practical means of defence and offence while the stout grey baton in the left hand is the sign of leadership carried from the days of the Greeks and Romans.

The secretary kneeling to take his Majesty's orders has used pen, ink and paper to turn a drum-head into a temporary table. His dress follows that of his Sovereign but is not so elaborate. One can now see clearly the buff coat or jerkin fastened in front with leather thongs. There is gold lace on the grey sleeves and they button at the cuffs to make a close fit. The pale blue sash, this time worn over the right shoulder, has a pendant at the knot, a crowned shield within the Garter. The rose-coloured waist sash has a narrow gold fringe on its edge and serves to cover the sword belt, the sling of which comes from below it. Grey breeches and gold lace disappear into leather boots which appear stouter than those worn by the King. Although prepared to write with one hand, it will be noticed that Sir Edward has his other hand ready to draw his sword in his master's defence.

The main forces of the King's army were the horse and foot. The gentlemen gravitated to the cavalry whereas the commoners went into the infantry. When the King's Life Guard of Foot was raised, gentlemen were also enlisted into a troop of horse which had the Prince of Wales as its captain. Being gentlemen volunteers these soldiers did not have the same problem of dress as poorer men and could vie with one another in style. Thus while lack of personal funds led to the provision of free dress—and uniformity—in the infantry, the cavalry appeared in feathers, lace and ribbons. The Prince of Wales's regiment of Horse dressed themselves in a uniform fashion, choosing red as their main colour. Horsemen were privileged in the dress fabrics, for a letter from King Charles is preserved authorizing a cloth mill in Gloucestershire to let a cavalry trooper collect cloth and canvas, the best of which was to be for the troopers (or horsemen) but the rest was for foot and dragoons, the latter being little more than mounted infantry.

Captain John Moore of Northampton's Horse in 1645 captured some red cloth which he was pleased to have as he intended to clothe his troopers in it. Lord Hastings, a Roundhead who had three troops of horse totalling a hundred men, had them uniformly clad in blue coats underlaid with leather.

As far as the cavalry went they were lightly armed and wore very little armour. The cavalier horsemen favoured speed of movement which called for lightness of equipment. At the commencement of the war we read of Sir Edmund Verney writing home asking for his gorget and pistol but his cuirass and head-piece were not needed. Open helmets, pots and barred helmets were worn but plumed hats were most common. The poverty of the combatants made it possible for any old piece of family heirloom to be taken into action provided it fitted. Closed helmets, though not popular, were worn as we know at Hopton Heath in 1643 where the Earl of Northampton was so fully armoured that when he was unhorsed, to kill him his enemies had to remove his helmet.

Visually the main distinction of opposing bodies of cavalry were the standards; these were plentiful at this time, having one per troop. It was usual for all in a regiment to be the same colour for ease of recognition when it was necessary to rally after a combat. Waist sashes were also worn by cavalrymen and so were field marks, but these are mentioned later.

The fully armed man, descendant of the men-at-arms, had his last lease of life in the Civil War. The heavy cuirassier was still in favour on the Continent but England preferred the lighter-armed man. Sir Edmund Verney, when summoned by the King in 1638 to fight against the Scots, was expected to appear as 'a cuirassier in russet armour with gilded studs and nails' but he rebelled at the thought of a campaign in full armour. The portraits that exist showing officers armoured to the knees may be accurate but the armour may not have been worn. To dress up in the family armour would make a much more convincing picture of a military career. As late as 1668 the *Compleat Body of the Art Military* had a description of the cuirassier who was to ride a horse of about fifteen hands (the lack of such a hardy strain of strong horses precluded the use of the heavy-armed men). The 'close casque, gorget, brest, pistol and caliver proof, the back, poldrens, vambraces, two gauntlets, tasses, cuisset, culet or guard de rain, all fitting the body' etc., were all specified for this antique soldier. The Parliamentarians were responsible for clinging to the outmoded armour, though whether by conservatism of outlook or fear of personal harm is not clear; there were two such bodies at least: Essex's Lifeguard and Haselrig's Horse. A contemporary account tells us that 'a regiment of 500 Horse under command of Sir Arthur Haselrig, which were so prodigiously armed that they were called by the other side the regiment of Lobsters because of their bright iron shells, with which they were covered being perfect cuirassiers and were the first seen so armed on either side, and the first that made any impression on the King's Horse who being unarmoured were not able to bear a shock with them, besides that they were secure from the hurts of the sword which were almost the only weapons the others were furnished with.'

Despite the advantages given above, one of Essex's Lifeguards, Edmund Ludlow gives an account of the Battle of Edgehill on Sunday, 23 October 1642, of which he writes, 'In which account, being dismounted, I could not without great difficulty recover on horseback again, being loaded with cuirassier's arms, as the rest of the guard also were.'

Between horse and infantry were those troops known as dragoons who began life as infantrymen mounted on horses, only for the reason of quick transportation from place to place. On arrival at their destination they were expected to dismount and fight like the ordinary foot soldiers. Apart from their boots and spurs, these mounted musketeers had little to distinguish them from their lower brethren, the footsloggers. Their distinctions occurred mainly in their flags, which were of the peculiar forked shape and known as guidons; they were small like the cornets of horse and also fringed, but in system followed that of the infantry. The cap of dragoons was also worn, being more manageable on horseback than the broadbrimmed hat.

It was the opposition offered to the King at Hull in 1642 that gave him the excuse for establishing a new and more militant bodyguard. According to Lord Clarendon, he bestowed this honour upon the regiment of trained bands under Sir Robert Strickland; there were six hundred men in this body who were paid regularly each Saturday and at the King's charge. Another version of the raising is given in the correspondence of

Lord Fairfax where it is stated that the King's Life Guard of Foot were raised from the Derbyshire Miners 'at our first entrance to this war'. The exact origin is not clear, but there is no doubt that the new troops wore red as their distinction.

The normal infantry troops were divided into pikemen and musketeers. The pikemen were proud men for they were specially selected for their height and strength; this was necessary, for eighteen feet of wood—the regulation length for a pike—called for considerable strength and agility. More often than not the pikemen lessened this length by using their stout swords to lop off four or six feet of wood from the butt end. The pikemen's duty was to form the central mass in a body of infantry where they lowered their pikes at the advance of the enemy, or when their own attack was to be made at 'push of pike'. For head-dress they wore the iron combe cap frequently with large curling plumes. The cheek-pieces were tied under the chin with ribbon. The pikemen of the Honourable Artillery Company who accompany the Lord Mayor of London on special occasions wear a costume of this period. The body was covered with a two-piece cuirass, back and breast, with tassets or thigh-pieces also of iron. The gorget was also worn on the neck as a piece of defensive armour. It is recorded in the list of stores at Oxford in 1642 and appears in a carving at Cromwell House. A buff leather coat was necessary below the armour to prevent chafing. Leather gloves with gauntlet cuffs were also worn by pikemen, so as to protect their hands from splinters in handling the long and awkward pike.

The white falling collar tied with strings was worn above the armour and the coloured uniform coat frequently had white cuffs. The loose knee breeches were sometimes of the uniform colour and tied at the knees with bunches of ribbons. Broad lace and buttons were also used to enliven the side seams. The stockings could be worn two pairs at a time, one pair drawn up under the breeches but the second pair 'for rowling' were worn loosely, either rolled or drawn part way up the calf; this casual appearance of loose hose may have had its origins in the affected raggedness of the German lansquenets who sometimes wore one leg covered and the other with the garment hanging around the ankle. The stout shoes had laces, sometimes tied with bunches of ribbons on the instep.

The musketeer was a small man and he was armed with a musket and rest. Usually the musketeers were positioned in two bodies on either side of the pikemen. They had no armour which permitted freedom of movement, and because of this were known to flee at the first shock of battle.

They wore broad-brimmed hats of felt or leather. The hat-band could be used to indicate their side—red or rose-coloured bands being used to indicate the Royalists. When money permitted, plumes of feathers curling around the brim were added for ornamental effect; white or black feathers were employed, but the dearer red ones were used to indicate the King's cause just as orange denoted the Roundheads. Field marks were also worn in the hat but they are described later.

The coats were made fairly short and hanging sleeves were common. These relics from Tudor times had been part of the doublet but were now dropping out of favour and becoming vestiges worn by musicians. White falling collars tied with cravat strings and cuffs were worn after the habit of the pikemen. Trouser wear was on the same lines.

Their firearm was the long musket firing twelve bullets to the pound. The rest was a slender rod of wood with a U-shaped top or fork to take the weight of the musket during firing. Across the chest was the bandolier, a leather strap with twelve wooden powder cases, nine in front and three behind, nicknamed the 'Twelve Apostles'. A small priming horn and a bullet bag were also worn on the right side. The length of cord or match needed to ignite the charge was worn in a twisted hank, on the bandolier, at the back or even placed inside the wearer's hat.

Firelock men were no more than foot soldiers armed with a light musket known as a firelock, using a flint for ignition and capable of being used without the troublesome rest. The straight sword was the common sidearm. The firelock which had no continually burning match was a safe weapon to carry when near open barrels of gunpowder and thus popular with troops guarding the artillery trains.

Halberdiers and targetiers were other types of soldiers appointed to special tasks such as guarding colours or high-ranking officers. They were equipped more or less as pikemen, but with their own special weapons. As to be noted from the Cromwell House statuettes, the round targets have a strap or guige and their surfaces were protected with plates of metal. The halberd was a stout staffed weapon with an elaborate iron head; a cutting edge to the front, a spike on the top and a hook at the back met the studded shaft at a juncture which was ornamented with a heavy tassell and fringe.

These figures from the staircase of Cromwell House, Highgate, are contemporary, for the house was refitted in 1646 when Oliver Cromwell gave it to his son-in-law, Ireton. The group of statuettes includes one which must have held a flag, but it is so broken nowadays that this aspect is not clear. There is little doubt that he is an officer for he wears boots with spurs. His simple coat and breeches are civilian in aspect and he wears no trace of armour. This ensign carries the usual sword and for head-dress has a broad-brimmed hat with curling feathers.

Two other figures are those of a drummer and a fifer; they both wear short coats open down the front to reveal a shirt. The drummer has a fancy collar and cuffs and carries his drum slung well around to the left side. The fifer has a fife case on the right hip and both carry swords, their only indication of a military career.

The officers could exercise a little more latitude with their dress depending upon their purse. Gold lace and thread ornamented hat and clothing, the higher the rank the more gold and ornamentation in many cases. A contemporary stained-glass window in Farndon church shows officers with rows of lace around the bottom of their trousers, the lowest rank having but one row and the highest with five; these do not seem to be regulation markings, for no order has appeared on this point and some commanders are noted for the plainness of their dress; but there is nothing to preclude such differences being pointed out in a local regiment.

Field officers are frequently shown with long white batons, the traditional sign of command from ancient days, but whether these wands were actually carried on the battlefield in the seventeenth century is not clear. High-ranking officers wore voluminous scarves over the left shoulder with the knot on the right hip; the ends were usually finished in gold fringe and frequently gold and silver thread was worked in patterns on the main ground. Lower-ranking officers wore their sashes around the waist where they would make a closer fit and not be an encumbrance in the heat of battle. Gorgets, destined to be the last piece of armour, were worn at the necks of officers, and the sword belts or baldricks were handsomely embroidered. A fad of infantry officers was to wear loose leather boots with spurs. A short staff with an elaborately pierced head was carried by officers as a leading staff—an example of which is still to be seen in modern times carried by the officer of the Honourable Artillery Company pikemen. Normal company officers had a partisan for a staff weapon. These weapons had a well-designed pointed head, sometimes richly gilt and protected with a fringed tassel. Sergeants carried halberds, also long staffed weapons with an axe-like head. Although these N.C.O.s may have had an embroidered baldrick for the sword, the use of a sash for them had not begun at this date. Swords were the sidearms for all, worn on a shoulder belt or baldrick for officers. The officers could choose fancy blades of their own purchasing but the other ranks had to be content with the crude issue sword.

Red uniforms were most popular on both sides but the King also favoured blue, another colour from the Royal coat-of-arms. In fact a report in July 1643 noted that at Oxford, he King's Headquarters, all the common soldiers were new apparelled, some all in red coats, breeches and monteros, and some all in blue.

Richard Symonds kept a diary during the Civil War and noted the uniforms at a rendezvous at Auborne Chase in 1644 and elsewhere. This Royalist noted many troops in red, the King's and the Queen's Life Guards, Colonel Apsley's regiment being among them. Replacement of clothing showed that a continuity of uniform was attempted. The Company of Drapers of Worcester appealed to King Charles II for the payment of a bill of over £453 for 'red cloth demanded by the Duke of Buckingham and the Earl of Cleveland from the Mayor and Aldermen, to clothe His Majesty's Life guard of Foot when he was in Worcester.' This was to be repaid by the raising of a tax, 'but before this was done, the army was defeated and then miserably plundered.'

We also know that blue was worn by the Regiments of Colonel Charles Gerard, Lord Hopton and Prince Rupert (the last was also commanded by Lunsford). It was at Naseby, 1645, that 'the blew Regiment oft he King's did fight most bravely and held out to the last man.' In 1644 Sir T. Dallison wrote to Prince Rupert saying that 'I have had 113 coats and caps for foot soldiers in the house of my Lord Powis, an 100 of which are blue which will serve very well for your Highness' Regiment of Foot.' This shows that clothing was interchangeable and that cloth caps were also of a uniform colour. The letter went on to say that the remainder of the coats were green which would serve for 'Col. Tylyer's.' Colonel Tillier's regiment which had come from Ireland wore green coats as we know from other accounts; so did the men of Lord Northampton and later still when the regiment came under Col. Legge. Legge, who had been a Captain in Northampton's, once made the dire error of mistaking the green coats of Hampden (a Roundhead) for those of his own regiment and so was captured. Broughton's men who also wore green coats, were an Irish regiment, as were Tillier's. This may indicate a national colour, or a survival from the days of Elizabeth.

The Royalist also had the unusual colour of yellow, for we know that the men of the regiments of Colonel Talbot and Colonel Paulet had coats of this bright hue. Much more understandable was the grey utilized by Bard's regiment, late Pinchbeck; this colour was no doubt an easy one to procure, being in common civilian use. White unbleached cloth was also used in an emergency, as in the case of the Marquis of Newcastle who had his regiment in white. This was apparently a temporary measure, for a Scottish paper of 1644 said that the 'Earle of Newcastle's white Regiment was dyed red', although this must have been an allusion to their blood being shed. Lord Percy's men were also clothed in white which was not a very suitable colour considering the duties they were to perform—that of Firelocks to guard the artillery—a rather dirty job. A hundred white coats of Colonel Hawkin's regiment were left by Henry Gage as a bodyguard to a Lord in 1644. Black coats were the unusual distinction of Colonel Blackwell's regiment—perhaps an allusion to his name.

The Commonwealth forces had as great a diversity of colours as the Royalists. Red was a popular colour with them also, for it was worn by the regiments of Denzil Holles, Lord Robarts and others. Blue was the distinction of Lord Saye, Col. Mandeville, Sir Arthur Haselrig and Sir William Constable. Green was chosen by the Colonels Hampden and Byng for their regiments. Grey, no doubt an easy shade, was chosen by Colonel Ballard, Colonel Meyrick and Sir John Gell. Major William Ryves, late of the King's party, had his company of grey-coats. One commander, Lord Brook, though not of the King's cause took into use the Imperial colour, that of purple.

The Parliamentary forces also favoured another style which was later to become more widespread—that of having their coats faced with a different colour; this meant that the inside was lined and only showed when the cuffs were turned back or the inner skirts were exposed. Material collars were not yet part of the coat.

The Earl of Manchester as early as October 1643 had 1,200 men in green cloth coats lined with red. Lord Halifax's regiment wore red coats lined with blue according to the *Perfect Passages* of May 1645. In 1644 Lord Montagu raised a regiment in Cambridgeshire and the Isle of Ely, which was clothed in red faced with white.

When the New Model Army of the Roundheads was organized, the clothing was made uniform. Red was the main colour for all, but the facings varied. The General chose blue facings and Cromwell's Horse as well as the infantry followed this rule. We read accounts of the Earl of Essex's men being in red lined with blue. An exception to the red coat was the dress of the Firelocks who protected the artillery and they wore coats of a tawny hue. The red coat was now firmly established as the sign of an Englishman. Skippon, when captured, wore a red coat and the coats of Lord Inchequin's regiment who served in Ireland were also red.

It may have been noted that both sides in this domestic conflict wore similar clothing and that colours of coats were not enough to differentiate friend from foe. There were other aids to this end.

Early in the war the Venetian Ambassador wrote to the Doge and Senate to tell them that the Royalists were distinguished by 'rose-coloured bands on their hats.' What shade this might have been is not very clear from the text and may have been the full red as we know the Royalist did have.

It was in the colour of the scarves that the opposing sides were best distinguished. Red scarves were worn by the King's men and orange by the Roundheads. A scarf which King Charles wore at the Battle of Edgehill was presented by His Majesty to Adam Hill of Spaldwick according to legend. This relic is preserved in the Victoria and Albert Museum and is eight feet nine inches long; it is a purplish hue and embroidered with silver: the original dye may have changed with the passing years and not be as first worn.

Abroad in the numerous conflicts that ravaged Europe, military personnel wore voluminous scarves, usually of a colour to denote the country of their origin. Sometimes taken from the national flag and sometimes from the national coat of arms, the basic colour of the silk had a fringe of silver or gold from the same sources. For England the Cross of St George had long been the national flag, thus giving red and white (or silver) as the colours of the scarves. An example of this usage is quoted in *Hakluytus Posthumus or Purchas His Pilgrims*, when the English at Bantam, in Java, celebrated the Queen's Coronation on 3 May, 1606. It says:

'Moreover, few as they were, they did not forget that they were English, for on the anniversary of the Queen's Coronation (who was dead at that time, albeit they did not know it) they suited themselves in new apparel of silk, and made themselves scarves of white and red taffeta, being our country's colours; also they made a flag with the red cross in the middle.'

But in July of the same year, when the Danish King came to London, the marshals of the City had their men 'suited in yellow fustian—and red scarves.' Other horsemen in the procession wore yellow and red feathers 'and their scarves very large, laced with fair gold lace at each end.'

The reason why red and yellow were now being worn could be accounted for by the fact that James I was originally King of Scotland and the coat of arms for that country is a red lion on a golden or yellow ground. Boutell tells us that the livery of the House of Stuart was gold and scarlet and for many years later red coats with yellow facings were the distinctions of Scottish troops. Even in modern times one can see the full dress sashes of officers like the Foot Guards, made of dark red and gold intermingled.

Thus red was the common colour for both England and Scotland and no doubt both Royalist and Rebel wore this colour at the outbreak of the war. The Earl of Essex made a departure by giving his troops an orange sash, which colour was also used for his cornets or standards. It is not clear why orange should have been used for a livery by the Earl of Essex, but it is interesting to note that the coat of arms for the first Earl of Essex, Geoffrey de Mandeville, 1139, is gold and red, which two colours mixed would produce orange.

The fact that the Parliamentarians used red scarves is substantiated by the diary of a Royalist defender of Pontefract Castle, where it is stated that among those killed was 'one of them supposed to be a Lieutenant Collonel or a Captain at least, in a gallant shuyt of apparell with a great redd skarfe.' The same account speaks of a commander who wore a black scarf, a fashion repeated by Captain Mason who appeared at the second battle of Newbury with a 'black scarfe about his middle.'

To return to the red scarf, the *Beating of the Rebels* at Chalgrove says 'now the reason why we killed no more was partly because diverse of the Rebells had red scarfes like ours and by following them were Mr. Howard and Captain Gardner unawares ingaged and taken.'

The wearing of scarves sometimes served its purpose too well as in the incident at Chalgrove where 'of the King's party, were some 10 or 12 slain and some of them through mistake being for want of scarfes or their not having the word readily.' But on the other hand the wearing of the scarf could be put to a more unusual purpose, as when Captain Smith is said to have rescued the Royal Standard from Essex's secretary. On this occasion, some Royalists disguised themselves with orange-coloured scarves and approaching the secretary pretended that it was unfit that a penman should have the honour of carrying the standard; they then took it from him and rode with it to the King. Another unusual case was when the men of Sir Faithful Fortescue's troop failed to throw away their orange-tawny scarves quickly enough when they came over to the King at Edgehill: this error cost seventeen or eighteen of them their lives.

Obviously the colour of the scarves was not sufficient a safeguard and other field marks were adopted, often a secret until the day of the battle. At the battle of Newbury, Essex's men wore green boughs in their hats, a habit no doubt brought from the Continent and which idea persisted well into the next century. At the siege of Bristol Prince Rupert ordered his men to wear green colours, either bows or suchlike, and every officer and soldier to be without any band or handkerchief about his neck. At Marston Moor, the Parliamentarians wore a white handkerchief or a piece of paper in their hats, while the sign of the Royalists was to wear no bands or scarves.

An example of the lax use of the field mark is pointed out in the tale of the officer who was killed in a newly-found hat, because he had failed to remove the green branch of the enemy and insert the white paper of his own side. Fairfax gives us an example showing how easy it was to misuse the field mark. At Marston Moor after the defeat of the cavalry he commanded, he took the white handkerchief out of his hat (which was the sign of the Parliament party that day) and being in the Royalist ranks 'passed through for one of their own commanders' till he reached his own troops.

The Royalist defender at Pontefract Castle, mentioned before, also noted of the enemy that 'many of theire foot were with Roasemary in theire hattes.' The whole of the Parliamentary Army wore green boughs in their hats on 20 September at the Battle of Newbury, and another account by a member of the Trained Bands gives on 15 September, 'all white handkerchiefs in our hats and the word "God" in our mouths.'

This latter comment brings us to yet a third method of distinguishing friends from foes: the field-word, pass-word or watch-word. Fairfax's bold action in passing through the Royalists might have failed had he been asked for the field-word. No doubt the great number of safeguards was too complicated a matter in the heat of battle. This secretly chosen word would no doubt soon be learnt by the other side, if not by accident then by traitors and isolated persons calling it out to the wrong side. A Roundhead account of the Battle of Naseby says that on this occasion 'The enemie's word was "Queen Mary", ours "God is our Strength" and so he was indeed. They had beane stalkes in their hats, we nothing: some of ours of their owne accord had white Linnen, or paper in their hats.' On another occasion, Walker, a Royalist officer, wrote 'I commanded the men to be ranged into battalions and riding up to every squadron, gave them what good words and encouragement I was able (though I confess it needed not, most of them being so well resolved of themselves) and delivered the word (St George) commanding every man to tie a white tape, ribband or handkerchief, upon their right arm above the elbow, which was the sign and word I had formerly sent to my Lord Marquess.'

There was an interesting occasion in June 1648 when at a skirmish near Bangor, both sides decided that their field-sign would be *not* to wear scarves, a coincidence which must have been confusing at the beginning.

INTERREGNUM 1649—1660

Although the interregnum developed into a military government and the Roundhead Army remained in force, there is not much information as to their appearance although there are many printed words as to what they said and thought—at least the teachers and preacher who were in every unit. But there were minor conflicts in various parts of the Kingdom and overseas which called for the armed forces.

PLATE 30. Trooper, 11th Dragoons.

PLATE 31. Light Trooper, 11th Dragoons.

PLATE 32. Drummer, 11th Dragoons.

PLATE 33. Farrier, 11th Dragoons.

When Wales did not readily knuckle down to full obedience of Parliament, Colonel Gryffith made what was called at the time a 'ridiculous Expedition with Silver Trumpets and Guarded Coats' but as he was totally routed at his first encounter, his display was of little avail.

Cromwell had to send a large army to Ireland to keep the natives under control. These he clothed with fifteen thousand cassocks of venice-red colour, shrunk in water, with a like number of pairs of breeches of grey or other good colour. Ten thousand hats with bands were obviously the head-gear for the 'soft' troops, but the pikemen would have had the iron pots or helmets.

The son of Oliver Cromwell, Richard, when he became Protector, continued to use red as the national colour for the coats of all the foot-soldiers, but as a mark of respect for his dead father he had these coats trimmed with black. Cromwell had his own Guard of Halberdiers which were a kind of Yeomen of the Guard; they were dressed in grey coats guarded with black velvet.

Although the Roundhead forces had been troops specially raised for the internecine campaigns, many of the units had a continuity of life when the warfare died down. When a Colonel died, another took his place and so, although reduced, many of the regiments continued in being right up to the restoration of Charles II. In Ireland many units were disbanded in 1649 and 1653. In 1654 many regiments were raised for service in the West Indies, no doubt a useful theatre for absorbing the troublesome soldiers who were unwilling to return to the more humdrum civilian life. These overseas troops with various reorganizations also lasted until the Restoration, as did the troops raised in 1657 for service in Flanders. It was a short time before this that the Royalists living in exile began to raise regiments on foreign soil.

In May 1657, Sir John Reynolds landed at Calais with six thousand men to fight the Spanish and 'every man had a new red coat and a new pair of shoes'. Charles II took the opportunity to strengthen his contingent of 2,000 men which was in the vicinity, with deserters from this Parliamentary force. The Royalists were now formed into six regiments: the King's Regiment of Guards being all English, four of them being Irish and the last Scottish. At the same time, the Duke of York took command of a body of cavalry a hundred strong. Thus can be seen the origins of the Household troops still in being today.

The opposing forces of the same Kingdom came in active conflict with one another at the battle of the Dunes 1658, which took place near Dunkirk. Although prints remain of this unusual occasion we have little information as to the dress apart from the red coat. The Duke of York with twenty of his Guards went boldly through the French lines, thus showing the similarity of dress.

CHARLES II 1649—1685

The carefully balanced and protracted negotiations which brought Charles II back to the throne had to take note of the powerful Commonwealth troops still in the country — once the actual rulers of the Nation. General Monk carefully manoeuvred possibly hostile elements into safe districts and made sure that his reliable troops were in London. Thus when the returning King made his first Regal procession through the streets of London, he was also accompanied by soldiers who had previously made their allegiance to Parliament alone. To quote a contemporary Chronicle these included 'five regiments of Army Horse with Back, Breast and Head-piece, which diversified the show with delight and terrour.'

This procession of 29 May, 1660 saw several troops of mounted volunteers also welcoming their newly returned Monarch. The Lord Mayor, Major-General Brown, led a troop of Gentlemen brandishing their swords and clad in cloth-of-silver doublets. Another troop wore velvet or plush coats and yet a third had buff coats with cloth-of-silver sleeves and green scarves; then followed a troop in blue liveries and silver lace. The Earl of Northampton had his own troop in liveries of grey and blue. But these were only temporary formations and passed away as did the Army Horse.

HORSE GUARDS

The troops in that procession who attained a permanent footing were the three troops of Life Guards with their kettledrums and trumpets. To be precise, the term Life Guards is of modern use, dating only from the eighteenth century. In Charles II's days they were known as Horse Guards as distinct from Foot Guards. 'Guards' was the term applied to all personal bodyguards, and cavalry men were called 'Horse'. There were these three troops of Horse Guards which at the time of the Coronation belonged respectively to the King, the Duke of York and Monk, created the Duke of Albemarle for his services in securing the King's return. The King's Troop wore white armour—that is to say, bright cuirasses— over their buff coats. In their hats were red and white feathers and around their waists were red scarves. The Duke's Troop had black armour, the same red scarves round the waist and red, white and black feathers in their hats, with the additional distinction of sword-belts in His Highness's livery. Red scarves are mentioned as being part of the dress of the Horse Guards during the Venner Rebellion of 1661.

A few years later further details were noted in the dress. The King's Troop was dressed in red faced with blue and richly ornamented with gold lace, but the hat feathers were now white alone. The Duke's Troop had the same dress without the gold lace and plain white feathers. Albemarle's Troop was dressed as the Duke's but instead of feathers, they wore ribbons of a crimson colour. A portrait of an officer of this period, Major-General Egerton, shows this elaborate costume. It will be noted that the troops wore 'backs, breasts and potts' when on active service or during troubles. This armour is shown in battle pictures and was the normal dress for 'Horse' who were sometimes called 'cuirassiers'. The 'pott' was an open helmet, usually having a movable nasal-bar and a laminated neck-guard.

When the Duke of Albemarle died, the troops were re-named. The King's Troop remained the first, but the second became the Queen's and the third was now the Duke of York's. The distinctions between these troops were as follows: the King's had blue ribbons and carbine belts and the red housings and holster caps bore his cypher. The Queen's Troop had green distinctions, this being Catherine of Braganza's colour; the ribbons were green and the carbine belts were covered with green velvet and ornamented with gold lace; a cypher was embroidered on the green housings and holster caps. The Duke of York chose yellow as his distinction, this being one of the Stuart colours, and used by him in other regiments which bore his name. The ribbons, carbine belts and housings were all of this bright colour.

A review of 1684 gives further information of these Royal troops. The King's Own Troop of Horse Guards had their carbine-belts of velvet laced with silver and gold; their cloaks were the same colours as the coats, scarlet lined with blue. The Queen's Troop had green velvet carbine belts laced with gold, but cloaks as the King's Troop. The Duke of York's Troop had carbine belts of yellow velvet, laced with silver, the rest of the costume as mentioned before. Each troop still had its own kettledrummer and trumpeters.

HORSE 1660—1685

Apart from the personal troops of the King, the Duke of York and the Duke of Albemarle, there was another body of horsemen who eventually achieved permanency and became the Royal Horse Guards (The Blues) of today. When the King returned to England he took the precaution of placing his own trusted officers in charge of the Parliamentary regiments. One of these originally under the command of Colonel Unton Crooke was taken over by the King and called the Royal Regiment. Although this Horse Regiment was disbanded, it was re-raised almost at once in January 1661 under the Earl of Oxford and adopted the livery which gave them the nick-name of the 'Oxford Blues'. These were the men that the Duke of Tuscany saw on his travels in 1669 and commented on the fact that the officers wore red sashes with gold tassels.

Later in the reign the Royal Regiment of Horse Guards was at a review on Putney Heath, on which occasion its dress was described in some detail. The account tells us that 'This Regiment of Horse-Guards consists of eight Troops, each of them having, besides — Commissioned Officers, three Corporals, Two Trumpets, forty-five private Men, distinguish't by their Carbine-Belts laced with Gold upon buff with a red edging, Hooses, and Holdster-Caps with the Royal Cypher, embroidered upon Blew, Coated and Cloaked Blew, lined Red.' The 'hooses and holdster-caps' were part of the horse furniture, the house or housing was a kind of shabraque or saddlecloth, while the holster-caps were the coverings of the pistol-holsters in front of the saddle. The King's troop of this regiment had a kettledrum.

A deserter's report speaks of 'tawny colour breeches': these articles and also the waistcoats were buff in this regiment for many years later.

Charles's marriage to Catherine of Braganza brought Portuguese territory to the nation. One of these new possessions, Tangier, on the north coast of Africa, was constantly being threatened by the marauding Moors and needed a garrison to protect it. The garrison of Dunkirk found men for infantry battalions but it was also deemed necessary to have a small proportion of cavalry, to engage the fleet Moorish horsemen who fell like a cloud of flies on any small detached group of white colonists. A hundred men destined to be the nucleus of the Tangier Horse, mustered on 21 October 1661, in St George's Fields, Southwark, near where the Imperial War Museum stands today.

These cavalrymen went to Tangier where they took over horses previously used by Portuguese troops. The country was not healthy for horses and the horsemen must also have felt the rigours of the African climate. The troops of horse which had numbered three in 1664 were reduced to two by the following year, and by 1668 only one troop remained. To help keep up the numbers two hundred Spanish horsemen were employed in the colony, but further efforts had to be made. In 1680 three troops were raised in

England and sent out to augment the dwindling Horse. The officers came from a recently disbanded regiment of Horse which had been commanded by the Duke of Monmouth. The horses themselves were taken from the troops of Horse Guards. Even with this supplement the numbers decreased rapidly and the abandonment of Tangier, in 1684, must have come as a relief to these sorely-tried horsemen. It was this handful of men who, on their return to England, made the first recruits of the King's Own Royal Regiment of Dragoons, now known as the Royal Dragoons.

No enlightened outlook was taken with the equipping of the cavalrymen for the strenuous tropical service and the troops were issued with backs, breasts, pots and carbines after the fashion of the home equipment. A contemporary picture shows these Tangier Horsemen in black triple-barred helmets and black cuirasses worn over red coats with black high boots covering the whole of the leg. The mounted officers in this review wear hats, as might also troopers in actual combat if we are to believe a picture by Wyck showing the defeat of the Moors in 1680. No armour at all is shown in this latter picture where the horsemen fall on the natives with swords and firearms.

HORSE GRENADIERS 1678—1685

A new type of soldier had been coming into being on the Continent—the grenadier. The grenade had long been in use but the new conception was to make a special body of troops, and complete companies were added to infantry regiments. The cavalry was not slow to adopt this fashion and in Spring 1678, the three troops of Horse Guards each had their own troop of Horse Grenadiers, the King's Troop having eighty men and the other two, sixty men each. Each troop mounted guard with the troop of horse to which it belonged, performed sentry duty on foot and also attended the King on foot when he walked 'abroad'.

Evelyn notes in his diary under the date of 5 December 1683, that they were a new sort of dragoons who carried grenades and were dressed after the Polish fashion. He further writes that they looked fierce and fantastic in their long peaked caps. The three troops were at a review in 1684 and were then noted in some detail. The grenadiers of the King's troop had red coats lined with blue and the loops of the buttonholes were blue with yellow tufts. The grenadier caps were lined blue and had a blue round mark on the outside—this probably being the representation of a grenade. The Queen's troop had red coats lined with blue but the coat loops were green with yellow tufts. The third troop, the Duke of York's, had similar coats but with all-yellow coat loops down the front. These grenadier troops sometimes acted together as one body and the Regiment of Horse Guards did not have a grenadier troop.

The Horse Grenadiers had hats as well as caps and, according to a drill book, only put on the caps when about to commence field exercises.

DRAGOONS 1660—1685

Finance, political considerations and small wars all played their part in the rapid creation of new units and in their sudden disappearance. Independent troops of dragoons, concerned mainly with internal security and police duties, appeared frequently on the home establishment, but complete regiments were few unless overseas service was envisaged. One well-known regiment was that raised for Barbados. Prince Rupert was the nominal commander, and under such an inventive and forceful man one can understand the contemporary 'modernity' of the order which specifies that each dragoon was to carry 'one bayonet or great knife.' These sidearms had been in use earlier but appear to have fallen into disfavour. As mounted infantry one may expect their sergeants to be carrying halberds, but to find twelve soldiers in each troop carrying these cutting weapons seems to indicate a high proportion. Matchlocks were the general issue weapon for the men, not an easy weapon to be managed on horseback. Nor for that matter would be the two drums per troop. The dragoon was still little more than an infantryman mounted for speedy movement from place to place, useful for patrols and keeping the peace in civil disturbances.

However, the status of dragoons was improving and they were becoming a lighter version of Horse, without the cumbersome armour and what is more important, much cheaper to maintain. When the remnants of the Tangier Horse returned from that abandoned garrison, they were converted into Dragoons and exist today as the Royal Dragoons. During the first year of their new life they were reviewed on Putney Heath and are described in a contemporary account as being 'coated and cloaked red lined blew; Hooses embroidered with blew and yellow upon red with the Royal Cypher: caps the same with Royal Cypher.' The red and blue are the Royal colours as used in other Royal Regiments. The 'hooses' and 'caps' are the usual horse fittings, housings and holster caps. Caps for the head were also worn by Dragoons; these were of different patterns, sometimes having an edging of fur as the one of blue velvet which was sent to Ireland as a pattern in 1684. Another of blue cloth lined red, was apparently the pattern for the private soldier.

The Scottish nation had its own military establishment, despite the fact that a Scottish King took over the throne of England in 1603. Detached troops of dragoons were raised there from time to time, usually disappearing from service after a short life. But two troops raised in 1678 achieved permanence and became later the regiment now known as the Royal Scots Greys. From the beginning there were nationalistic tendencies and, as might be expected, the men wore Scottish bonnets. The coats were made from the 2,436 ells of stone-grey cloth which was imported from England in 1683, specifically for clothing these troops. It may be pointed out that the Royal Scots Greys wore grey coats long before the idea was conceived of riding horses of a single grey colour. Under their head-dresses, dragoons wore an iron scull-cap, their sole item of armour. The usual armament for dragoons was the infantry musket but reduced by having four inches cut off the barrel, thus sometimes acquiring the name of carbine. Leather slings were strapped to the musket so that it could be carried across the body, leaving the hands free. Later an attachment was added by which means it could hang from a belt going over the left shoulder.

FOOT GUARDS 1660—1685

When Charles II left Holland in June 1660 to return to England, the opportunity was taken to make it a military occasion. A contemporary oil-painting at Hampton Court shows this colourful scene and in the foreground are troops which have been considered as the King's Foot Guards. The musketeers are dressed in red uniforms with blue trimmings which are the colours one would expect for a Royal regiment. The red jacket as shown has hanging sleeves at the back and the actual arm coverings are shown as buff in colour, possibly indicating a buff leather jerkin worn below. The red breeches have cloth buttons of a similar colour down the side seams and knots of red ribbons at the knees. The red hose are kept up by garters of red edged with blue. The black shoes have red bows and heels. The polished steel helmet they wear is not the head-dress usually expected for English musketeers, but no doubt Dutch influences must have prevailed, as also in the case of the officer who wears a dark blue coat with red cuffs. This officer has a bunch of red ribbons on the point of the right shoulder which might serve to keep his sword baldric in place. Another officer wears a short jack-a-napes coat of yellow with a decorative over-pattern; this might represent cloth-of-gold material as worn by a Guards officer of a slightly later period. This second officer wears blue breeches, blue ribbons at the waist and on his hat. His cravat is tied with strings which end in two heavy tassels. His white hose have the tops turned down in what was no doubt considered an elegant style. His black shoes have blue ribbon bows and red heels and soles. Although he bears a sword on his side from a silver baldric, in his hand he has a stout cane.

A drummer from the same group wears red with red, yellow and blue ribbons at the knees and waist, while a bunch of ribbons helps to keep his silver-grey sword-sling in place. His shoes are buff leather and also have the fancy red heels of the period. An account of October 1661 shows that a pound was paid for embroidering each drummer's red tunic. Besides the accounts for the twenty-four drummers, there is mention of 783 red tunics for the musketeers and 505 buff coats, presumably for the pikemen. The troops thus provided were part of the Garrison of Dunkirk, for at that time we still had a foothold on the Continent which lasted until 1662. The King's Foot Guards were divided into two parts, one in London and the other at Dunkirk.

The original Foot Guards were not considered as solely ceremonial nor as a fighting body but fulfilled a variety of duties as the occasions demanded, often sending their men away as reinforcements to distant places. Companies were raised for garrisoning of the Tower of London; six hundred men in 1664 were employed on sea service and odd companies were sent to Tangier, to remain there more or less permanently. The Guards were also employed to impress visiting nobility and to make a fine show when necessary. In 1669 Cosmo, Duke of Tuscany, visited this country and wrote in his diary that he saw the soldiers of the King's Own Regiment of Foot Guards. There were ten companies of eighty men each, all dressed in red coats turned up with light blue (which was the colour of the Royal livery), except the pikemen who were distinguished from the others by wearing coats of a silver colour turned up with light blue.

The issue of new uniforms in 1678 was to be 'a cloath coat lyned with bayes, a pair of kersey breeches lyned, with pocketts, two shirts, two cravatts, one pair of shoes, one pair of yarne hose, one hatt edged and hatt band, one sash and also one sword and belt for non commissioned officer and soldier'. It will be noted that cravats are now being worn instead of the falling 'Peter-Pan' collar. These cravats were cloths which were worn around the neck; sometimes two of contrasting colours were worn; the ends were made to tie, sometimes in distinctive fashion and to fall down in front. The mention of the sash as a general issue is worthy of note as being worn by all ranks of soldiers and not peculiar to officers.

There was a regiment raised in 1642 which is an ancestor of the Scots Guards: it was re-raised in 1662 after Charles had returned to his Kingdom. A command from Whitehall in May 1669 tells us that the men of this regiment wore 'red coats lyned with white and belts.' In 1682, the few grenadiers attached to each company were formed into their own company but precise information of their early dress is lacking.

It may surprise some people to know that there were Irish Guards as early as this reign. Unfortunately this is another instance where the dress is not clear. In December 1661 Lord Ossery wrote a letter asking if it might be possible to clothe the King's Regiment of Guards in Ireland in red trimmed with green with green buttons. Whether this was permitted is not clear, for the next year's accounts only mention scarlet coats. These Irish Guards left British service at the end of James's reign.

INFANTRY 1660—1685

The internal state of the Kingdom on Charles's return was most disturbed. There were many plots and attempts against the Throne which necessitated the action of troops. The military government of the Commonwealth had been unpopular yet many of the old Roundhead troops were still in arms. When regiments were disbanded, further discontented and unemployed men were added to the turmoil. The weak state of the country was encouraging to an uprising like that of the Millenarians' insurrection of 1662. Thus troops had to be hastily re-raised as in the case of the Governor of Essex who raised a regiment of foot and clad them in red coats, which shows that red was still a national colour.

Throughout the period of Parliament rule, there appears to have been little change in costume, but the return of the King brought new fashions from the Continent which showed a tendency towards luxury although the low state of the Exchequer acted as a brake. Pictures of soldiers about 1660 show the tall crowned hat still in use, but it soon became reduced in height and narrowed in the brim. Paintings of officers serving in Tangier show quite small hats with narrow brims and bunches of ribbons around the brim, but these were more or less a tropical version.

The body garment worn by soldiers at the time of the Restoration was a short jacket, but officers soon brought into use continental styles, and a long cassock, surtout or overcoat was worn on top. Within a few years this coat was the main garment and the undergarment was becoming a sleeved waistcoat. The loose surtout had the cuffs turned back to reveal the facings or linings which were to become so important a part of regimental distinctions.

The coat hung straight down without much acknowledgement of a waist, for a waistbelt was not used and the necessary belts were suspended from the shoulders. However, by 1678 the infantry coats were girt around the middle with sashes for all ranks; these sashes varied in colour for the different regiments. The Royal Regiment of Foot Guards had white sashes with blue fringes. The Coldstream Regiment of Foot Guards had white sashes fringed with green and the Royal Scots had all-white sashes. The wearing of these sashes apparently led to the habit of leaving the coat unbuttoned to the waist.

The falling linen collar remained in use for several years longer—the troops at Albemarle's funeral in 1670 are shown wearing them but the officers wear the cravats or neckcloths of lace. A short while later the neckcloths were being worn by the ordinary soldiers.

33

Concessions for climate were now being made. The troops in Tangier wore clothing lighter in weight and the armour of pikemen was practically discontinued. Undress clothing was worn even at home to save the red coat for important occasions. Grey clothing is to be noted in the fine collection of water-colour sketches which the famous artist, Wenceslaus Hollar, made at Tangier. The officers are shown wearing loose grey coats differenced by the colour of the ribbons, facings, baldrics and strings. These colours are blue, crimson and light yellow or buff. Although one can make guesses as to which regiment wears which, there is no conclusive proof.

There are a few sketches of ordinary soldiers wearing close-fitting grey coats with cuffs of the colour of the regimental facings. Grey clothing is frequently quoted as being worn by deserters in the notices which appeared in the *London Gazette* and other newspapers of the time. These grey coats are sometimes noted as having black facings even for regiments which are known to have other colours. The inference to be drawn is that there was a more or less general undress garment in common use.

There was a regiment which had black facings, a rare event, and it was the short-lived body of troops raised by Lord Chesterfield in 1667. He states that the reason why he gave his troops red coats lined with black was 'I then did because I was at that time in mourning for my mother.'

The garrison at Tangier had to be constantly reinforced. The original battalions dwindled in strength, were amalgamated into one, received new reinforcements and they too would be incorporated into the steadily reducing force. But out of these constant changes, two regiments emerged—the Governor's Regiment, the Old Tangier Regiment which became the 2nd Foot or Queen's and the other, the New Tangier Regiment which became the 4th Foot or the King's Own. Little sure evidence exists of the dress of these regiments during their stay in that now lost outpost of the Empire, but if we can trust the contemporary oil-painting by Dirck Stoop, both the Tangier Regiments wore red coats with red linings with breeches and hose to match. The Regimental Colours of the Old Tangier Regiment have a green ground, which colour was used later for a regimental facing: but the figures are so small that the artist may have had to simplify the costume. Officers are sometimes shown in this artist's work wearing blue coats or even the undress greys.

To make a review before the Alcade Omar more imposing, the sailors from the fleet were sent ashore and dressed in blue and white striped linen coats; these appear grey in the contemporary picture, as do the men's hose. They formed Lord Dartmouth's own battalion of seamen, and two other battalions each of two hundred seamen were clothed in 'such clothes as the Scotch shall provide.' These men appear to be wearing all red coats but a larger portrayal of a soldier by Stoop shows us what the Royal Scots, the regiment in question, should wear. We also know from a newsletter of 1677 that Lord George Douglas departed for Spain with his regiment of 1,600 men and they took with them cloth to make coats of red lined with white: it is this type of coat that the large Tangier picture shows. White hose and a white sash were also part of the clothing of a pikeman on sentry duty. He wears no armour and has a broad-brimmed black hat. The white sashes fringed with white were still being worn in 1684 as an account tells us. The breeches and stockings are noted as light grey.

The Holland regiment, now the Buffs, had been in Dutch service since 1572 but they had been recalled to England in 1665. Cosmo, Duke of Tuscany, said in 1669 that they wore red coats with yellow facings but at the review of 1684 they were noted as being in red coats lined with a flesh colour. The description of a deserter in a *London Gazette* of 1685 mentions red coats 'lined with a buff coloured lining.' These coats had cross pockets with scalloped flaps, and large pewter buttons.

There was also in being the Lord High Admiral of England, His Royal Highness the Duke of York and Albany's, Maritime Regiment of Foot: it was raised in 1664 to serve at sea and was disbanded early in 1689. Intended to serve on board ship these soldiers were armed with firelocks and had no pikemen. The firelocks were flintlocks and not the dangerous matchlocks. During the reign of Charles II the regiment was clad in yellow with red linings, a combination which at least distinguished them from the usual red coat of the normal land soldier. Yellow was the colour favoured by the Duke of York who gave it to his troop of Horse as a distinction, and it was, of course, part of the colours of the Royal Stuart livery.

GRENADIERS 1677—1685

Horse grenadiers have been mentioned before but a more numerous and popular soldier was the foot grenadier. These were gradually added to each infantry regiment and as a specialized type of soldier remained in being for nearly seventy years after the horse grenadiers disappeared, although the name was nominal rather than practical. The high honour attached to a grenadier is to be noted in the fact that the premier regiment of Foot Guards is known today as the Grenadier Guards.

A warrant was issued on 19 May 1677, ordering that two soldiers of each company of infantry then serving in the Tower of London should be trained as 'grenadiers'. These were from the two Regiments of Foot Guards and made a total from each regiment of fifty-four and twenty men to be trained. In April 1678 a warrant was issued in which a grenadier company was to be added to the eight eldest regiments of foot. The equipment was to be fuzees—flintlocks—with slings to each one, cartridge boxes on girdles (this was a departure from the common practice of having the pouch on a shoulder belt) and grenadier pouches, as well as hatchets and bayonets. The grenadier was to be a special man to go forward in the attack, to be able to use his hatchet for breaking down obstacles, and use his grenades boldly to clear away the enemy. These men in their day must have had much of the glamour of a commando about them. It was at the Hounslow camp in June 1678 that the diarist John Evelyn noted the 'new sort of soldiers who with a pouchful of hand grenades were skilful in throwing them at the enemy.' He also described them as wearing 'furred caps with coped crowns like Janizaries, which gave them a fierce expression: while some wore long hoods hanging down behind, as fools are pictured. Their clothing was piebald, yellow and red.' These comments are hardly kind and it is not clear which regiments are meant. The yellow and red has been thought to represent the yellow coats of the Maritime Regiment. There is no doubt that the dress of the grenadier was made something special. Seventy grenadiers of His Majesty's Own Regiment of Guards had special cravats of 'fox tails', no doubt made with fancy lace or pointed ends, which were tied with scarlet ribbons.

When the garrison came home from Tangier, the returned Guardsmen were formed into additional grenadier companies of the Foot Guards. The captain of the one added to the 1st Foot Guards was Francis Hawley, whose uniform we know for the next reign. The warrant for the equipment as authorized on 28 April 1684, more or less repeated that authorized in 1677.

An account of the time tells us that the 1st Foot Guards wore red coats lined blue, blue stockings and breeches. Their caps were lined with blue and had the Royal Cypher and Crown embroidered in front; the tuft of the cap was said to be blue and red. The Coldstream Guards had red coats lined with green, with red stockings and breeches. The caps were lined green with green tassels on top. The grenadiers of the Royal Regiment of Foot, better known today as the Royal Scots, wore red coats with white lining and their caps also had white lining and the device of a crowned lion's head embroidered in front. The reconstituted 'Old' and 'New' Tangier Regiments had grenadiers but details are not available. The Duke of York and Albany's Maritime Regiment and the Holland Regiment, had no grenadier companies at the parade described so fully.

MILITIA 1660—1685

The militia of this period wore uniforms similar to the Regular Army. The Duke of Beaufort when he made a progress through Wales in 1684 had a writer, Thomas Dinely, record the happenings and scenes of the journey. Descriptions of the troops which came forward to greet the noble lord give us a picture of auxiliary forces. Thus we learn that at Brecon the foot soldiers were in new hats, had blue cassocks, white sashes edged with blue worsted fringe, and red yarn stockings. In Flintshire Captain Roger Mostyn had his company clothed in red also lined red, with white sashes, red stockings and new hats which were edged and turned up on the sides with buttons. Another regiment in Glamorganshire wore purple lined with red and had white sashes around their middles. Red stockings were the netherwear in this case.

The militia of Surrey at the same period wore red coats as did the militia of St Helena. The Essex militia had red coats with white linings for the 1st Regiment, blue linings for the 2nd or Colchester and green linings for the 3rd or Chelmsford. The Somerset militia is said to have had red coats with yellow linings.

The Scottish militia had their own colour for their coats. A ballad of Bothwell Brig tells us that

> 'The Lowdien Mallisha they
> Came with their Coats of Blew
> Five hundred men from London came
> Claid in a reddish hew.'

The Earl of Lauderdale in 1669 was modest regarding his own troops, and writes 'but if the Militia regiment of this Shire had not been mine, I would say they looked the best because all, both musket and pikemen were in blew coats lined with white, which made a good show.' It will be noticed that the blue and white combination matches the white saltire of St Andrew on the blue field of the national flag. Blue bonnets were the headdresses of the common Scottish soldiers of the Covenanting period, according to writings, but no doubt the Lowlanders, not being true Highlanders, managed to find hats for headgear.

MUSIC 1660—1685

Distinctions of the dress of Charles I's days which can still be seen perpetuated today on special occasions, are in the State dresses worn by the band of the Household Cavalry and the Drum-Majors of the Foot Guards. This striking gold-laced clothing was no doubt a legacy from the days that Charles spent in exile in France where he would have seen elaborate liveries such as he would have liked to have had in his own Court. It is difficult to realize that the garment which strikes one as being all gold is basically a red coat with blue velvet cuffs and facings. The broad gold-lace covers, first of all, the main seams and then follows all the edge of the garment. In places it is laid on double, and in between a chain tracing is placed to fill the blanks. Originally the lace was silver then gold and silver but eventually it became entirely gold.

On the back where the sleeves join the shoulders were two pieces of cloth still to be seen on the State clothing of the musicians of the Household Cavalry. These remnants which hang down to the waistbelt where they are tucked in, are the vestiges of the old doublet or outer garment. The outer sleeves were slit so that the arms could pass through freely and in time these sleeves dwindled in size until they remained no more than strips of gold lace, with their original purpose forgotten. The bills of Charles's reign describe the coat in some detail: it is of crimson velvet trimmed with silver and silk laces with silver buttons and loops, richly embroidered with His Majesty's letters and crowns on the breast and back. No mention is made of gold in these early accounts. The original garments were lined with chamois leather and the waistbelts were also of soft leather, edged with gold lace.

JAMES II 1685—1688

Officers

James seems to have wished to appear as the head of an important nation. He was pretentious in many of the customs he adopted from abroad and did much to offend the populace. Prints and portraits of him show a supercilious curl to his nostrils. He is shown in heavy armour with lace ruffles at his wrists. A more probable costume is the equestrian print which shows him on a rocking charger: his hat has a profusion of feathers and rich fringe on the edge; a mass of curls hangs on the shoulders of his heavily laced coat; a bunch of ribbons on the right shoulder indicates the coming fashion of epaulettes.

The ample and loosely tied sash encircles the waist allowing the coat to be partly open to reveal an elaborate waistcoat. We get a glimpse of puffed breeches which disappear into long boots, still used with an inner lining. The horse furniture employs bows and ribbons and the saddlecloth an embroidered crown and cypher.

An unusual vehicle to show contemporary uniform is the life-size marble statue of Sir John Clobery which is in Winchester Cathedral. This officer raised one of the short-lived regiments of Charles II's reign. He died in 1687 and his memorial statue shows the elaborate dress of the period. He wears a large full wig which rests on his shoulders; his neck is hidden by a voluminous lace cravat. The long skirted coat has much embroidery down the front, around the pockets, the cuffs, the arm holes and down the seams of the sleeves. His middle is girt with a many-folded silk sash, the two ends of which end in many tassels. His netherwear is not observable because his long soft boots reach right up to the lower edges of the coat-skirts. The hard stiffened boots were just coming into fashion. The sole 'weapon' of his rank is the long baton which he holds in his right hand—perhaps the absence of a sword is a concession to the hallowed place where the statue rests.

CAVALRY 1685—1688

When James came to the throne he wished to appear every inch of a King and his Coronation was to be a minutely worked-out affair, recorded in detail and pictures. The 1st Troop of Horse Guards, now belonging to the new King, is described taking the words of Sandford, the Herald, who wrote the history of the occasion as:

'The Officers of this Troop were richly Habited, either in Coats of Crimson Velvet Imbroidered with Gold and Silver, or of Fine Scarlet Cloth Imbroidered or Laced with Gold or Silver, or both intermixed. They wore Scarfs about their Wastes, either of Gold or Silver Network, or Crimson Taffata, richly Fringed with Gold or Silver on the Edges, and with a deep Fringe of the same at the Ends. Their Cloaks were also of Fine Scarlet Cloth, Imbroidered on the Capes and down before with Gold or Silver, or both intermixed. In their Hats they wore Tours of White Feathers; Their Housses and Holster-Caps, being of Crimson Velvet, were richly Imbroidered and Embossed with Gold and Silver: And the Manes, Cruppers and Tayls of their Horses were garnished with large knots of broad Blew Taffata Ribband.

'The Gentlemen of this Troop (Two Hundred in Number) were all new Clothed in Coats and Cloaks of Scarlet Cloth, lined with Blew Chalon: The Facings of their Sleeves, of the same Stuff, were laced about with a figured Galoon of Silver (edged with Gold) two inches broad: Their Buttons were of Silver Plate; They had each of them a good Buff Coat, and a large Pair of Gantlet Gloves of the same: And in their Hats (which were Black and turned up on one Side and edged about with a broad Silver Lace) they wore Blew Knots of broad Taffata Ribband; which Blew being the Distinguishing Colour of their Troop from the others, the Heads of their Horses were adorned with knots of the like Ribband. They were extraordinary well Mounted, and excellently well equipped, having their Housses and Holster-Caps of Scarlet Cloth, Imbroidered with the King's Cipher and Crown within a Border of Foliage. Each of these Gentlemen was armed and Accoutred with a good broad Sword, and large Buff Shoulder-Belt, a Case of Pistols, a Carabine, with a Carabine Belt of Blew Velvet five inches broad, bordered with figured Silver Galoon (edged with a narrow Gold Lace) in bredth two Inches, so that not above an Inch in bredth of the Velvet appeared.'

The Officers of the 2nd Troop, now belonging to the new Queen, were dressed and equipped 'in like manner as were those of the First Troop, from whom they differed only in the Colour of their Housses and Holster Caps, which were of Green Velvet; and in the garnishing of the Manes, Cruppers and Tayls of their Horses, which was with Green Taffata Ribbands, whereas the Distinguishing Colour of the First Troop was Blew.

'The Gentlemen of this Troop, were also 200 in number, all new Cloathed, Armed and Equipped in like manner as were the First Troop, differing only from them in the Lace of their Hats, of their Sleeve-Facings, and their Carabine Belts, all which was Gold edged with Silver, and in the Colour of their Ribbands in their Hats and Horses Heads, which were Green as were also their Housses and Holster Caps and Carabine Belts; only the King's Cipher on the said Housses and Holster Caps was within a Border.'

38

The 3rd Troop was similar in dress to the other with the difference in the colour of the carbine belts, housings and holster caps which were of yellow velvet. Yellow taffeta ribbons were used on the manes, cruppers and tails of the horses. The men's lace was of silver instead of gold or gold and silver.

Each of these troops had its own grenadiers. Those attached to the 1st Troop wore coats of fine red cloth, lined and faced with blue shalloon decorated with buttons of white metal hatched with silver. On the body, arms, and facings of the sleeves were large loops of blue worsted edged and tufted with black and white. The crowns of the caps were raised high to a point and fell down at the back; the blue plush lining was turned up in the front and the back on which latter part was placed a grenade as a distinction. The holster caps and housings of the horses were of red cloth scalloped at the edges and embroidered with foliage, the Crown and the Royal Cypher. The 2nd Troop of Horse Grenadiers had green distinctions, that is to say, for the housings, holster-caps, linings, facings and worsted loops; these last-mentioned items had edgings and tufts of black and white like the 1st Troop, but the buttons were gilt and the hat lace gold. The 3rd Troop of Household Cavalry had yellow distinctions in place of the blue of the 1st and the green of the 2nd. The buttons were white metal hatched with silver and the hat lace was of silver.

His Majesty's Royal Regiment of Horse—the Horse Guards Blues of modern days—was not described in these coronation records but the Earl of Oxford, their commander, saw fit to issue in 1686 orders for the clothes of the officers of his regiment. These tell us the differences between the different grades, which system may have been applied to other regiments. These orders state that 'all the Captains coats are to be of blue cloth faced with the same, the lace of the said (coats) must be of gold, laid double upon every seam and slits with a gold foot between the two laces. The buttons of gold thread with a gold fringe round the sleeves, under which must be laid the same lace as down the seams. All the Lieutenants' and Cornets' coats must be the same as the Captains', only a single broad lace on each seam and slits and sleeves, the fringe excepted. The Quartermasters' coats must be the same cloth as the rest of the Officers' with a gold edging down before, at the pockets, slits and round the sleeves, with a broad lace round the sleeves, as the Lieutenants and Cornets, and gold buttons as the rest of the Officers. The pockets of all the coats must be of the same fashion, viz., with two long slits on each side. Each officer must have a black hat edged with a gold lace and a white feather. The trimming of the hats must be yellow as also the cravat strings.'

HORSE 1685—1688

The threatened rebellion of Monmouth prompted James II to raise new regiments, in particular Horse regiments. Some were raised before the actual rebellion took place and others taking longer in their process of forming, were only completed after the trouble had died away. But James did put this national upheaval to a practical purpose and achieved a result and success not enjoyed by Charles II, for most of these new regiments were put on a permanent footing and descended down to the present day.

The new regiments of Horse were those belonging to the Queen, the Earl of Peterborough, the Earl of Plymouth, Lord Dover, the Earl of Thanet, the Earl of Arran, the

Earl of Shrewsbury, Princess Anne of Denmark, and the Queen Dowager. Lord Dover's regiment was disbanded in 1686 and the Earl of Thanet's and Princess Anne of Denmark's disappeared a few years later, but the others eventually became the King's Dragoon Guards, the 2nd Dragoon Guards (the Bays), the 3rd Dragoon Guards, the 4th Dragoon Guards, the 5th Dragoon Guards and the 6th Dragoon Guards.

It is not until the next year that good information appears as to the distinctions of these newly raised regiments. At a review in June held at Hounslow, the Queen's wore red coats lined with yellow, Peterborough's wore red lined with red, the Earl of Plymouth's red lined green, Major-General Worden's red lined blue, the Earl of Arran's red lined white, the Earl of Shrewsbury's red lined buff, Scarsdale of the Princess Anne of Denmark's red lined yellow and the Queen Dowager's red lined sea-green. It is interesting to try and deduce why the facing colours were chosen. The Queen no doubt continued to use yellow distinctions used previously by herself and her husband when he was Duke of York. The Earl of Arran had argent or white as the main colour of his coat of arms. The Earl of Shrewsbury had a red field to his coat of arms but there was also a yellow lion in his arms which hue he inclined towards in the lining. The Queen Dowager continued the sea-green which she had used as Queen Catherine of Braganza. Princess Anne of Denmark had the yellow of that country.

Of the other short-lived regiments of Horse raised by James to support his tottering throne, very little is known of their dress. A troop of English Catholics formed in September 1688 under the Earl of Salisbury, were arrayed in red cloaks lined with orange. The Earl of Galmoy's Horse wore light-grey coats lined with red and ornamented with brass buttons; their black hats were laced with galloon, a cheap tinsel lace and some of their horses were grey in colour.

DRAGOONS 1685—1688

James II began his reign with a Regiment of Dragoons in England and another in Scotland, the Royal Dragoons and Scots Greys. New regiments of these mounted infantry were raised in 1685 two of which achieved permanency but one which had a fairly long life, the Irish Dragoons, faded away later. The two which have descended to our time are the Queen's Dragoons and the Princess of Denmark's Dragoons, later to be known as the 3rd and 4th Hussars.

Later when James raised his army in Ireland to fight against William of Orange, many new dragoon regiments appeared. On the defeat of the Irish Army the regiments were dispersed, although many elected to accompany the King into France, in exile. The Dragoons of Viscount Clare were one such body and they were called the 'Yellow Dragoons' it is said, on account of their facings. They later formed part of the Queen's Dismounted Regiment of Dragoons serving under the departed King. But generally speaking little information remains about the dress of the dragoons of this period.

FOOT GUARDS 1685—1688

By contrast the details of the uniforms of the Foot Guards are voluminous. The herald, Francis Sandford, tells us much about the dress of the First Regiment of His Majesty's Foot Guards at James II's Coronation. He says:

'The Officers of this First Regiment of Foot Guards were exceedingly richly habited; some in coats of cloth of gold, others in crimson velvet imbroidered or laced with gold or silver; but most of them in fine scarlet cloth, buttoned down the brest, and on the facings of the sleeves with silver plate. Their scarffs (which they wore about their wastes) were either network or gold or silver, or taffatta richly fringed with gold and silver, and their hats were adorned with tours of feathers. The captains were distinguished by corslets or gorgets of silver plate double gilt; the lieutenants by corslets of steel polished and san-guined and studded with nails of gold; and the ensignes had their corslets of silver plate.

'The private soldiers were all new cloathed in coats of red broadcloth, lined and faced with blue; their hats were laced about with silver, turned up and garnished with blew ribbands. Their breeches were blew broadcloth and their stockings of blew worsted. The musquetiers were armed with snaphaunce musquets, with sanguined barrels, three foot eight inches in length; good swords in waste belts and collars of bandiliers; and the pike-men with pikes sixteen feet long, each headed with a three-square point of steel and good swords in broad shoulder-belts, wearing about their wastes, shashes of scarffs of white worsted, fringed with blew. The granadiers were clothed as the musquetiers, but distin-guished by caps of red cloth lined with blew shaloon, and laced with silver galoon about the edges: and on the frontlets of their caps (which were high and very large) was im-broidered the King's Cypher and crown. Each of these granadiers was armed with a long carabine strapt, the barrel thereof three foot two inches in length, a cartouch box, bionet, granada-pouch and a hammer-hatchet.'

The mention of officers in cloth-of-gold coats is reminiscent of the officers who appear to wear a garment of this material at the departure of Charles II from Holland. No doubt this would be the dress of a colonel, for the same Coronation account tells us that Lt-Col John Strode wore a coat of cloth of gold, richly embroidered with silver. The lower grades appear to have worn crimson velvet coats embroidered with gold and silver. The all-gold sashes or waist sashes may also indicate the higher grades and also be graduated down-wards by decreasing richness.

The use of the word 'corslet' as a distinction for officers had originally meant the 'back and breast' of a cuirass, but as this armour was obsolescent or even obsolete, the term is applied to the last relic of armour, the gorget. It will be noted that although the pikemen are distinguished by white scarves fringed with blue as worn in the previous reign, the musketeers had no such finery.

The 2nd Regiment of His Majesty's Foot Guards called the 'Coldstreamers' was also described in the same Coronation account.

'The officers of this second Regiment of Foot-Guards were exceedingly richly habited, but differing in their imbroideries, laces and fringes, which were of gold, and their buttons of gold thread, from the officers of the First Regiment of Foot Guards, which had them of silver. The captains, lieutenants and ensigns were distinguished by corslets or gorgets as those officers of the First Regiment, and their hats were also adorned with tours of white feathers.

'The private soldiers, viz. musquetiers, pikemen and granadiers were in all points armed and accoutred as the First Regiment and agreeable to them in clothing except their breeches which were of red broadcloth and their stockings of red worsted. Their hats were black turned up and laced about with gold galoon in which they wore red ribbands and the shashes or waste-scarffs of the pike-men being of white worsted were fringed on the sides, and at the ends with red worsted. The granadiers had their caps lined and faced with blew shaloon and laced with gold galoon, and imbroidered on the frontlets with the King's Cipher.'

It seems unusual for gold embroidery to give place to silver, but it may be that the silver was genuine whereas the gold may have been a gilded or substitute metal.

The Monmouth Rebellion provided a reason for the Regiment of Guards in Scotland to be brought to London. When they appeared on review in 1686 they wore red coats lined with white, as well as white breeches and stockings. A more serviceable colour was chosen later for we know that in an account of May 1686, 560 pairs of grey stockings were sent to the regiment.

The Regiment of Foot Guards in Ireland remained loyal to James when William of Orange arrived and, in fact, went into exile when the former monarch went to France. Even in French service they continued to wear the old red coat with Royal blue facings and although they suffered structural changes, continued in being up to the Napoleonic Wars.

Good evidence of the uniform of a grenadier officer in this short reign is to be seen in a portrait of an officer of the First Foot Guards. The cloth cap is still small and had not acquired the typical mitre-like front; the little flap has the Cypher of the King under a crown. The grenades and decoration of later styles had yet to appear and a few golden stars are sufficient decoration for this early cap. The main body is bright blue with gold lace.

The red coat has facings of bright blue and the small cuffs are of the same colour. The buttons are shown as yellow. The waistbelt which holds the bayonet is bright blue with gold lace and embroidery. The plug-bayonet in its elaborate cloth scabbard is a sign that grenadier officers carried a fuzee or good type of flintlock musket. The pouch on the right side is to hold grenades and such a weapon is seen to be part of an officer's equipment, for this Captain Hawley holds one in his right hand while lighting it from the burning match held in his left hand. The large white cravat about his neck has a gold fringe and embroidery.

INFANTRY 1685—1688

The threat of the coming Rebellion prompted James to create new infantry regiments, nine of which attained permanence. The first in precedence was the Royal Regiment of Fuzileers. These men had a special task to perform—to guard the train of Artillery and for this dangerous post, every man carried a snaphaunce or flintlock instead of the matchlock. The burning match of the latter weapon would have been exceedingly unsafe near exposed gunpowder. Although there were no pikemen in this regiment their lack was made up by a special invention called turnpikes; these were carried by the men in parts and set up as a defensive hedge in time of action. The Regiment had another novelty, a company of miners. The regimental commander Lord Dartmouth, was also the Master General of the Ordnance and having been responsible for the miners at Tangier knew their worth. The uniform of the 'fuziliers' (practically any spelling seems to have been employed at that time) was a red coat lined with yellow, grey breeches and stockings. The men also had strapped muskets with bright barrels three feet eight inches long and the miners had extraordinary hammer-hatchets.

PLATE 34. 4th Queen's Own Dragoons, 1808. Oil Painting by Reinagle.

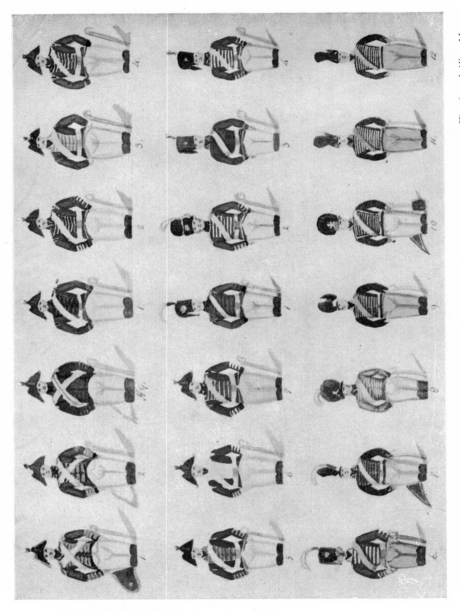

PLATE 35. 1st and 2nd Life Guards, Royal Horse Guards, 1st to 7th Dragoon Guards, 1st to 4th and 6th Dragoons, 7th to 12th Light Dragoons, *circa* 1800. Original watercolour by C. Hamilton Smith.

PLATE 36. Royal Scots Greys, 1807. Original watercolour by C. Hamilton Smith.

From Goddard & Booth Military Costume of Europe, 1812

PLATE 37. The Marquis of Anglesey, G.C.B., Colonel of the 7th Regiment of Light Dragoons, Hussars.

PLATE 38. Royal Scots Fusiliers, 1742. From the *Representation of Cloathing*.

PLATE 39. 41st Regiment of Foot, 1742. From the *Representation of Cloathing*.

By gracious permission of Her Majesty the Queen

PLATE 40. Grenadier of 40th Foot, man of Invalids' Regiment, and grenadier of Black Watch, by David Morier.

PLATE 41. (*Left*) Corporal Samuel McPherson,
Black Watch, 1743.
After a print by Bickham.

(*Below*) Highlanders. *After a German print.*
British Museum

The Princess Anne of Denmark's Regiment which became the 8th Foot and is now known as the King's Liverpool Regiment, had yellow linings, representative of Denmark. Francis Cornwall's Regiment which became the 9th Foot and is now known as the Royal Norfolk Regiment, adopted orange-coloured linings to their red coats. This orange colour is sometimes claimed as being worn in honour of the Prince of Orange, but it will be seen that this colour was worn three years before he came to England to become William III. Grey breeches and white hose are also noted in deserters' notices of the time as being part of the dress in this regiment.

The next regiment in precedence is that of the Earl of Bath, which became the 10th Foot and still later the Royal Lincolnshire Regiment. They had the distinction of blue coats, and although this colour for a garment was common a few years later when William III brought his Dutch troops, it was most uncommon in James's reign. The linings, the breeches, the waistcoats and the stockings were all red. This colour may have been chosen because the Colonel, John, Earl of Bath, had a red field to his coat of arms. Captain Granville's company of grenadiers wore the same coat with red and white loops as extra distinctions. 'Large red whiskers' were also noted as part of a deserting grenadier.

The Marquis of Worcester, son of the Duke of Beaufort, raised a regiment which became the 11th Foot or the Devonshire Regiment. A red coat lined with tawny cloth, with tawny-coloured breeches and stockings was their striking dress. Tawny is described at the same period as being feuillemort, philemot or dead leaf, which had been the livery of the Beaufort family from the time of John of Gaunt.

The Earl of Lichfield's regiment (later the 12th Foot and Suffolk Regiment) wore red coats lined with white cloth but the stockings and waistcoats were blue. The field of the Earl's coat of arms was argent which gives the clue to the white facings. The Earl of Huntingdon's regiment (later the 13th Foot and the Somerset Light Infantry) wore red coats lined with yellow and had breeches to match the facings but the stockings were the more humble shade of grey. As to the other regiments raised in this reign which achieved permanence, we have little contemporary details.

To avoid the complication of a large English establishment which was not favoured by the home government, Charles II was glad to have regiments serving abroad as mercenaries under foreign powers. We have already mentioned the Holland Regiment (The Buffs), but there were also others in the service of Holland. There were three English and three Scottish regiments which, in 1688, were in the service of the States General. They were called to England at the time of the Monmouth Rebellion but returned to the Continent when that trouble was over. These were the men who were to return to England later, but when James made a second call for them in 1688 he was refused.

MUSIC

Although the numbers of troops were small, little opportunity was lost in making a brave show with musicians. Trumpeters and drummers served as necessary adjuncts on special occasions when an impression was to be made. Abroad, these musicians were unavowedly in the livery of their commanding officer. In the United Kingdom this allegiance was not so apparent but at least the King's own men did wear the Royal livery of red and blue, which although the same as the fighting man, was distinguished by a profusion of lace and embroidery. At James's Coronation the trumpeters and drummers appeared in their State dress. The trumpets were adorned with banners fully embroidered with the Royal Coat of arms and cherubs. The kettle drums also had similar banners and one saw the unusual method of carrying the kettle drums on foot. One man trudged with his back bent and carrying the two drums by means of a strap and had little enjoyment of the procession, while the drummer walked behind free and untrammelled to strike the skins whenever he thought appropriate. The King's letters appeared on the chest and hanging sleeves were worn. A sword at the side lent a martial appearance, but the respectful absence of head-dress was uncommon although little headgear seems necessary with a hair style that involved so elaborate a mass of curls. Head-dresses were worn; either the broadbrimmed black hat properly laced and ornamented or the jockey cap. This peculiarly shaped head-dress was covered with dark velvet and survives, slightly altered, to the present day.

THE REBELLION 1685—1688

Besides the Royal forces there were other military units in the Kingdom in this reign. When James II came to the throne he openly favoured the Catholic religion. James, Duke of Monmouth, taking advantage of the tide of public feeling, set himself up as King, and operating in the West Country, organized large forces against the legal King. The latter hastily raised new forces, but in the meanwhile Monmouth's army began to move around the countryside. It included some six hundred horsemen known as Grey's Horse and presumably followed the current practice and appeared as light-armed cuirassiers, for such armour was found abandoned after the battle of Sedgemoor.

The infantry were known respectively as the Blue Regiment, the White Regiment, the Red Regiment, the Green and the Yellow; these were no doubt named after the flags or colours, but may have referred also to the colour of the facings or other distinctions. We know that red coats were worn by the rebels because they were mistaken for the Royalist troops. Many of the local Militia soldiers joined Monmouth's cause and they too would have worn red coats. The similarity of the opposing forces led to the necessity of a field sign: the distinguishing sign of the rebel army was a green bough in the hat. Field words were also used for recognition purposes, and it may be that Monmouth's men did not have all the uniforms that they may have wished, and looked no more than armed peasants.

Weapons were scarce and hastily constructed arms were brought into use. Scythes on poles, miners' picks and forks as well as flails and bludgeons were found from civilian sources. Of Monmouth's own personal adornment, items of which are still preserved and said to have been used during the rebellion, there is a plume of black ostrich feathers, a silver buckle, a gold thread button from his cloak and a pair of gauntlets. These do not indicate a very military dress but he is said to have led the foot battalions into battle with a pike in his hand. But with the crushing defeat, the rebels faded away and little knowledge of their appearance remains.

CHAPTER III

STUARTS (PART 2)—WILLIAM III TO QUEEN ANNE

1688—1714

WILLIAM III 1688—1702

CAVALRY

WILLIAM of Orange was requested to come to England and take over the Kingdom. His wife Mary, being a daughter of James II, gave him a reason based on relationship, but the careful Prince did not move until he was very sure of his reception. When he did land at Brixham (note the choice of the sympathetic West Country) he was accompanied not only by his own troops but also by the English troops in the Netherlands service. Apart from some minor skirmishing, the change of power was soon effected. Had pitched battle been attempted it is doubtful whether the home forces could have been victorious for not only were the invaders numerous, but well equipped.

The Dutch troops which William brought with him stayed to fight for his cause in Ireland, and later to remain in the country as part of his standing army. William had his own Life Guard or *Gardes du Corps* and when taken on the establishment, they replaced the old fourth troop of Lord Dover which had gone over to James. The dress of this troop looked quite English, having crimson coats with dark blue linings and facings. The contemporary oil-painting preserved in the Palace at Hampton Court, shows them in red cloaks with black bows to their white cravats. The hats are grey with yellow tape or lace on the edge of the brim. The steel of the cuirasses can be seen through the opening of the cloaks. The barrels of their muskets or carbines are polished. Many grey horses are to be noted in the troop. One officer appears to be in a cloth of gold coat and his black hat has gold lace and red feathers. The trumpeters have white coats with black loops and white feathers in their hats.

There is also a Regiment of Horse Guards known as the *Gardes te Paard* which numbered some 480 men under the command of William Bentinck. These men are also shown in the same oil-painting at Hampton Court, but they are clad in blue coats and wear plain black hats. A portrait of William III apparently shows this regiment in the background, but here the hats are buff laced with gold; this may indicate a change of fashion just as we know the trumpeters later had crimson coats heavily laced with gold and silver. This regiment also fought in Ireland where it is said that the garrison of Waterford 'blew up in a mine the whole Dutch Guard of Horse'. They were, however, not wiped out and continued on the establishment until nearly the end of the century when they returned to Holland with the remainder of the Dutch troops.

The entry of the Prince of Orange into Exeter was striking, if we can credit the accounts of the time. The Earl of Macclesfield led a troop of two hundred horsemen equipped with bright armour consisting of headpieces and cuirasses. They were accompanied by 'two hundred Blacks brought from the Plantations of the Netherlands in America' who were dressed in fur-lined embroidered caps ornamented with plumes of white feathers. Another picturesque body was the Dragoon Regiment of the Duke of Courlander who were called 'Finlanders or Laplanders in Bearskins taken from the wild Beasts they had slain, the common Habit of the cold Climat, with black armour and broad Flaming Swords.' The oil-painting at Hampton Court shows a body of horsemen in black with fur-edged caps having long flying hoods. These may be the same troops but they did not remain long in England.

Apart from the volunteer cavalry under the command of the Earl of Macclesfield, others were willing to serve William's cause. Thus on 31 December 1688, the Earl of Devonshire was given a commission to raise a regiment of Horse; this was ranked as the Tenth Horse and later became the Seventh Dragoon Guards. It would appear that at first a blue uniform was chosen in compliment to the Dutch colour, for 153 dark blue coats lined with white flannel were furnished to the Earl of Devonshire at this time. By 1690 the uniform had changed to red, still lined with white. When the famous black facings were adopted and gave them the nickname of the Black Horse, is not clear, but it is interesting to note that the first two colonels of the regiment had black and white as the main colours in their coat of arms. The white has been noted already as linings, but it is not until forty years later that we know black velvet is being used for facings.

Although the early abdication of James seemed to presage an easy change of occupant to the Throne, the outbreak of the war in Ireland led to the creation of new regiments. Independent troops of militia were regimented together and one such was that formed in Inniskilling under Colonel Wolsley and having twenty-five troops. This body was split into the 1st and 2nd Inniskilling Regiments of Horse and although all wore red coats, the 1st Regiment had linings of red and the 2nd of green. Their red cloaks were lined with similar distinctions and red breeches were also worn. Another regiment was created from the five troops of horse made up from soldiers trapped in Londonderry during the siege and placed under the command of the Governor, Colonel H. Baker.

Armour which had been falling out of favour was ordered in December 1691, to be provided for the regiments of Horse serving in Flanders. With back, breast and head-piece, the troopers must have presented a similar appearance to the cuirassiers of Bavaria and Austria. A list of clothing for a regiment of horse in 1695 quotes coats of crimson cloth, but specifies cloaks of red cloth.

DRAGOONS 1688—1702

William brought many regiments of dragoons with him on his entry into the Kingdom, but for the most part they were foreigners and soon left the country and so had little effect on the dress of English dragoons. Scotland raised several independent troops of dragoons to support the new King's cause, and these were eventually grouped together or regimented. Two such regiments were those of Richard Cunningham and of Conyngham. Although these regiments were reduced in 1714 they were re-raised as the 7th and

8th Dragoons, now known as the 7th Queen's Own Hussars and the 8th King's Royal Irish Hussars.

The dragoon was becoming more and more a cavalryman and not just an infantryman mounted for transport reasons only. One step which gave the dragoon a higher status came when he acquired some of the glamour of the newly raised grenadiers. The grenade pouch became part of the equipment of the dragoon, which also brought about a modification of the head-dress for it was inconvenient to throw a grenade in a hat. The broad-brimmed hat gave way to a dragoon cap with a pendant cloth bag as can be seen in the bills of the time. The infantryman wore shoes and stockings, the horseman had high stiffened boots and so the dragoon wore something in between—high boots, but of a soft leather which permitted a certain amount of freedom when dismounted.

The very name of dragoon indicates that the weapon he used was a musket or carbine and, although swords were issued, they were not used yet as the battle weapon in the same manner as those in Horse regiments. Heavy cavalry were noted for their crimson coats, but Northcote's dragoons followed this practice by having crimson coats faced with green. A sergeant of this regiment had silver lace down the seams and brass buttons.

Colonel James Wynn and Sir Albert Conyngham both organized regiments of dragoons in Inniskilling during the Irish wars, and these two regiments became the 5th and 6th Dragoons, more modern descendants being the Royal Irish Lancers and the Inniskilling Dragoons.

INFANTRY 1688—1702

William brought with him the English and Scottish infantry regiments which had served side by side with the Dutch—the troops for which James had asked in vain. The three English regiments were commanded respectively by Tollemache, Babbington and the Earl of Pembroke: they became the 5th Foot or the Royal Northumberland Fusiliers, the 6th Foot or the Royal Warwickshire Regiment and Cutt's which was disbanded in 1699. The three Scottish regiments were under Mackay, Ramsay and Balfour. They continued to serve the Dutch troops until disbanded late in the eighteenth century; all appear to have worn red coats. The three Scottish regiments originally may have had white facings but a list of 1689 gave Mackay's red linings. The Earl of Pembroke's Regiment wore red coats lined with 'Isabella', a shade of buff, and the grenadiers had loops of black and white. Precise evidence of the other regiments is not known, but traditionally they were yellow or orange in honour of the Prince of Orange.

William also brought with him Dutch troops like the *Garde te voet,* or Foot Guards. This regiment, some two thousand strong, accompanied him in his landing and fought in many battles in the last quarter of the seventeenth century. The uniform coat was dark blue with orange-yellow cuffs, waistcoat, breeches, and stockings. The officers also wore orange-coloured sashes around their waists instead of the red normal in England. In 1698 this regiment was ordered to be clothed in red in order to assimilate their appearance with the rest of the army. But foreign troops were not popular and they returned to Holland before the close of the King's reign.

The other various Dutch regiments mainly wore blue coats faced red or white, but certain had red coats lined buff or yellow.

A few companies of Foot in Ireland had been under the command of Arthur, Earl of Granard, in 1684, and at the time of the Irish War were transferred to the English establishment under Lord Forbes. This regiment of Foot became the eighteenth in precedence and known as the Royal Irish. Troops were raised in great numbers for James when he took the war to Ireland, but one must not forget that there were also many volunteers, especially in the North, for King William's cause. In Inniskilling three regiments were formed, the first being under Colonel Zach. Tiffin; the second under Col Thos Lloyd and the third under Col Gustavus Hamilton. Lists of clothing in 1689 show that these men (the first regiment later became the 27th Foot or Royal Inniskilling Fusiliers) were to be issued with red coats, no doubt with blue linings and breeches of the same colour. A doubt arises as to whether the clothing was actually issued, as a confidential inspection report of 1689 speaks of them as not clothed. White coats were also ordered for all as surtouts, and the officers were distinguished by having blue coats.

The blue coat besides being a distinction of the Dutch troops, was also adopted in compliment to the new King and newly raised troops took this sombre hue. A newsletter of April 1689 said that all the Royal Regiments were clad in blue and ready to march to Ireland. Colonel Fleming writing in July of the same year, tells us that 'all the soldiers and staff officers in our regiment must have new hats, coats, breeches, stockings all of blue, new buff belts, new scabbards to their swords and sashes.' Newly raised regiments were Lord Herbert's Welshmen (later the Royal Welch Fusiliers), Deering's regiment, Lord Lisburne's Foot (later Coote's), Ingoldsby's from Staffordshire and the Duke of Bolton's—all of whom wore blue coats. White linings were worn by Lord Herbert's men, orange by Lord Lisburne's and no doubt the others had their own hues.

Red coats were soon taken into wear again and even captured clothing was worn. When the Jacobites were defeated at Belturbet on 18 June 1689, it was agreed that they should surrender their red coats, but only sufficient were available to clothe two companies as the rest were new levies clad in grey coats. These grey coats were also worn by the Inniskilling troops, for a contemporary writer speaking of their part in a skirmish near Dundalk 1689, informs us that 'every man of them stripped off his coat, so that instead of a grey regiment they appeared in white, being their usual way of fighting to enable them for better action in the service.' Grey coats were worn by Lord Castleton's Regiment of Foot. These apparently had purple facings, for the drummers wore coats of this colour. Although a clothing contract quotes grey breeches for the drummers, red breeches are mentioned in a deserters' notice. The Jacobites also wore grey coats as might be expected, for they were fighting side by side with the French who were clad in off-white or white coats.

A list of the Army at Tillroy Camp 1689, gave the regiment later known as the 16th Foot, a red uniform lined with red, but a list of the troops at Gerpines camp 1691, gave the lining as white which is what one would expect for a regiment raised by an ex-officer of the Royal Scots.

The Earl of Mar's Fusiliers changed from the Scots establishment to the English in 1689, and later became the 21st Regiment of Foot or the Royal Scots Fusiliers. Thus at Tillroy camp, now under O'ffarrell, they are noted as wearing red coats lined with red, a fact which is repeated in a list of 1691. The nickname of this regiment gives a clue to their netherwear for they were called the Earl of Mar's Greybreeks. Regarding the dress of fusiliers, a command was sent to troops on the English establishment in December 1695, regarding alterations which had 'introduced in our army contrary to our Royal intentions', and that 'none of our regiments or companies of foot do wear capps, excepting only the Royal Regiment of Fuzileers, the Regiment of Scots Fuzileers and the grenadiers of each respective regiment.'

A series of bills gives us much information as to the clothing of a regiment raised in Scotland in 1694 by Lord Lindsay. The men wore coats of white Galloway cloth, the grenadiers being distinguished by forty-five loops on each coat. The sergeants wore stone-grey cloth coats, and the twenty-five drummers had red cloth coats faced with blue cloth and also laced with blue. The sergeants wore red breeches and hose, the sentinels or men, white breeches and red hose, while the drummers had blue breeches and hose. White and black double cravats were worn, but the sergeants also had ones of red, and the drummers cravats of blue. The drummers' caps were faced with blue and the Drum-Major's was made finer than the rest. The regiment appears to have been equipped as a fusilier regiment without any pikemen, for the privates had caps for head-dress as did the sergeants, although the latter's were better made. The equipment and waist-belts were made of buff leather and each grenadier's belt and bag had a badge.

The close-fitting long coat worn in James's reign was continued in the new King's reign and the buttons down the front were left undone to reveal the waistcoat, the shirt and the cravats. The double cravats now being worn were no doubt popularized by the troops of William. The British troops had favoured a plain white neckcloth, sometimes laced or fringed, but abroad, red or black cravats had been worn, no doubt as being better suited not to show the dirt and toil of service. French dragoons had worn white and blue cravats combined.

Although it might appear that each regiment was dressed in a distinctive uniform, the same dress was sometimes applicable to two regiments. A letter written in 1691 begged that if Beaumont's Regiment (the 8th Foot later) was broken, it might be broke into Colonel Hastings Regiment (later 13th Foot) 'they being the same livery'—red with yellow linings. The buying and selling of clothing and equipment of disbanded regiments was popular, for it not only helped to clear up the complicated debts of the regiment closing down but helped another regiment to purchase 'new' material at a reduced price.

Although we know that some infantry officers wore blue coats lined with blue in 1692, as in the case of Brigadier Stewart's (later 9th Foot), they also had all scarlet or all crimson coats as in G. Hamilton's 1691, Bellaysis' 1692 and Drogheda's 1692. The lace seems to have altered with the rank of the officers, silver for the subalterns and gold for the higher ranks. Thus officers did not display any strong regimental connexion, a fact which must have been helpful to their purses. Promotion was achieved by purchase and if one quickly took up a vacancy in another regiment, it was useful to have a uniform which agreed with the other officers and was not a new expense.

MUSIC

Many examples are available in this reign of the practice of drummers wearing coats of 'reversed colours', that is to say a coat of the colour of the privates' facings but with cuffs and linings of red, the normal coat colour. For example, a drummer of Hastings' regiment (later the 13th Foot) in 1692 is noted as having a yellow coat laced, and lined red. The drummers of Farrington's regiment were newly raised in 1694 and later became known as the 29th or Worcestershire Regiment. They had '26 surtout coats of yellow kersey faced with blue bays.' Lord Castleton's regiment, according to a clothing warrant of 1693, were to have purple coats with badges and grey breeches.

Hautboys or oboe players are occasionally mentioned: one in 1696, of the regiment which was to become the 10th Foot, had a blue coat lined with red, and down all the seams was a narrow silver lace; he wore red stockings and breeches and besides having silver lace on his hat, his waistbelt was laced with silver. A hautbois of Coote's regiment in 1692 wore a green coat lined with orange, very much decorated with orange chain lace on the seams, six dozen froggings of lace, white metal buttons and badges as well.

QUEEN ANNE 1702—1714

STAFF AND OFFICERS

Valuable information of the uniforms of the troops of Marlborough's army comes down to us in a set of tapestries made at the Duke's instructions, and still preserved to the present day in his ancestral home, Blenheim Palace. They were designed by L. de Hondt and Ludocus de Vos, Belgian artists, and woven only a few years after the actual events. A request was made by the Duke in 1713 for the Duchess to pass through Brussels to note the progress being made in the manufacture.

The Duke of Marlborough figures prominently in many of the tapestries. His scarlet coat had gold lace down the sleeve seams, round the pockets and elsewhere; a waist sash is worn around his middle. Over his left shoulder he wears the sash of the Order of the Bath and in his right hand he usually carries a baton—the sign of his command. Distinctive features of the Duke's dress are the high gaiters which he wears on horseback. Normally, mounted officers wore high stiffened jack-boots, but in these tapestries Churchill is shown with stiff gaiters coming well above the knee and buttoned all the way down; spurs are worn on top of them. Such a dress for an officer must be correct for we know of the close watch the Duke kept on these tapestries.

Staff officers are shown in pictures and tapestries as wearing an all red or all blue coat, and the profuse lace is either gold or silver. Even officers in charge of regiments did not always wear the regimental dress and could easily be confused with civilians, who not only sported a dress of military cut, but also carried a sword. The exact method of suspension for the sword of an officer is not clear; indeed in some cases the hilt of the sword suddenly appears above the left side pocket and the scabbard peeps out below the skirt as though the sidearm is pushed through a hole in the coat. The side of the coats of this period was made to button up and thus the sword could go through the slit, but the waist belt which must have been worn under the waistcoat is rarely shown.

The hats worn by staff officers are turned up on three sides and have lace around the brim; sometimes this is plain, in others it is fancy and scalloped; the turn-up on the left side is secured by a loop and a button. In none of the Marlborough tapestries is a cockade shown, although cockades are invariably shown in the hats depicted in the murals in Marlborough House. It may be that the murals were painted in the reign of the Georges when the black cockade was worn. Although a fringe of feathers was worn in the brim of some officers' hats, the tapestries depict hats without them in most cases. At the surrender of Lille in 1708, Marlborough is shown with a feather fringe going all around the brim.

In the tapestries of Donauwerth and Bouchain are shown footmen clad in fringed clothing. These were the runners used by the Duke of Marlborough to carry messages of lesser importance and only for short distances. The costume is a little reminiscent of the dress of the American backwoodsmen. As a sign of their authority these runners carried long staves with brass heads. Their little jockey caps appear to have golden tassels.

CAVALRY 1702—1714

On one of the wall paintings in the Taniers or Malplaquet Staircase in Marlborough House in Pall Mall, are cavalrymen of the Life Guards. The lacing on the cuffs and general style agrees with an engraving of the funeral of Marlborough where the Life Guards are similarly dressed but with the addition of a crown and garter on the housings. The three-cornered hat has yellow or gold lace. The red coat has blue cuffs and yellow or gold lace on the seams and buttonholes. A blue bandolier to take the swivel of the firearm has three rows of lace. A blue and red cloak is rolled behind the saddle; the blue housings have gold lace and fringe.

It is strange that for all the fighting and number of troops that existed in Queen Anne's time, there is very little precise information regarding individual regiments, a sad lack for this most colourful period. One scrap of information comes from a deserter's report and tells us that Cadogan's Horse (now the 5th Irish Dragoon Guards) in 1711 wore red coats faced with green, had green waistcoats and shag breeches. The sleeves of the coat of this particular deserter were laced with broad silver lace and his hat also had silver lace. Under his saddle was a green horse cloth—that is to say a shabraque—of the regimental facings.

These campaigns brought armour back into wear and as a letter from Marlborough quotes, cuirasses were being worn in 1707 by regiments of horse. The Queen's Regiment of Horse on active service wore 'Brestpieces' which may have indicated that they wore the front piece only, as was a continental fashion. By 1714 these relics of armour were going back into store.

Dragoons were now acting more as light cavalry and not only as mounted infantrymen, but they still retained many of their earlier distinctions like drummers on horseback. The drummers and hautbois of the Scots Greys were noted as having new coats faced with blue and with slashed sleeves and collars; this means that the music of the Scots Greys did not wear coats of reversed facings. The Royal Dragoons on the other hand, *circa* 1708, had blue coats for their hautbois.

The Scots Greys having the opportunity of acquiring the clothing of Colonel Guis-cart's regiment, made it up to match their own by altering the facings to blue. The drummers of the Queen's Dragoons (later the 3rd King's Own Hussars) wore the Queen's own livery and had blue feathers in their hats. There are cavalrymen shown in the tapestry of Donauwerth which are called the Scots Greys. The men wear buff coats but the officers have scarlet and they all are mounted on grey horses. Each man carries a large fascine or bundle of branches on his saddle bow. The long lines of cavalry all converge to a point in the rear of the infantry. These fascines were to be used in filling the moat and ditches when the infantry stormed the town. The cavalrymen have their red cloaks made into long rolls and placed behind the saddles. The wide bandoliers over the left shoulders have swivel attachments to retain the firearm, the butt of which goes into a bucket.

Grenadier troops were added to some dragoon regiments. It was logical that if infantry had grenadiers then dragoons being mounted infantry should have mounted grenadiers. Although grenadier and such élite companies continued in being in the continental cavalry, they passed out of fashion in the British Army. Two regiments which kept the tradition as long as possible were the Scots Greys who eventually became entirely equipped with the grenadier head-dress and the other, the 5th or Royal Irish Dragoons, who late in the eighteenth century made claims to this distinctive item of dress.

The musicians of cavalry regiments when depicted are shown in heavy regiments with one kettledrummer and two trumpeters, thus following closely the practice of the earlier Civil War times.

INFANTRY 1702—1714

The Foot Guards figured prominently in Marlborough's campaigns and they appear to good effect in the tapestries and wall-paintings. The long red coats have buttons and large loops all the way down the front; the wide cuffs have lace around the tops and the buttons which keep the cuffs turned back also have large loops; the horizontal pocket-flaps, placed low at the sides have similar loops and on the small of the back just below the waistbelt are two pairs of loops. The wide loose skirts of these coats permit full freedom to the lower limbs. A cape or collar is a feature of the dress of these guardsmen and the upper part of the coat which is left unbuttoned, is faced with blue cloth and turns back slightly giving promise to the elaborate revers or lapels which developed a few years later.

A newspaper account of 1712 describes a soldier of the Coldstream Guards as being in regimental clothing, red lined with blue and brass buttons, waistcoat lined with yellow and his hat with yellow worsted lace. The grenadiers wore their specially embroidered caps with the low blue turn-ups and the pointed fronts also of blue; the small turn-up had embroidered on it a flaming grenade or crossed swords; the main frontlet had a crown and below that the red cross on a white ground in the midst of an eight-pointed star; at the uppermost tip was a tassel or tuft of short threads. The red waistcoat was also looped with lace at the buttonholes. From the left shoulder hung the cartouch belt of buff leather, while the cartouch pouch itself had a black leather flap with a large device of the Garter star on it. The sword was suspended from a waistbelt closed in front with a large brass buckle. The tapestries show guardsmen in gaiters and the wall-paintings favour the white hose, caught below the knees with garters. Black shoes with high tongues and fastening with buckles were the common footwear. The grenadier sergeant carried a halberd, had a sash around his waist and had lace or braid around his arm-holes, down his back and elsewhere. Officers had waist sashes, gold lace on the seams and down the fronts of the coats.

Queen Anne was quoted in later years as being the first monarch to make regulations on the issue of clothing, but these refer to the scale of issue rather than the distinction between regiments. In 1706 it was laid down that a well-lined coat was to be issued and to serve the following year as a waistcoat. A pair of kersey breeches, a pair of shoes, a good shirt, a neckcloth and a hat well laced were the remainder of the minimum requirements. This issue was improved in later years but it was a good beginning to protect the common soldier. Sergeants and drummers were to be clothed after the same manner but everything was to be of its kind better. The recruits were to be supplied with a new waistcoat, one shirt and one neckcloth more than the old soldiers 'who have some linen before hand'.

The infantry wore coats of the style already described for the Foot Guards but with their own distinctive facings and less lace. Infantry hats are not always shown as being bound with tape on the edge of the brim, although later this was the invariable practice. The buff equipment was similar and although some pouch flaps had a cypher of a device, poorer regiments had to be content with a plain flap.

The grenadiers are always shown as leading the main mass of the infantry with three regimental colours following behind them. One tapestry shows a grenadier with a camp kettle slung on his left hip, a homely though necessary adjunct in wartime. Grenadier caps while still following the general pattern, had variations: the main bag or head covering was of red cloth, the small back and front turn-up as well as the frontlet were of the facing colours. While the smaller turn-up was used to diplay swords, muskets, grenades, laurels and the like, the main frontlet was utilized to display the devices of the Colonel. Here might be embroidered the charge from his coat of arms, the crest of one so entitled or even the full coat of arms from a rich or lordly Colonel. The Colonel, being not only the 'father' of a regiment but also the head of commerical enterprise, could provide his troops with such splendour as he thought he could afford and the grenadier caps, the drums and the regimental colours were the places where he could display his ownership.

Fur caps were also worn by grenadiers at this period, but in Britain the embroidered cloth cap was the fashion until later in the century. There is an exception in the case of a deserter from the grenadier company of Wynn's regiment who had a cap faced with bear skin, but others in the regiment had red cloth caps faced with yellow and a wolf's head embroidered thereon.

The discontinuance of the pike as a weapon of war led to a change in the composition in infantry regiments. For some time past it had been common to raise regiments without pikemen. Regiments raised for sea-service had no pikes and those regiments converted to marines had their pikes taken away. But the large expense of fire-arms compared with the few pence necessary for a pike made the general change-over a slow and unattractive process for those who had to foot the bills. Fusiliers to guard the artillery were permitted the dearer weapon and as the match-lock went out of fashion so entire regiments equipped with fusils appeared. The sling on the fusil permitted the fire-arm to be slung on the back but also made the wearing of a hat difficult: thus the early fusiliers wore caps similar to the grenadiers. Later when the fusil became the common weapon, existing regiments did not change their hat for a cap and thus the term fusilier became one of tradition rather than distinction of service.

MUSIC

To give the marching rhythm to infantry marching from place to place all over Europe was the duty of drummers. The two men per company carried much larger drums than now in use. The drummers of Royal regiments wore the same red coat as the infantry soldier because both wore the livery of the Monarch. The other line regiments favoured the reversed colour system, an example being that of Lord Lucas's regiment in 1702 when the drummer wore a light grey coat lined with red, the reverse of the men's coat, red faced with grey. Red breeches and waistcoats were also worn by these drummers and the coats had crimson worsted loops and white metal buttons. On the back of the coats were embroidered the devices of the colonel, in this case a coronet and a griffin's head. The drummers in the Marlborough pictures show the hat still being worn, a habit which was to change later.

CHAPTER IV

HANOVERIANS (PART 1)—GEORGE I AND GEORGE II

1714—1760

GEORGE I 1714—1727

THE arrival of George of Hanover to be the King of Great Britain was the prelude to the introduction of certain continental fashions in the way of army life; the Hanoverian army had for many years past made its own mark in German history and it is little wonder that the new King felt some of its idiosyncrasies were worth introducing. From the uniform point of view the widespread use of the White Horse and the black cockade were two well-known features, persisting even to the present day; the White Horse being part of the Arms of Hanover appeared on head-dresses and on regimental colours and standards; the black cockade was a general feature of the cocked hats and still appears on military cocked hats, to say nothing of private head-dresses. Even the adoption of the blue coat for the Artillery seems to be a Hanoverian idea. Unfortunately the documentary evidence of clothing from a regimental point of view is very small, in fact hardly anything from government sources and the evidence must be found from pictures, and odd scraps of information.

A portrait which exists of William P. Ashurst shows an unusual dress for the King's Own Regiment of Horse (later King's Dragoon Guards) in this reign. The officer is mounted and wears a long scarlet coat with a yellow waistcoat and breeches. Silver lace and buttons make a truly military appearance but the peculiar long cuffs which button up to the crook of the arms are most unusual; but as the coat is entirely red without any use of yellow distinctions, it may be an informal garment.

The dress of the dragoons was assuming a more distinct fashion and gradually departed from that of the infantry. One item of dress is noted in this reign: the shoulder-knot. In 1715 a contract for the clothing of the Earl of Stair's Dragoons (later the Royal Scots Greys) noted shoulder-knots of silk for the six sergeants and the 'hautboys, Drums, Corporals and Private Dragoons' all had this showy appendage. But a more picturesque regiment was that which became the 4th Dragoons, for a newsletter of November 1715 stated that the writer 'scarce thought there is a more showy regiment in Europe'. There were six companies of dragoons which were drawn up in two squadrons and 'each company had a farrier, or hatchet man, with a very high black furred cap on, and a pock [pocket or bag] hanging behind tipped with fur. Instead of a sword, they had a saw at their side, and a shovel in place of their slinged carbine. They carried axes in their hands, and a hatchet under their belt instead of pistols. There were fixed two large things likest to muff cases where their horseshoes and nails were. They have clean white aprons and white gloves, and rode upon good grey horses. The six Drummers were Moors, with brass drums, and the Hautboys and they rode upon grey horses'.

The writer further added that never in his life had he seen so many fine black horses. 'The officers' led horses were extraordinarily fine, with fine decks of different skins to cover them. There was something very shog and neat in the appearance of the regiment as footmen and the servants that led the deck horses'.

INFANTRY 1714—1727

There is little direct pictorial evidence of infantry dress of this reign although the wall-paintings in Marlborough House may depict more accurately the dress of this time rather than the wars of Marlborough, which were becoming history. There are, however, several objects which show the uniform well. Two leaden figures said to have been in the Old Chelsea Bun-House are in existence, as is a third lead figure recently acquired by the Scottish United Services Museum. The figures are as boy-soldiers and show coats without lapels or turnbacks to the skirts. From the cloth caps they wear they may be grenadiers of a Scottish regiment or even fusiliers in a Scottish unit, possibly in Dutch service. Hogarth made sketches of the Bun-House figures but made them appear as grenadiers of the later Georgian pattern, so they may have been altered by paint at a later date. Being about three feet high these figures have certain moulded features which have not been changed. The cloth cap has a central portion finishing in a tassel, then comes a turned-up front on which is moulded a large thistle—not crowned as one would expect if the regiment was on the British establishment—and below that is a small flap; this small flap is painted plain blue in modern times but once it had the White Horse of Hanover. The wide-skirted red coats have blue cuffs although they have a greenish tinge, possibly due to age. The front of the coats are buttoned down to the lowest edge of the skirts and loops to correspond are on the left side; there are buttons to the side pleats and the side pocket-flaps are loose with buttons below; the back slit has loops of lace strengthening it at the top. The hose are gartered below the knees and the light-coloured stockings are ornamented with clocks.

The waistbelt holding the sword and the pouchbelt are both of narrow leather unlike the wider pattern which came in later. The sword has a stout knuckle-bow and is straight. At the open neck can be observed the white shirt which has a pleated ruffle. It was in 1718 that Colonel Crosby ordered every private soldier in his regiment, the 18th Foot, to wear ruffles at the bosoms and sleeves of their shirts, which custom was never known before in England according to a contemporary journal.

The ordinary soldiery were dressed much the same but with three-cornered hats. A contemporary drawing of the Tower of London in 1720 shows the coat with double loops at the back and the cuffs turned back low on the forearm.

A good representation of grenadiers *circa* 1725 is that of men of the Buffs depicted in enamel on the memorial tablet of Sir Charles Wills in Westminster Abbey. The two supporters to this gentleman's coat of arms hold lighted grenades in their hands. The red coats are open to the waist revealing red waistcoats; the front of the coat does not yet have revers but has loops on both sides down to the waistbelt. The very pale buff of the regimental distinction is on the cuffs, the belts, the front of the cap and on the buttoned gaiters, but this latter might be artistic portrayal. The most interesting feature is the grenadier cap. The little flap is buff with a black grenade spouting red flames: the large front has the crest of the Wills family—a demi-griffin azure, a coronet or about the neck, holding in its claws a battle axe or, the whole being placed on an argent and azure wreath. The coat of arms of Sir Charles Wills included three griffins passant, wings expanded azure. These creatures are very reminiscent of the dragon which we know nowadays as the badge of this regiment.

The wearing of part of the Colonel's coat of arms on the head-dress was not only carried out by grenadiers and fusiliers but also by marines. Shannon's Marines (later the 25th Foot) were in Deal in 1715 and in a cellar was found a chest of cutlasses and grenadier caps, the crest being a 'tigers head on yellow on the front of the caps'. Actually it should have been a lion's head, for that was the crest of the Shannon family. A few years later a consignment of material for the same regiment included 124$^{1}/_{2}$ yards of gold-coloured cloth for facing the sleeves of the said regiment, which still seems to indicate that the lapels had not been introduced. The transport of cloth and material gives us useful information as to other regiments. In 1726 we learn that Lord John Kerr's regiment (later the 31st Foot) had scarlet cloth, and buff cloth with linings of scarlet and buff shalloon with silver lace and trimmings. Another regiment, that of Colonel Lanoe (later the 36th Foot) had buff cloth for facings, buff shalloon for linings and silver lace and buttons.

Life-size cut-out figures of soldiers were popular during the first half of the eighteenth century: there are references to about half a dozen different examples of these throughout the country and in every case the description is that of a grenadier. They are variously called picture boards to fill a corner, a fireplace ornament or even a target for musket practice. But there remains a more useful purpose—that of recruiting. When the small recruiting parties toured the towns and the countryside looking for likely men, the group could be as little as an officer, a drummer and an odd man. The officer would take up his abode at an hotel while waiting for men to come along to take the King's shilling. A silent wooden sentinel placed outside a door would indicate the nature of the business to be transacted. The fact that many of these picture board figures were found at hotels seems to indicate that they had been abandoned by recruiting parties. The grenadier would be chosen as the most showy soldier at that time.

Some picture boards remained in private hands, where they may have come by purchase or by virtue of a previous connexion with a regiment. Sir Henry Dryden in the nineteenth century had one of these full-scale soldiers in Georgian dress. The uniform depicted appeared to be that of the 3rd or Scots Guards, although it may be that over-painting may have been applied to convert it into that regiment. The large buttons grouped in threes, a practice which was not adopted until many years later, look as though they are added, especially as they are placed on top of the grenadier pouch. The high-fronted red-cloth cap has the cypher 'GR' on the little flap and the main device below the crown is the St Andrew's Star. The full-skirted red coat has Royal blue for the linings and cuffs; although the fronts of the coat are open the turned-back lapels are not yet developed. The single-breasted coat is buttoned down to the bottom; the loops on this and the cuffs are white and square-ended. The waistcoat is red, the white stockings are gartered below the knee and the footwear is buckled shoes. The grenade pouch had the 'GR' cypher within foliage and the shirt does not have a ruffle. The 'flaming' sword with its basket or enclosed hilt has the wide blade associated with the shable.

A pair of picture boards which afford the most important information are those preserved at the Depot of the Queen's Royal Regiment. They had been in hotels in Carlisle for many years but were eventually purchased by a Colonel of the Regiment and returned to the appropriate home. Once again they are grenadiers and as such contain the details which identify the regiment and place a date. The little flap instead of bearing the White Horse as in all other English line regiments, has a white lamb and the motto around the edge is *Pristinæ Virtutis Memor* which applies to the Queen's alone. The front of the cap is red and carries the device of the three white feathers, the coronet and motto *Ich Dien,* usually taken to indicate the Prince of Wales, but in this case the Princess of Wales, whose title the regiment bore from 1715 until 1727 when she became Queen: thus the date is placed in the reign of George I. The red coat has facings which prior to cleaning, appeared as green, but after restoration appeared blue. It is not the deep cuffs which claim our attention so much as the definite plastron-shaped lapels. These innovations are edged with white braid and the buttonholes are also looped in pairs. The regimental lace or braid figures largely on the pockets and cuffs; this is white with the green, now blue, threads running through it. The feet are not very clear and so it is difficult to decide whether gaiters or hose is being worn. The tall swelling grenadier cap is much different from the cap of Queen Anne's time and is more like that worn later in the century. The grenade pouch is now plain without embroidery, but the bayonet is still worn hanging in front.

The buttoning of the coat to the bottom hem is discontinued, a possible saving of money and buttons at the waist were sufficient to keep the coat fastened.

GEORGE II 1727—1760

It has been noted that George II on coming to the throne continued the reforms begun by his father but concentrated on the uniform aspect, possibly in an attempt to vie with his brother-in-law, Frederick William of Prussia, who was considered at that time 'the greatest military tailor in Europe'. George came to the throne in June 1727, and by October an order had been issued to the effect that 'the King being desirous that all his regiments should have a fixed clothing and that each regiment should differ in their facings or otherwise . . . . the several Colonels to consult together and prepare patterns before they make up the next clothing which they are to show His Majesty and then orders will be given that the regiments continue that clothing and that they do not presume to make any alteration whosoever shall come at the head of the corps.'

New clothing was to be put on by the Army on 11 June 1728, the Accession Day, and some of the new regulated clothing might have been on view for the first time. As the reign went on so the regulations increased, but they will be dealt with in their proper place.

HOUSEHOLD CAVALRY 1727—1760

Although much activity went on in the military world, the regulations were more concerned with the quantity to be issued per man. But much work must have been done behind the scenes, for it was apparently the Duke of Cumberland who had the idea of

PLATE 42. 15th Light Dragoons, 1760. Print by F. Jeffreys.

PLATE 43. George III reviewing the Composite Battalion of Foot Guards on Wimbledon Common, 1788

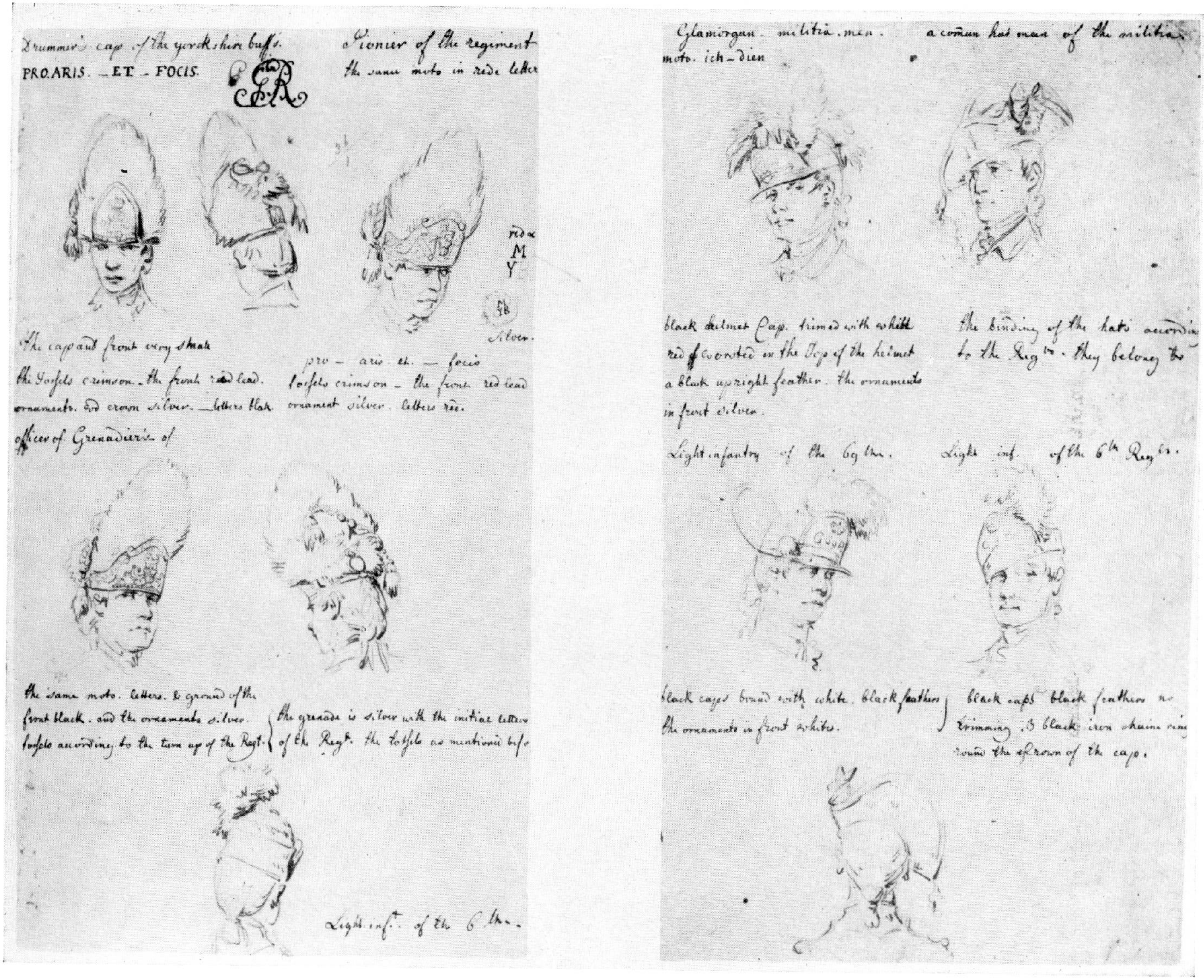

British Museum

PLATE 44. Sketches of Infantry, 1778, by P. J. de Loutherbourg.

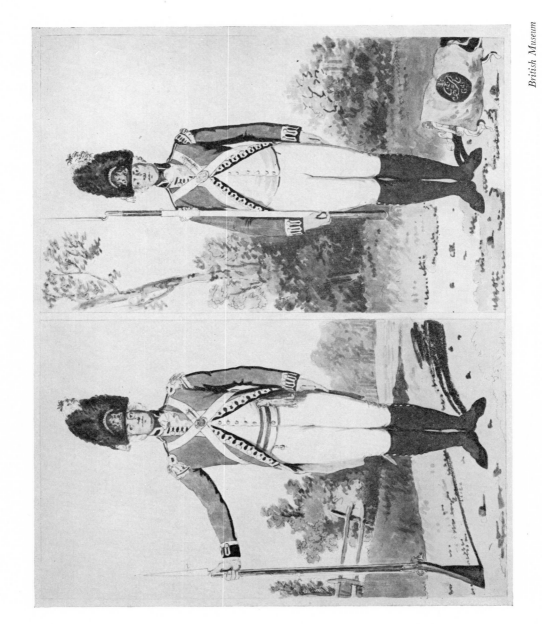

PLATE 45. 1st Foot Guards. Grenadier serjeant and grenadier, 1792. Print by E. Dayes and T. Kirk.

setting on record the uniform of each unit in the army. Thus a fine series of copper plates were engraved and hand coloured to represent a man from each regiment of cavalry and infantry. These were bound into a book and named *A Representation of the Cloathing of His Majesty's Household and all the forces upon the Establishments of Great Britain and Ireland 1742*. The date on this title page is no doubt that of the completed work but the compilation must have begun many months previously for the detail in the lace, arrangement of buttons and other minutæ, must have involved a vast amount of work.

The four troops of Horse Guards and the two troops of Horse Grenadier Guards take precedence of the other cavalry as might be expected. Then follow the Royal Horse Guards (the Blues) then known as the 1st Regiment of Horse, the remaining seven regiments of Horse, later converted to Dragoon Guards and the twelve regiments of Dragoons in being at that time complete the cavalry.

This work shows only the dress of other ranks and for that of officers we have to look elsewhere. Portraits which have been preserved in families and elsewhere show the officers dressed more like private gentlemen than fighting soldiers. The all-red coat with very full skirts was favoured. The cuffs were deep but no facing nor regimental colour was employed. Gold lace of elaborate pattern is shown on the hat, the pockets and buttonholes in a portrait of Captain J. Miller. Another officer of the same period, Captain Richard Giffard, is depicted without this lace but he wears a coat of a puce colour which may be an undress version.

The *1742 Book* shows that the troopers of the four different troops had their own distinctions. Although the same basic print is used the differences are carefully made. They all wore red coats with blue turned-back skirts and although they did not wear lapels, a small piece of blue material was turned back at the neck. Elaborate patterns of gold lace on the cuff and down the front made the coat an elegant garment.

The waistcoats and breeches were light buff in colour and above the high black boots can be seen the white knee pieces—an invention to prevent the surface of the thick breeches from being rubbed and defaced by the stiff boots; these short bands of white were fastened below the knees with string and fastened on to the breeches by means of a loop or other attachments. The distinction between the four troops were the stripes of the carbine belts: each had two stripes of the colour that had been their distinction since the last century, red for the first, white for the second, yellow for the third and blue for the fourth. The holster caps and housings were of a common pattern having gold fringe and the Royal Cypher on red inside a Garter and surmounted by a Crown, but the colour of the cloth followed the colour of the belt-stripes; these stripes were no doubt the fore-runners of the flask-cords of modern times.

In 1746 the same wave of economy which put the three regiments of Horse on a lower establishment also reduced the four troops of Horse Guards to two. Of the remaining troops the fine series of oil-paintings by David Morier painted *circa* 1751 and preserved at Windsor, show only slight differences from the pictures of 1742. The small blue patch on the collar is shown more clearly and the troopers look fatter and more prosperous but that may have only been this Swiss artist's preference. The First Troop still have the two red lines in their carbine belts but the second now has two blue stripes instead of the white. The change to blue may have indicated a link with the 4th or Scots troop with the wish to preserve a connexion with the Northern Kingdom as had been done in the case of the Second Troop of Horse Grenadier Guards.

The horse furniture of the Second Troop was now red like that of the First. The pointed loops down the front of the coat were in pairs for both the troops, although another painting said to have been made by Parrocel shows the First Troop with equally spaced loops. The lace on the furniture of the First Troop was yellow with a red central line and that of the Second was yellow with a blue line.

A series of small oil-paintings also preserved at Windsor shows a dismounted trooper of the Second Troop of Horse Guards going through the evolutions of the musket exercise. His golden loops are in pairs and his belt has two blue lines. In these pictures the coat is closed from the neck, part of the way down, but it cannot be closed all the way because of the large iron basket hilt of the sword on the waistbelt worn below the coat.

The *1742 Book* employs the same basic print for both of the Horse Grenadier Guard troops, the difference between the English and the Scots troops being quite marked. The basic dress is common—a tall embroidered grenadier cap, a full-skirted red coat with blue cuffs and turned-back skirts, pale buff waistcoats and breeches, boot cuffs or knee pieces, and stiff black boots. The embroidered caps differ; the First having a blue front, small red flap and the back all red, and the Second a red front, small blue flap and an all-blue back. The central devices are the 'GR' cypher inside the Garter with the Crown overall but the small flap of the English troop does not have the White Horse of Hanover as might be expected, but an indecipherable double scroll. The Scottish Troop, true to form, has the Thistle and appropriate motto. The right arms of the mounted grenadiers hold muskets in the advanced position permitting the cords on the right shoulder to be seen. Above the large flap of the cartridge pouch can be seen the powder horn which is secured to the belt by means of a coloured cord; the First Troop had blue flask-cords and the Second had red: these cords or strings were attached so that the powder flasks could be moved freely towards the muskets, yet fastened so that they could not be dropped or lost. The horse furniture, housings and holster caps were blue for the First and red for the Second Troop with the Cypher, Garter and Crown devices.

A portrait of Captain Hopkins of the Horse Grenadier Guards, shows him in a gold-laced hat, and in his case the blue cuffs and the small blue collar patch show clearly amid the gold lace on his red coat. The coat skirts are not turned back which seems to be a fad of officers, for the men are usually shown with the skirts turned back except for night duties, etc.

There are in the Royal Collection at Windsor several oil-paintings about 1751 of the Horse Grenadier Guards by Morier and Parrocel, which show the details of the dress very clearly. The cap of the First Troop is still blue with the 'GR' cypher and the little red flap has a grenade within a trophy of arms—this is possibly the device on the 1742 cap. The Second Troop cap is as mentioned before but the back of the cap is red with the turn-up of blue; one main difference is that the tuft which was once at the apex of the mitre now appears lower down, no doubt because the bag at the back is folded. The back view of a standing Grenadier shows that the red shoulder-strap retaining the pouch-belt is placed down the back practically on the left shoulder blade. The dress at the end of the reign was more or less the same but the horses had taken to long tails, a prelude to the fashion that was adopted soon after by the rest of the cavalry.

The Royal Regiment of Horse were still more allied to the regiments of Horse rather than Horse Guards at the beginning of the reign, but were considered a very special regiment. The King reviewed his Royal Regiment of Horse in 1728 on Datchet Common. It was, to quote a contemporary account, 'a glorious fine day and the ground we reviewed upon was like a bowling green'. The Regiment had new Trophies or Standards and trumpet banners, most of the men had new boots and horse furniture, while the officers made a good showing by having red feathers in their hats.

A picture of their dress in this reign comes in the *1742 Book* which shows a trooper in his blue coat with turned-back skirts and cuffs of the same colour. The coat is very simple in cut with yellow metal buttons. The waistcoat is red, the breeches are blue and the 'boot cuffs' are white as usual. The hat lace is indicated yellow. A red cloak is rolled behind the saddle and the housings are red with scroll embroidery and the Royal Coat of Arms on the holster caps and housings. The man is mounted on a black horse and the buff cross-belts are to be noted as having a red flask-cord running through the swivel-belt. This is for the priming horn and is a distinction which this regiment has worn up to the present day.

When some regiments of Horse were converted to Dragoon Guards in 1746, it was the old 5th Horse which became the 1st Horse. Thus the Blues lost this number and became specially honoured. They had engaged in fierce fighting on the Continent up to 1745 and then the King took them for extensive personal duties both as escorts for his journeys abroad and for attendance in the Court, thus performing the duties of a Royal Guard rather than that of a Line regiment.

The Morier painting of 1751 shows very little different in the actual dress of the man, but it is now clear that the red lapels extend to the bottom of the coat as was the fashion then for all regiments of Horse. The buff cross-belts are now made narrower and more elegant and it can be seen that two blue shoulder straps retain them in position. The waistcoat is still red and the breeches are altered to agree, being red instead of blue. In the horse furniture, however, a great change is made: although still with a red base, the elaborate foliated embroidery around the edges is discontinued and simple rows of gold lace are borne instead. The devices of the holster caps and housings are the 'GR' cypher in the Garter with the Crown on top. The horse is black in colour as is the harness.

In 1753 John, 1st Earl of Ligonier, became their Colonel and an equestrian portrait of him by Reynolds shows him in the uniform of the Blues. The long red lapels have gold edging and buttonholes in pairs; his gold-edged waistcoat, breeches and gauntlets are buff. He wears a gold knot on the right shoulder and, although he wears a cuirass beneath his coat, this is not part of the regulation dress of this regiment at the time, but rather an indication of his high rank and command. The crimson horse furniture is heavily embroidered and fringed with gold, once again indicating his rank.

The Marquis of Granby, famous for his 'bald-headed charges', became Colonel in 1760, and his portraits show a similar dress to that of the previous Colonel, the cuff still being very full and round with vertical loops and buttons to keep it fastened back. An oil-painting of the same period and prints based on it show the dress of a trooper which is very similar to the earlier Morier, but a strange omission is the red flask-cord. The men still have red breeches.

HORSE 1727—1760

In 1729 a board of senior officers proposed new regulations for clothing, but this referred mainly to length of time each article was to last. However, we learn that troopers were to have a new cloth coat well lined with serge, a waistcoat, a laced hat and a pair of large buff gloves. Other items mentioned included cloaks lined with the livery of the regiment, and buff or buff-coloured cross-belts.

In May of the same year we get details of material needed for Ligonier's Regiment (the Black Horse) for they had red cloth, black velvet, buff cloth and gold lace. It will be seen that the red coats were lined with buff, had gold lace on the sleeves, etc., while the large quantity of black velvet indicated that lapels were being worn as well at the cuffs. The 6th Horse (later 5th Dragoon Guards) in 1731 had silver lace and buttons sent to them, and the 7th Horse in 1737 had scarlet coats lined with yellow and the lapels were of yellow velvet. It will be noted that the use of velvet for facings was a distinction of horse, and this material later became the mark of Dragoon Guards regiments.

For the completest picture we next turn to the *1742 Book*. The 1st Regiment of Horse has already been dealt with as the Royal Regiment of Horse and the 2nd Regiment, the King's Own Regiment of Horse (now the King's Dragoon Guards) was dressed in a similar fashion but with the red coat, blue cuffs, linings and breeches. The distinction of Horse, a flask-cord in the belt, was in this regiment of a blue colour.

The Third Regiment, the Queen's Regiment of Horse (now the Bays) wore a red coat with white cuffs and linings, buff waistcoat and breeches. The red housings bore, instead of the Royal Arms of the previous regiment, a trophy of flags, drums and weapons. The 4th Regiment of Horse (now the Carabiniers) also wore white facings with their red coats but the hat lace and buttons of this regiment were silver colour instead of gold as had the three senior regiments. White waistcoats, red breeches, white rolled cloaks with the red edges showing, white housings with full coloured trophies were further distinctions.

The Fifth Regiment of Horse (now part of the 4/7 Dragoon Guards) wore red coats, blue cuffs, linings, waistcoats and breeches. The blue cloaks were rolled with the red edge showing. Their buff equipment had a blue flask-cord. The lace and buttons were yellow and the blue housings had the full Royal coat of arms. The 6th Horse (later the 5th Dragoon Guards) as became an Irish regiment wore green facings to their red coats. Green waistcoats, breeches and cloaks followed the usual patterns and the red housings had the embroidered trophy device.

The King's Regiment of Carabiniers (later the 6th Dragoon Guards) had light yellow as their distinctions, applying equally to facings, equipment, waistcoats, breeches, cloaks and housings, the latter having the trophies. Buttons and hat lace were white. The Eighth Regiment of Horse (later the 7th Dragoon Guards) were also known as the Black Horse and had regimental facings of black on their coats. The skirt linings were buff in the 1742 period as were the waistcoats and breeches. Buttons and hat lace were yellow.

As mentioned, 1746 saw the conversion of the Second, the Third and Fourth Horse into the First, Second and Third Dragoon Guards; the First became separate and the remaining four regiments were re-numbered the First to Fourth respectively, making such alterations as the Third Irish Horse or Carabiniers.

There was a Royal Warrant in 1751 which laid down what was to be the regulation clothing, and had been reached after years of deliberation and adjustment. It repeated the order that the lapels of Horse were to reach to the bottom of the coat; it further gave the distinctions of the First Horse as pale blue with silver, the Second as full green with gold, the Third as pale yellow with silver and the Fourth as black with gold and in all cases the buttons were to be in pairs. The waistcoats and breeches were the colouring of the facings, except that the Fourth had buff instead of black.

DRAGOON GUARDS 1727—1760

There is no doubt that the Scottish Rebellion had been an expense to the nation and the Government siezed the opportunity to economize when they reduced three regiments of Horse to Dragoon Guards, for despite the fact that the title might sound more imposing, it was a down-grade step. Regiments of Horse had originally been equipped as Cuirassiers and parallel formations on the Continent continued as such; but in the United Kingdom the equipment of Horse had lightened and that of the Dragoons had veered away from that of infantry and approached to that of the Horse. Thus the change in appearance was very little and to compensate for the loss of pay, the elaborate title was given. At first only the Second, Third and Fourth Horse were converted to the First, Second and Third Dragoon Guards.

The Royal Warrant of 1751 was actually draughted in 1747 and thus gives us early information on the Dragoon Guard dress. The coat was to be lapelled only to the waist with the colour of the regiment and lined with the same colour. Previously the Horse were lapelled to the bottom of their coats and the dragoons had no lapels at all. Thus the new kind of cavalry man adopted a half-way fashion which in point of fact became so popular as to spread later. The sleeves had slits up the forearm to permit the hand to pass throught the cuff which was of the regimental colour. The cuff of cavalry previously had a three-buttoned flap but now the slit went nearly up to the elbow and fastened with several buttons set in chevron-shaped loops of lace or tape. The pockets, which were called long pockets, were placed vertically and closed with buttons and chevrons in the same manner as on the sleeve. The loops were placed in pairs or threes and by making them white or yellow, sufficient variations were found so that no two cavalry regiments with the same colour of facings had exactly the same uniform.

The 1st Dragoon Guards had blue facings, the 2nd buff and the 3rd white, all the same as before conversion and all had yellow or gold lace, depending on the rank. The waistcoats and breeches remained the colour of the facings. The corporals of Dragoon Guards were distinguished by narrow gold lace on the top of their cuffs and the sergeants had similar lace as well, on the lapels and pockets. The sergeants also had the added distinction of gold shoulder-knots and of worsted sashes around their waists; these sashes were an unusual combination of colours, that of the facing and of the lace stripes in the housings. Thus the 1st Dragoon Guards had blue, the 2nd buff and blue, and the 3rd white and red. Quartermasters also had sashes around the waist but these were entirely crimson in colour. Officers had clothing made as the men but with gold lace or embroidery to the binding and buttonholes. Their crimson silk sashes were worn over the left shoulder.

DRAGOONS 1727—1760

The Regulations of 1729 specified cloth coats lined with serge, waistcoats, breeches, laced hats, large buff-coloured gloves with stiff tops and boots. Dragoons at this time were to have buff or buff-coloured shoulder and waistbelts. The shoulder-belts had pouches for ammunition but the sword which was carried from a shoulder-belt in the case of Horse was, in the case of dragoons, worn on a waistbelt which also had a place for the bayonet.

Grenadier troops are mentioned in this reign as being part of cavalry regiments, no doubt wearing the appropriate head-gear. Cavalry officers were now distinguished by shoulder-knots. In the 5th Dragoons these were gold and in the 8th they were silver. Sergeants were also recognized by their shoulder-knots. In the case of the 8th Dragoons they were silver as for the officers and in the same regiment the corporals wore silver and yellow silk knots.

But it is the *1742 Book* which gives us the greatest information, and a description of the Plates now follows. The Royal Regiment of Dragoons wore red coats with blue distinctions. The cuffs and skirts were turned back with blue and although lapels were not yet worn, the collar had a small blue patch. The buttons and button-holes down each side of the front were yellow in colour. The cuffs of dragoon regiments which were Royal, appear to have had a distinctive cuff with a long flap and five buttonholes; this pattern is shown on the Royal Regiment of Dragoons, the King's Regiment, the Queen's Regiment and the Royal Irish Dragoons. The print of the Royal Regiment of Dragoons does not show the white boot cuff, but two upright loops of yellow or gold braid at the side of the knee may indicate where these protections may have fastened. Flask-cords are shown in distinctive colours for the regiments of dragoons as they were in the horse, and Royal Regiments had the colour of blue.

A yellow or gold shoulder-knot is shown on the left shoulder, perhaps being an indication of an N.C.O. rather than a regimental practice; this is the only example in the dragoon prints. The saddlery is blue with the Royal Cypher, Crown and Garter.

The Royal Scots Greys are shown in the book wearing their grenadier cap, but the Fifth Irish Dragoons who also claimed the privilege are depicted with the normal hat. Actual cloth caps of the Scots Greys still exist in Paris. One pattern, that of an officer, has a red velvet front with the device of the St George's Cross inside a garter, these devices being set on an eight-pointed cross; the little flap is the colour of the facings and not only bears the national Thistle for Scotland, but the motto *Nemo Me Impune Lacessit* around the edge. The other cap is of a slightly later period: the front is now blue with the device of the Thistle moved to the centre on a red circlet surrounded by a garter with the Scottish motto; a crown above and a union spray on each side fill in the embroidery. The dress is very much as of the previous regiment but on the right shoulder is a white knot, a practice adopted by many of the other dragoons as shown in these prints.

The 3rd Dragoons had blue facings and yellow lace; thus the cuffs, coat lining, flask-cord, waistcoat and breeches were of the former colour and the hat lace and buttons were of the latter. White boot cuffs are shown with only one pointed tab to keep them fastened to the breeches. The horse furniture is red with a garter device. At the Battle of Dettingen, Thomas Brown of this regiment, had two horses shot from under him and two fingers of his bridle hand chopped off, after which he regained the regimental standard from the gendarme who had captured it. He then shot the Frenchman through the head and made his way through a lane of the enemy, exposed to fire and sword. For this rescue the doughty Yorkshiremen was rewarded and much recorded in print. One engraving shows him in the dress as in the *1742 Book*. The butt of his musket rests in a bucket on the off side of the horse, and the small powder horn used for priming is to be seen on the belt which crosses over the left shoulder.

The 4th Dragoons had green and white distinctions carried in the same manner as for the previously mentioned regiments, the 5th Dragoons had blue and yellow and the 6th or Inniskilling Dragoons yellow and white. The Inniskilling Dragoons had red breeches. The holster-caps and housings, although of the facing colour, were unusual in having a striking geometrical pattern around the edge—yellow diamonds flanked by red and black half-diamonds.

The 7th Dragoons, the Queen's Regiment, had white for their regimental colour; the purity of white had been symbolic of previous Queens, and the buttons were also of white metal. The cuff-slash had the five buttons which distinguished other Royal Regiments.

The Eighth Regiment of Dragoons are shown with distinctive equipment. They had claimed the privilege to wear 'crossbelts' on the grounds that they had overthrown an entire regiment of Spanish Horse at the Battle of Almenara and had taken into wear the heavy pouch belts of these prisoners. The Duke of Cumberland forbade these pouches and for a short while the crossbelts were not worn, but remonstrances from the Colonel regained permission for their wear. The regiment also had the 'horse' pattern of hilts for the swords instead of the normal dragoon pattern. The 1742 print shows a broad belt over each shoulder and the normal flask-cord is omitted. The dress of the 8th Dragoons had other peculiarities. Instead of the narrow loops on the coat, the print shows very wide white loops. The cuffs, skirt lining, waistcoat and breeches are shown as an orange colour which does not make much contrast with the dark red of the coat. Incidentally, yellow had been noted in 1735 as being the regimental colour. A narrow white knot is shown behind the right shoulder. The 1751 warrant and the Morier oil-painting show that yellow was back in wear, for the linings, cuffs, waistcoats and breeches are this colour with white lace. The regulation now specifies the arrangement of the button-holes as to be set on three and three.

The 9th Dragoons had buff collar patches, cuffs, linings, breeches and saddlecloths with buttons and white lace. The 10th Dragoons had full yellow distinctions and white metal buttons, while the 11th had white facings and waistcoats but were differenced from the 7th Dragoons by having red breeches with the yellow lace and buttons. The 12th Dragoons were dressed as the previous regiment, but differed by having white lace and buttons. The 13th Dragoons had green facings and distinctions while the 14th had light yellow cuffs, skirt linings, etc., with white buttons and lace.

The Duke of Cumberland's book shows Dragoon regiments numbered up to fourteen, but at the time of the Scottish Rebellion of 1745 new regiments were raised.

LIGHT CAVALRY 1745—1760

At the time of the '45 Rebellion, a regiment of cavalry was raised at the personal expense of a group of gentlemen and known as the Duke of Kingston's Light Horse. On the Continent, Hussars had been a popular adjunct to cavalry since the seventeenth century, and now an attempt was made to introduce something similar into British service.

These new-style cavalrymen were mounted on light horses with swish or 'nick'd tails'. All the accoutrements were made as light as possible and the armament included a carbine slung at the side by a 'moveable swivel to run up the shoulder belt'. Pistols were also carried and the swords were very sharp 'and rather inclined to a wave', which was after the fashion of Hussar blades.

This was not a show regiment alone but one which performed good service at Culloden. It was then due to be disbanded, but so successful had been the experiment that the Duke of Cumberland obtained leave from his father to take this regiment with himself as Colonel. A painting by David Morier preserved at Windsor, shows the uniform of a ranker. The black hat has yellowish lace with what appears to be a green plume. His red coat has green cuffs and turnbacks and a green patch on the collar. A yellow knot on the right shoulder may indicate that the wearer is a non-commissioned officer. His waistcoat, breeches and gloves are buff-coloured and his boots are the high black stiffened variety as normally worn at that time. The housing and holster-caps are green with a yellow and green lace on the edge. The embroidered devices are the Lion of England inside the Garter. Scarlet coats with green facings and gold lace we know were the Duke's livery, for it is as such that a newspaper of 1746 describes the dress of drummers of this regiment. Although taken within the numbering system and called the Fifteenth, the regiment was disbanded in February 1749.

Several years elapsed before the need for light cavalry was again recognized. It was in the latter part of 1755 that it was decided to add light troops to eleven cavalry regiments: the King's Dragoon Guards, the Second Dragoon Guards, Third Dragoon Guards, the First, Second, Third, Fourth, Fifth, Seventh, Tenth and Eleventh Dragoons. Although called Hussars in the periodicals of the time, they were never referred to as such by the authorities.

Their method of fighting differed from that of the heavy cavalry, for they used their firearms on horseback as well as on foot; thus the equipment had to be altered accordingly. The side pouch which went over the left shoulder of heavy cavalrymen was altered to a belt and swivel which clipped on to a ring on the carbine, thus following the practice of continental Hussars. The carbine had a bar and sliding ring for attachment and a bayonet was also carried. At first one pistol was deemed sufficient, but later two were issued. The dress was modified and the most striking feature was the head-dress: instead of the cumbersome black hat, a cap or helmet was worn; this was made of strong black-jacked leather with bars down the sides and a brass bar on top. Not only would this headgear serve as a crash helmet, but it would stand up to the enemy's sabre-blows. Ornamentation was not forgotten: the front was red with pierced brass work, the crown over the Royal Cypher and the regimental number. An additional distinction was the tuft of horse-hair placed behind the front piece; this hair, according to regulation, was to be half red and half the colour of the facing of the regiment, but the oil-painting by Morier of the private of the Light Troop of the Eleventh Dragoons belonging to the Earl of Pembroke, shows what appears to be an all-white tuft. The tan equipment of the man shows clearly in this picture as do the shorter boots. These troops were mounted on small horses which led to the comment of one observer as seeing 'monkeys mounted on cats'.

The simple helmet was improved just before these light troops were disbanded. There was a rolled-up leather flap which could be lowered down over the neck in bad weather on the old cap, but the new pattern had a turban rolled around the lower part and made to perform the same function and to tie up with two tassels at the back when not in use.

These light troops were employed with great success on an expedition to the coast of France in 1758, and this emboldened the authorities to raise complete regiments of light dragoons. Unfortunately this sounded the death knell of the light troops and being deemed unnecessary, they were disbanded in 1763.

In March 1759 the 15th Light Dragoons were raised, another regiment, the 16th Light Dragoons, following in August of the same year. In November the 18th were raised, and in the last month, the 17th and 19th were raised. In January of the next year the 20th was raised and in April the 21st was raised. The 17th, 20th and 21st did not have a long life and in 1763 were disbanded, thus allowing the 18th to become the 17th and the 19th to become the 18th.

The 15th Light Dragoons when raised, wore green facings on their red coats. The clothing as approved in a letter of April 1759 ran as follows: 'a short coat lapelled and turned up with dark green, white lining and white waistcoat with a green collar; white buttons and button holes, two white shoulder straps, two pair of white linen breeches; jockey boots and spurs, the cloak with a green cape and lined with white . . . a green saddlecloth after the Hungarian manner, laced with white lace and a red stripe, . . . instead of a hat, a copper cap enamell'd with black, crest with white and red hair, the front turned up with the King's Cypher and Crown. . . .' The regulation cap for Light Dragoons was to be ornamented in the front with His Majesty's Cypher and Crown in brass and the number of the rank of the regiment.

The Sixteenth Regiment, Burgoyne's, wore red coats with black facings and white linings, buttons and lace. A Morier oil-painting in the Royal Collection confirms this dress. The trooper is depicted firing his pistol from horse-back and his carbine hangs at his side by means of a swivel-belt. A turndown collar and the cuffs are black, but there are no lapels on the front of the coat which is looped with pairs of white lace button-holes; the lining of the coat is white as are the waistcoat and breeches. The horse furniture is white with a red and black lace. Portraits of officers show the black turned-down collar to the double-breasted waistcoat. The swords carried by officers seems to vary in every picture. The early head-dress is difficult to make out, but it appears to have an edging of black fur in some pictures, but always with the crowned cypher and the letters 'L.D.'.

Hale's Regiment, now well known as the 17th Lancers, had red coats with white linings, buttons and lace but the latter had a black edge. Hale, who raised the regiment, had served in America with Wolfe, whose heroic death made a great impression on this officer. The black edge of the lace was adopted in mourning for the dead hero and the idea of 'Death or Glory' was incorporated in the regimental devices. The skull and crossed bones with 'or Glory' was carried on the regimental guidons and later on the buttons. Morier also made a picture of this regiment *circa* 1759, and this is also preserved at Windsor. In this case the helmet is bright brass in the skull with a white plume for the crest; around the edge and over the frontlet is a band of black fur; the small red front has the regimental device of the skull, cross-bones and 'GLORY'. The coat is red with white lapels, cuffs and turnbacks. No collar is worn with this dress. The waistcoat and breeches are white as are the flounces over the holsters. The horse furniture is red, with a white lace containing two black lines. The regimental device is on the fore and hind parts.

The 21st Light Dragoons commanded by the Marquis of Granby, were known as the Royal Regiment of Foresters. A deserter's notice of 1762 tells us that a private dragoon went off 'in his red Regimental jacket faced with blue, laced with a white lace and lined with white, white waistcoat and leather Breeches and long Black spatter-dashes with white Garters.' The horse furniture of the officers was white bearskin. The holster-caps had patches of blue cloth on which was embroidered in silver the initials 'R.F.' The men had white goatskin with the cypher and '21' on their blue patches. The farriers wore black bearskin caps with horseshoes in the fronts and although Light Dragoons wore helmets, the trumpeters wore hats and feathers.

An oil-painting by Morier from the Royal Collection at Windsor, shows us a trooper in a red coat with a turned-down blue collar and round cuffs. This regiment had applied for permission to wear half-lapels but they are not shown in the painting. White epaulettes are worn, an unusually early example of this type of distinction. This may be a later version of the uniform, for an actual coat of the regiment is preserved which carries a shoulder knot on the right. The waistcoat, breeches and linings are white, and the horse furniture is of white fur, with a six-sided panel on the forepart.

The helmet is the most interesting part of the dress. The front is an asymmetrical shape rarely seen in this country, but worn by the Hanoverian Light Dragoon regiments of the period. The front shown in the Morier painting is black, but an actual example of this head-dress preserved in Berlin before the war had a red front, and other pictures show the red front. The brass badge on the front consisted of a crown and 'G.R.' with the letters 'R.F.' and the motto *Hic et Ubique*. The motto was hardly true, for the regiment remained peacefully in England and was disbanded in 1763.

FOOT GUARDS 1727—1760

Although little information is available about the regulations of dress and uniform in the earlier part of the reign, the small trickle gradually increases until a mass of information flows from the authorities. For the Foot Guards there are scattered pictures. There are in the Scottish United Services Museum five original water-colours by Bernard Lens, dated 1731 and called 'A View of a Camp taken at Hampton Court Green.' These show soldiers performing the arduous task of erecting a tent, not forgetting the rest period afterwards. The dress of the sentries is that of the Foot Guards, apparently that of the First, for the Royal Badge on a regimental colour is that of the Royal Oak. The three-cornered hats have white tape on the edges, and black cockades. The white shirts are plain at the neck and the red coats are not shown with the skirts turned back. The wide well-rounded lapels of bright blue have only four large loops of lace on each, and this white lace also goes down the front and around the pocket flaps. There are double loops of lace on the back, presumably to strengthen the coat split. Blue breeches are worn and the hose are white. The sentry who guards the colour and the pile of drums, carries scabbards for both sword and bayonet on his waistbelt, and the weapon in his right hand is not a musket, but a straight sword.

Another picture by Bernard Lens in the Royal Library, Windsor, shows grenadiers. This has been dated *circa* 1740 and still does not show the skirts fastened back. The lapels have many more loops and the double row of lace on the sleeves is in evidence. The grenadier caps have red fronts, the larger having the Cross and Garter in a rayed star, with the White Horse on the smaller. The badge of a crown and 'GR' is on the black cartridge box. The *1742 Book* shows much the same dress for a private of the battalion companies, but the skirts are fastened back.

Whereas the coats in the earlier part of the reign are closed down the front, they were now allowed to part and reveal the red waistcoat. The buff leather waistbelt kept the coat from flying loose. In 1750 an order was issued regarding the number of loops on the waistcoat, which numbered nine only on each side for men under five feet eight inches, and up to twelve loops for all grenadiers of five feet eleven inches and upwards in height.

The 1751 paintings show the fronts of the coat quite open, allowing the loops on the waistcoat to be fully observed, and in these pictures at least, the waistbelt for the sword and the bayonet is worn under the coat but over the waistcoat. Coats were made short in this year, and were to be measured by being within four inches from touching the ground when the man was kneeling on both knees.

The dress of the Second Foot Guards was at this period very similar to that of the First Guards. The main point of distinction was in the side pockets: whereas the First had horizontal scalloped pocket flaps, the Second had theirs vertical and made like a branched tree. This pattern is shown clearly in the *1742 Book* and in the Morier paintings of 1751, where all three Guards units are shown side by side for useful comparison. An Army List for 1755 points out that the Coldstream Guards are distinguished by 'slash pockets'.

The grenadier cap as depicted in 1751, is the same for all three regiments of Foot Guards. The front is blue with white edging and scrolls; the embroidery has at the top a yellow crown with a crimson cap. The central device is a red St George's Cross on a white saltire (for St Andrew) all on a blue ground within the garter. The little flap is regulation, having the White Horse on a red background.

Morier's pictures of grenadiers are obviously taken from living soldiers because the features are so distinctive in every case. Painted as they were, for a Royal patron, there can be little doubt that the artist was careful to show the details as in use at the time. Thus it is surprising to see how similar is the dress of the three regiments of Foot Guards. Red coats faced with blue, red waistcoats, blue breeches, long white gaiters and white lace are common features. The buttonhole loops of the First Regiment are shown as square-ended but the others are pointed. The Coldstream Guards are shown with many loops in the side pleats of the coat, the other Guards not being clearly shown in this part. A notice of 1753 specifies that the Coldstream Guards had slash pockets. The Third Regiment of Foot Guards is noticeable as having no loops on the waistcoat.

The brass cover of the match case carried by all grenadiers so that they might have a ready light for their grenades, is to be seen on all the pouch belts. The brass 'GR' Cypher and Crown, a distinction of the Guards, is to be noted on the black flap of the pouch.

INFANTRY 1727—1760

As soon as George II came to the throne, he had thoughts as to the better regulating of the uniform of his Army. This interest might have been expected for was he not a brother-in-law of Frederick William, King of Prussia, with the reputation of the 'greatest military tailor in Europe'? Many of the continental fashions were adopted by the British —such as powder, pig-tails and tight clothing. An order of 1727 stated that 'the King being desirous that all his regiments should have a fixed clothing and that each regiment should differ in the facings and otherwise . . . the several Colonels are to consult together and prepare patterns before they make up the next clothing, which they are to show His Majesty, and then orders will be given that the regiments continue that clothing and that they do not presume to make any alterations.'

There was always a delay between the using up of old clothing and the introduction of new. For example a letter written in February 1728 from the Colonel of the 29th Foot remarked '. . . you want directions about the next clothing. I thought that matter was so plain that you needed no directions but to go on this year and show patterns as you did for last; for we shall not want to make a real clothing until the year 1729, for what we have will do till then.'

In November 1729, regulations were issued for the clothing of the forces and the foot soldier was to have a good full-bodied cloth coat, well lined (which was to act as a waistcoat in the second year), a waistcoat, a pair of breeches, a pair of stockings, a pair of strong shoes, two good shirts and two neck-cloths, besides a hat well laced. The second year's issue was slightly less complete. The rest of the necessaries were not listed in this order.

The same letter mentioned above gives us the additional information that the soldiers' coats were 'faced in the breast and sleeves' and that a collar was turned down about two inches. This does not seem to indicate that this regiment was wearing lapels and that the old collar was still in use in some regiments. Additions to coats, especially those of grenadiers, included those items known as wings. These pieces of cloth added to the point of the shoulder, served to add width to the chest and no doubt aided in keeping the shoulder-belts in position. At first, only some regiments wore wings, but in May 1730 an order was issued stating '. . . . on viewing the patterns of clothing, we caused such as had wings or lacings on their sleeves to be taken off and made plain.' The warrants of 1747—1751 made no comments on wings, but their use was being condoned, for the Morier pictures *circa* 1751 show that some nineteen regiments were wearing them, but not including the Guards. These additions gained favour and in December 1752, it was ordered that the grenadier coats of marching regiments of infantry were ordered to have 'the usual little ornament' on the point of the shoulder.

The style of the infantry coats in the Duke of Cumberland's *1742 Book* is by no means the same for all, although most had now adopted the wide lapels instead of the plain fronts. The collar is practically out of fashion and only shown for the Invalid battalion which unit preserved the older fashion of not turning the coat skirts back. The book shows many variations of cuffs, arrangement of lace or braid loops and many patterns of lace.

The soldiers' breeches were usually either blue for Royal regiments or red for the others. For full dress occasions long white gaiters were essential; these were worn over the shoes, stockings and lower part of the breeches. For marching, the white gaiters did not stand up well to the rigours and dirt of country roads, etc.; thus special marching gaiters were worn. In 1744 colonels were to provide each man with a pair of grey gaiters for marching and other duties. Even shoes were not standard and had to be regularized. The shoes of certain fusiliers had high quarters which were deemed necessary; however, in 1749 it was ordered that shoes of all infantry should be of this pattern.

By 1747 an attempt had been made to make the infantry appear more like Royal forces than private armies bearing the distinctions of their colonels. At the same time as this revolutionary step was taken, the opportunity was not missed to regularize and make more uniform the cut of the clothing. The drummers' coats are specially mentioned in the warrant of 1747 which said that all drummers (other than those of Royal Regiments) were to be clothed with the colour of the facing of the regiment, lined, faced and lapelled with red. It seems that the addition of lapels was meant to be general, for a letter of November 1749 ordered 'that all the coats of infantry to be lapelled that are not already so.' The varying pockets were to be made uniform in style and the same order said 'that all the coats be made with the same sort of pocket as the Scotch Fuzileers vizt., in the plaits of the coat'. As already mentioned, there was always a time lag— waiting for new uniforms to be completed and for uniforms already in use to be worn out. Thus in November 1751 a new order said firmly that 'the soldiers' coats of the Infantry were directed to be lapelled on the breast and fully looped, the form of the loops being left to the colonel. The same is now to be observed and carried into execution.'

These new regulations were now issued as a printed Warrant dated 1 July 1751, and the magnificent series of oil-paintings by David Morier, now preserved in the Royal Collection at Windsor, illustrates the dress of grenadiers at this date. In December 1752 it was made clear that infantry regiments were to be 'lapelled on the breast with the colour of the facing of the regiment' and to have 'white or yellow buttons and holes according as the clothing of the officers is laced with silver or gold.'

After the 1745 Rebellion the troops in North Britain were occupied in performing useful work—that of road-making. Although the troops frequently wore their red coats, General Wolfe in 1749 gave orders to Captains and Commanding Officers to provide a coarse shirt for the men to work in and 'to preserve this better linen', but no 'check shirts' were to be bought. It was a little before this that it was discovered that the regiments of General Wolfe and Colonel Rich had somewhat similar uniforms. To make a difference, General Wolfe was to adopt a white lace with a deep yellow stripe or worm. Colonel Rich was to continue to wear his normal lace which he had several years before General Wolfe, and the next year he was to take over any remaining lace that had been provided for General Wolfe's regiment.

The Foot Guards had been developing traditions and customs peculiar to themselves, and the infantry—now that some measure of permanency had been established—were consolidating their distinctions. Certain Royal regiments were under the patronage of regal commanders and achieved certain privileges or grants. Other regiments became dignified with the title of 'Old Regiment'—no doubt an idea prompted by the example of the French Army which had six *vieux corps* as well as *petit vieux* as early as Charles II's reign. It is in the Warrants of 1747 and 1751 that we find details of the selected regiments. The 2nd Foot (the Queen's), the 4th Foot (the King's Own), the 7th (the Royal Fusiliers), the 8th Foot (once the Queen's and later the King's) are obviously in a class to have Royal Patrons. The Royal Scots, the Buffs, the 5th Foot (later the Royal Northumberland Fusiliers) and the 6th Foot (the Royal Warwickshire of later date) although of as ancient a lineage, no doubt felt the lack of distinction and the Royal Warrant not only named these as Old Regiments, but gives them distinctive badges. It must be made clear at this point that these were not metal badges worn on the head-dress as we know them, but they were even more striking: these devices were borne on the regimental colours, were embroidered on the fronts of the grenadier caps, on the drums and the bells of arms.

This list of 'The badges or devices allowed to be worn by the particular corps' began with the Royal Scots. Here the King's Cypher in the circle of St Andrew was the main device, but in the corners of the second colour the regiment was permitted the Thistle and Crown. For the 2nd Foot the main device was the Queen's Cypher, and taking second place was the Lamb. The Buffs had the Green Dragon with the Rose and Crown as a subsidiary device. The 4th or King's Own Royal Regiment had the King's Cypher within the Garter and also the Lion of England, now worn as a cap badge. The 5th Regiment had the device of St George killing the Dragon, the 6th the Antelope, the 7th the Rose within the Garter, the 8th the White Horse within the Garter, the 18th the Harp, the 21st the Thistle within the circle of St Andrew, the 23rd the Prince of Wales's Feathers and the 27th a Castle to represent Inniskilling.

It will be seen that in the main, the permitted badges were those used by Royalty. All possibility of displaying private arms was abolished. The colonel's arms or devices on the colours were replaced by a regimental number or a permitted badge. The fronts of grenadier caps no longer carried personal attributes and in the absence of a permitted badge, carried the Royal Cypher. The drastic restrictions of Henry VII had given way to private markings but once again the wheel had made a full turn and the Royal distinctions were the rule.

INFANTRY UNIFORMS IN 1742
from
Representation of Cloathing

Regiment	Facings	Lace
1st Foot	Blue	Plain white
2nd Foot	Green	Black and Yellow stripes
3rd Foot	Buff	Red worm and buff stripe
4th Foot	Blue	Blue zigzag
5th Foot	Pale dull green	Plain white

Regiment	Facings	Lace
6th Foot	Yellow	Red zigzag and sprig
7th Fuziliers	Blue	Red zigzag
8th Foot	Blue	2 Blue stripes
9th Foot	Deep yellow	Red zigzag and yellow stripe
10th Foot	Bright yellow	No lace
11th Foot	Medium warm green	Yellow and green pattern
12th Foot	Light yellow	Yellow stripe
13th Foot	Bright yellow	Yellow zigzag and sprig
14th Foot	Pale buff	No lace
15th Foot	Yellow	No lace
16th Foot	Light yellow	Red worm
17th Foot	Greyish white	Double blue zigzag
18th Foot	Blue	Plain yellow
19th Foot	Green	Green figure and yellow stripe
20th Foot	Yellow	Plain white
21st Fuziliers	Blue	Blue worm and yellow stripe
22nd Foot	Pale buff	Buff stripe
23rd Fuziliers	Blue	Yellow stripe, blue stripe and red cross-stripes
24th Foot	Olive green	One green stripe
25th Foot	Yellow	Red and green worms
26th Foot	Yellow	No lace
27th Foot	Buff	2 Yellow stripes
28th Foot	Yellow	Plain white
29th Foot	Pale Yellow	No lace
30th Foot	Yellow	Plain white
31st Foot	Buff	Yellow zigzag
32nd Foot	White	Green stripe and red worm
33rd Foot	Red	Plain white
34th Foot	Yellow	Yellow and blue pattern
35th Foot	Orange	Plain white
36th Foot	Green	Green figure
37th Foot	Yellow	Plain yellow (no lace on lapels)
38th Foot	Yellow	Plain white
39th Foot	Pale green	Green worm
40th Foot	Buff	Small black worm and small buff worm
41st Foot	Light green	Plain white
Invalids	Blue	No lace
42nd Highlanders	Buff	No lace
43rd Foot	Lightish green	No lace
44th Foot	White	Black stars
45th Foot	Yellow	No lace
46th Foot	Deep bluish green	Green stars
47th Foot	Yellow	Yellow worm
48th Foot	White	Blue stars and blue stripe
49th Foot	Buff	Green figure and yellow stripe
50th Foot	Black	Plain white

GENERAL VIEW OF THE FACINGS OF THE SEVERAL MARCHING REGIMENTS OF FOOT

from the

1751 *Royal Warrant*

Colour	Rank and title of the Regiments	Distinctions in the same colour
Blue	1st, or the Royal Regiment	
	4th, or the King's Own Regiment	
	7th, or the Royal Fusiliers	
	8th, or the King's Regiment	
	18th, or the Royal Irish	
	21st, or the Royal North British Fusiliers	
	23rd, or the Royal Welch Fusiliers	
	41st, or the Invalids	
Green	2nd, or the Queen's Royal Regiment	Sea Green
	5th Regiment	Gosling green
	11th Regiment	Full green
	19th Regiment	Yellowish green
	24th Regiment (lined with white)	Willow green
	36th Regiment	
	39th Regiment	
	45th Regiment	Deep green
	49th Regiment	Full green
Buff	3rd Regiment, or the Buffs	
	14th Regiment	
	22nd Regiment	Pale buff
	27th, or the Inniskilling Regiment	
	31st Regiment	
	40th Regiment	
	42nd Regiment	
	48th Regiment	
White	17th Regiment	Greyish white
	32nd Regiment	
	43rd Regiment	
	47th Regiment	
Red	33rd Regiment (white lining)	
Orange	35th Regiment	
Yellow	6th Regiment	Deep yellow
	9th Regiment	
	10th Regiment	Bright yellow
	12th Regiment	
	13th Regiment	Philemot yellow
	15th Regiment	
	16th Regiment	
	20th Regiment	Pale yellow
	25th Regiment	Deep yellow
	26th Regiment	Pale yellow
	28th Regiment	Bright yellow
	29th Regiment	
	30th Regiment	Pale yellow

From Goddard & Booth Military Costume of Europe, 1812

PLATE 46. Officer of the 18th Regiment of Hussars in review order.

PLATE 47. 2nd Foot Guards. Officer and battalion serjeant, 1792.

From Goddard & Booth Military Costume of Europe, 1812

PLATE 48. 1st Regiment of Life Guards

PLATE 49. 5th Regiment of Dragoon Guards. February 1800.

PLATE 50. The King's Dragoon Guards attacking French cavalry at Waterloo. Watercolour by A. Langendyck, The Royal Collection, Windsor.

PLATE 51. A Private of the 13th Light Dragoons, 1812. By C. Hamilton Smith.

PLATE 52. (*Left*) The 10th (or the Prince of Wales's Own) Regiment of Light Dragoons. (*Right*) The 8th (or the King's Royal Irish) Regiment of Light Dragoons, October 1800.

From Goddard & Booth Military Costume of Europe, 1812

PLATE 53. (*From right to left*) A serjeant of Highland Infantry. A dragoon of 1st Regiment or Royals. A grenadier of the 4th or King's Own Regiment of Foot.

From Goddard & Booth Military Costume of Europe, 1812

PLATE 54. Officer of 25th Regiment of Foot, or King's Own Borderers.

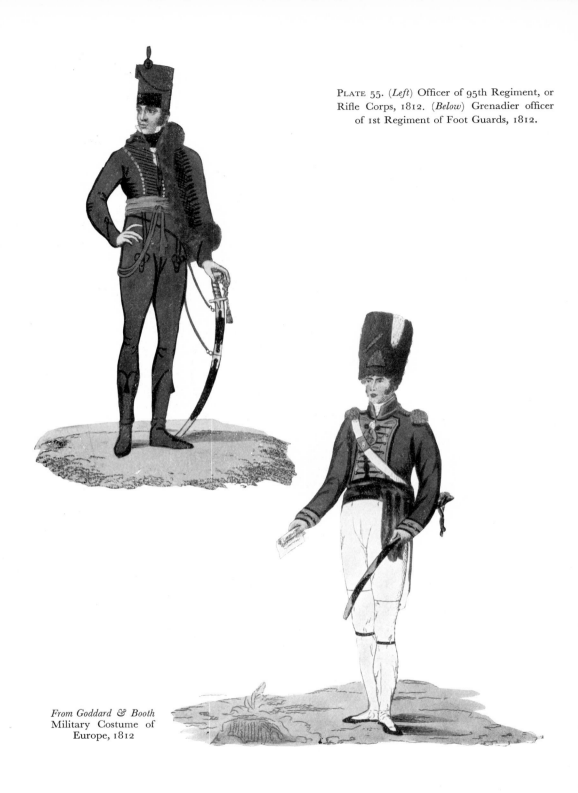

PLATE 55. (*Left*) Officer of 95th Regiment, or Rifle Corps, 1812. (*Below*) Grenadier officer of 1st Regiment of Foot Guards, 1812.

From Goddard & Booth
Military Costume of
Europe, 1812

From C. Hamilton Smith Costume of the British Army

PLATE 56. Grenadiers of Coldstream, 1st and 3rd Foot Guards, 1812.

PLATE 57. Infantry drilling, 1807. Print by Atkinson.

An Officer faced to the *Left* in the act of fronting.

An Officer facing to the *Right About*

PLATE 58. (*Left*) 76th Regiment of Foot. (*Right*) 42nd Regiment of Foot. January 1801.

From C. Hamilton Smith Costume of the Army

PLATE 59. 42nd and 92nd Highlanders, 1812.

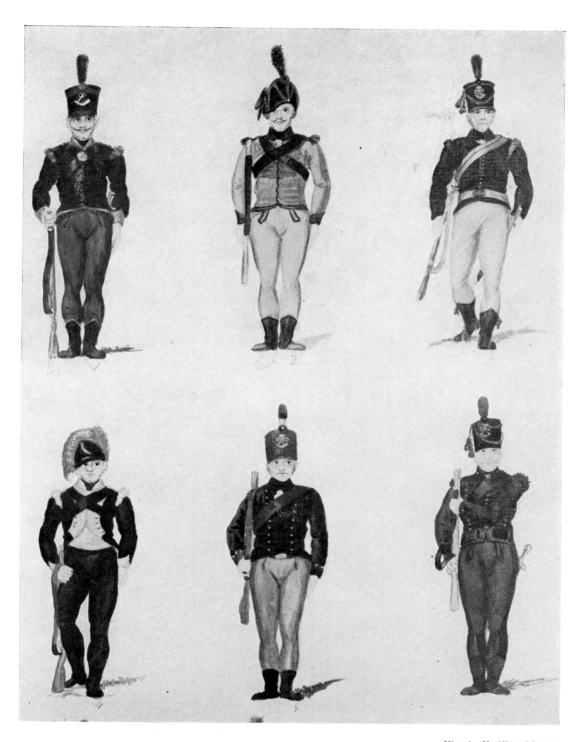

Victoria & Albert Museum

PLATE 60. (*Top row from left to right*) 5th Battalion 60th Foot (later King's R.R.C.). Lowenstein's (disbanded). 6th Battalion 60th Foot (later King's R.R.C.). (*Bottom row from left to right*) York Rangers (disbanded). Heyde's (disbanded). Coote's (later Rifle Brigade). *Circa* 1800. By C. Hamilton Smith.

From Goddard & Booth Military Costume of Europe, 1812

PLATE 61. (*From left to right*) Rifleman of 95th Regiment. Dragoon of 23rd Regiment Light Dragoons. Soldier of 43rd Regiment Light Infantry.

PLATE 62. Infantry, undress uniform, *circa* 1826

By courtesy of the Parker Gallery

PLATE 63. Drum Major, 87th Regiment, or Royal Irish Fusiliers, 1828. Print by E. Hull.

PLATE 64. Officer, Light Company, 62nd Foot, 1828. Print by E. Hull.

PLATE 65. Officers and other rank, 19th Lancers, 1819. Print by Henry Alken.

Colour	Rank and Title of the Regiments	Distinctions in the same colour
Yellow	34th Regiment 37th Regiment 38th Regiment 44th Regiment 46th Regiment	Bright yellow

HIGHLANDERS 1739—1760

In 1739 a new regiment was added to the establishment of the British Army—one which was to achieve much popularity and fame—the regiment now known as the Black Watch or Royal Highlanders. To take the wild Scottish mountaineer and make him into a regular soldier was a startling conception, but independent companies of Highlanders had been employed from 1667 to 1681, from 1682 to 1717 and from 1725 onwards. The independent companies of the last establishment formed the basis of the new regiment, first known by the name of the colonel, the Earl of Crawford and then Lord Semple. They were originally given the precedence of 43 but on the disbandment of another regiment became the 42nd.

So unusual a dress as that worn by the Highlanders had to be seen by the King for approval. Men of the Black Watch came to London and performed a broadsword dance before His Majesty. The King signified his approbation of the agility by presents of gold coins—which they promptly handed to the doorman on the way out.

The dress of the period consisted of a blue bonnet or flat cap, a short red coat, the plaid and kilt. The Duke of Cumberland's book of coloured prints shows this regiment to the extent that the artist was capable of dealing with the intricacies of Highland dress and tartan. The bonnet at this early period did not bear the diced band, and is either depicted plain or with a small piece of white tape with a red stripe and a black cockade on the left side. The early colourations of the Black Watch tartan are as much a problem to the moderns as they seem to be to the artist of the day, but it would appear that besides the well-known combination of dark green, blue and black, a red stripe was sometimes added, possibly to denote a grenadier company. It was the combined kilt and plaid that determined the shape of the coat. In wet or cold weather the plaid which fastened at the waist could be drawn around the body and used like a cloak; when not used for such protective purposes it was drawn back and the end fastened behind the left shoulder. It is obvious that the normal infantry coat with its long and full skirts would not be suitable for such usage. Thus the distinctive short Highland jacket was used, made with the military red cloth and small turned up cuffs of the buff facing colour.

The sword belt worn over the right shoulder was of black leather, a hue peculiar to the Black Watch. The cartridge pouch was worn on the waistbelt as was the bayonet. The big-hilted Scottish broadsword hung from a frog on the left side. Besides a musket, all-steel pistols were favoured by these Scotsmen. A loop over the right shoulder permitted these small firearms to hang on the left chest.

The hose were of red and white squares and gartered at the top. The turndown of the chequered material over the gartering presented an indented appearance. The lowcut Highland shoes or brogues had brass buckles. Prints published in London in 1743 show the dress very well. The crowned cypher is carried on the cartridge boxflaps. Dirks were also popular, also hanging from the overburdened waistbelt. The sporran or purse is of plain leather with a snap fastening at the top—the elaborate tassels and bells, to say nothing of the hairy surface of the later pattern were not considered at this time to be a military adjunct. Corporals are shown with a shoulder-knot at the back of the right shoulder, and a print of a regimental piper shows him clothed as the other members of the regiment, although with but a lone broadsword for his defence.

Although it is not until the 1751 warrant that printed orders appear for regiments to be known by the number of their ranking, these numbers had been in use previously. The actual warrant was drafted in 1747 and lodged two years later. Grenadier caps exist with numbers which can only refer to regiments prior to the re-numbering in 1749 when some were disbanded. Thus there is in private hands a grenadier cap with '43' on the back and having buff velvet on the front; this would appear to have belonged to a Black Watch grenadier officer prior to the change of numbers. Grenadier caps are mentioned in the draught warrant of 1747, but as a special distinction, differing from all other grenadiers, the Black Watch were permitted black bearskin caps with the King's Cypher and Crown on a red ground on the flap.

When five transport ships were wrecked in 1749, the troops marched across France, and the records of Caen give descriptions of the Highlanders who were among the shipwrecked men. There were '449 English and Scots wrecked on the coast both men and women; including two companies of Scots without breeches; one company of which wore small blue bonnets and blue stuff like scarves, the others bonnets ornamented with skins with the letters 'GR' in gold embroidery on the frontlet.'

The Morier painting of the grenadier of the 42nd Foot *circa* 1751, shows the fur cap with a red frontlet, although the warrant finally published in 1751 makes no mention of the red front. The short coat finishes square cut just below the lower edge of the waistcoat and has pointed loops of lace down each side of the front opening. The pattern of the lace is two red stripes on white. This lace also goes around the scalloped pocket flap and the slash at the cuffs. A turndown collar of the regimental buff colour is also laced and a plain red shoulder strap serves to keep the black sword belt in place. The waistcoat is red and is edged all around with the regimental lace. The sporran is now shown with leather thongs and fancy tassels.

For their excellent fighting record in America, the regiment was in 1758 called the 42nd or Royal Highland Regiment of Foot. The light buff facings were now changed to the Royal blue.

A second Highland regiment was raised in 1745 by the Earl of Loudon and, although it had fighting service—at Bergen-op-Zoom—it was disbanded in 1748. This is the other regiment referred to in the 1747 warrant which specified fur caps for the grenadiers of the Highland regiments. This regiment also wore the short red coats of the Highlanders with white facings. The tartan as shown in a portrait of the Earl of Loudon by Allan Ramsey, appears to be like that of the Black Watch but with the addition of red stripes.

The way was now open to raise other Highland regiments, and before the end of the century, many had been raised—and disbanded. In 1757 the 77th or Montgomery

Highlanders, and the 78th or Fraser's Highlanders were raised, the former having firstly red and then later green facings, and the second regiment white or very light buff facings.

In 1759 the 87th or Keith's, and the 88th or Campbell's Highlanders were raised and both fought and achieved fame in Germany. A portrait of Keith shows him in a red coat faced with green and laced with gold, but as the picture was painted some years after the regiment was disbanded, the evidence is not very reliable.

The 89th Highland Regiment was raised in 1759 as a Gordon regiment, and thus took light yellow facings, this colour being popular in the Gordon family.

MUSIC 1727—1760

The drummers' clothing of this reign was still of 'the reversed facings' system, as we know from a letter of 1728, where the drummers of the 29th Foot are mentioned as having coats of yellow cloth laced.

Royal regiments, of course, continued to wear the King's livery, red coats with blue facings, a point made clear in the Draught Warrant of 1747. Here it is stated that 'the drummers of all the Royal Regiments are allowed to wear the Royal Livery, vizt., Red, lined faced and lapelled on the breast with Blue. The Drummers of all other regiments are to be cloathed with the colour of the facing of the regiment, lined faced and lapelled with Red and laced in such manner as the Colonel shall think fit for distinctions' sake, the lace, however being of that on the soldiers' coats.'

The drummers of the Foot Guards had 'hanging sleeves', relics of the old doublet, and in November 1751 it was ordered that the drummers of the Regiments of Foot were to have the same sleeves and, as well, they were to wear caps. The Warrant of July 1751 had not been clear about caps for infantry drummers, although describing the drummers' cap for cavalry in some detail. These caps were cloth made up somewhat on the lines of fusilier or grenadier caps but not so tall; the front was to be the colour of the facings, with the particular badge of the regiment embroidered on it, or in lieu of that a trophy of guidons and drums; the little flap was to be as that of grenadiers, a white horse on a red backing and the motto *Nec Aspera Terrent*. The back part of the cap was to be red with a tassel hanging down. The turn-up was to be the colour of the facing and embroidered in the middle of the back with a drum and the rank of the regiment.

The Morier paintings of 1751 show us the dress of the drummers, the style of which more or less followed the regulations. The cap has the trophies of flags and drums with a crown above. The drummer of the 18th Foot has a grenade at the back of his cap instead of the regulation drum. The sleeves of the coat as well as the dummy hanging sleeves, carry many chevrons of lace and the body of the coat is so laid upon with vertical rows of lace that the red base is much reduced.

The fife, which went into disgrace in Cromwellian times, was at first only re-introduced to Royal Regiments like the Foot Guards. The famous picture by William Hogarth of the 'March of the Guards to Finchley' shows a boy with a fife. The regiments of foot began to have fifers again in 1747. The 33rd Regiment of Foot were in 1748 permitted four fifers instead of four drummers, and in 1750 three drummers of the 20th Foot were noted absent from an inspection owing to the fact that they were away 'learning to play on the fife'. The 1751 Royal Warrant still refers to 'cloathing' of drummers only, but that may have only been due to a slow realization of changing times.

The cloth caps of the Foot Guards at this time had a dark blue front edged with white. The embroidery on the front included a crown, two pairs of colours and two drums, with the White Horse of Hanover on the little red flap. The cuffs came to a point apparently known as a tip and for the Foot Guards the drummers' lace as worn on the the coat was blue edged with gold.

Besides the drums and fifes introduced mainly to give rhythm and then cheer to the marching soldiery, more elaborate music was being encouraged and the creation of military bands had begun. The Guards, the first to undertake the new idea (as they were also the last to abandon an old favourite), had a band of eight performers, according to an old print of 1753, which shows these musicians leading the troops across the expanses of the Horse Guards Parade. Their cocked hats had scalloped lace on the edges, the red coats were laced and appeared more like those of officers than privates. White hose and shoes completed the netherwear.

CHAPTER V

HANOVERIANS (PART 2)—GEORGE III

1760—1820

HORSE GUARDS AND LIFE GUARDS 1760—1799

THE reign of King George III was a long one and many changes took place in the sixty years. It will be more convenient to divide this period in two, stopping the first section at the change from formal clothing to something more suitable for warfare. But the full dress was now becoming very elaborate especially in the Royal troops.

Several oil-paintings of officers of the troops of Horse Guards show that *circa* 1770 the red coats had long blue lapels and very elaborate loops of gold embroidery quite unlike those previously in use. The cuffs now were of the smaller round type with gold embroidery on the upper edge, a long bar of lace up the forearm and three chevrons of lace branching from it. The epaulettes were complicated patterns of gold chain embroidery with a thin fringe hanging over the point of the shoulder. The sword-belt was worn under the coat, over the waistcoat but under the crimson waist-sash. The long straight sword was in a black leather scabbard.

In 1788 the separate troops were abolished and the two troops of Horse Guards and those of the Horse Grenadier Guards were made into two regiments of Life Guards, by which title they are known today. The loops of lace on the lapels of the full dress coat were now made so wide that they practically covered the narrow blue strip. For all their like of expensive trimmings the Life Guards were one of the first regiments to adopt the new style of wearing coats with the front closed down to the waist. The regimental pattern of 1797 was to have ten buttons on the facings including one on the collar. Prints of 1798 show the blue lapels joined down to the waist with gold lace on the edges and buttonholes. The blue collar was laced all round with gold and each blue cuff had a loop on it, with other loops above on the sleeve. The waistcoat no longer showed and the hat, which now had a white and red plume, was soon to lose the gold lace around the edge. The white cross-belts worn by the men had rectangular brass plates. In 1798 the white knee tops which had been worn for so many years, were ordered to be discontinued.

ROYAL HORSE GUARDS 1760—1799

The blue coat of the Royal Horse Guards continued to be a favourite in portraits: there were several of the Marquis of Granby made early in the new reign which show him with a variety of backgrounds but always the same pose. The costume is nearly the same as that worn previously. The coat is now made with half lapels which could button over or flap back, but in point of fact worn unbuttoned and flapping in a negligent manner. The gold aiguillette is worn on the right shoulder. In November 1766 the men changed the colour of their waistcoats from red to buff, thus making them match those of the officers which had changed some time previously.

A portrait of Sir George Cooke by Copley, shows another change of style. The blue coat, red lapels and gold lace are still in use as they were many years later, but a gold epaulette authorized in 1764 is worn on the left shoulder.

In 1770 the Marquis of Granby was succeeded by H. Conway who later became a Field-Marshal. A fine portrait of Conway shows the new pattern cuff, small and round, as mentioned in the 1768 Warrant for cavalry. There are four gilt buttons set on chevron shaped loops on the forearm. The gold lace does not now go around the lapels and is in the main restricted to the buttonholes and hat. There is a single gold loop on each side of the turned-down collar. The single gold epaulette is still worn on the left shoulder. The waistcoat and breeches are buff, as is the swordbelt which is worn under the coat but over the waistcoat. The belt has a simple buckle and is held securely in place by a crimson waist sash. The lining of the officer's coat is buff.

A portrait *circa* 1780 shows the epaulette of an officer with some detail; it is on a scarlet cloth ground with an interlaced pattern of gold and having a flat gold fringe. The hair style had changed and was worn powdered and brushed high, with 'rolls' over the ears. A long white frill was worn on the chest.

Prints and pictures about 1790 show troopers with red-tipped plumes in their cocked hats. The carbine belt is shown with swivel clip and the red flask-cord. The turned-back skirts of the coat are shown as white. The hats were soon to lose the lace around the edge, and a sketch of 1793, showing the Blues as they arrived in Flanders with French prisoners, omits it.

In fact, the other ranks were noted for their lack of lace or tape on their clothing. Even the four gilt buttons on each side skirt and each forearm lacked those chevrons so distinctive in the Dragoon Guards' dress. The old soldiers' tale that the Blues had run away and so had their gold lace taken away to mark their disgrace was a contemporary tale without any truth. But the Duke of York spoke in their defence, told of their distinguished services and gave the reason that 'a splendid parade uniform was thought inconsistent with the services and duties of active service and a plain coat was accordingly issued to them. On their return, it was necessary to re-establish uniformity, and the colonel unwilling to be at greater expense in clothing his Regiment than were the Colonels of other Regiments—ordered the gold-laced uniforms and furniture to be laid aside, and in order to render their appearance still uniform with the rest of the army, the brass ornaments on the horses' bits were also ordered to be taken off.'

HORSE GRENADIER GUARDS 1760—1788

The Royal Warrant of 1768 which made fur caps a general issue to grenadiers of foot, made no comment on the dress of the Horse Grenadier Guards, but we know that they also had the black fur cap with the Royal coat of arms on the front plate. The coat also took the slimmer line of cut with narrow cuffs and a small turn-down collar. Epaulettes were worn on the shoulders. Four loops of lace made chevrons on each sleeve and loops were on each side of the front opening of the coat.

A print of 1777 shows the pouch flap with the design of a grenade on it, but the rest of the uniform is much as before. Portraits of officers of the same period show them wearing fur caps with heavy gold tassels. The crimson waist sashes had on the right side a large knot. They wore wrist-length white gloves and the men have gauntlet gloves. The buttons and buttonholes were in pairs.

The sword-belt of officers was worn at first under the coat with only a plain buckle and tip, but this was changed to a belt worn over the coat and with a most elaborate belt plate. The regimental initials were in gold on a red enamel ground, surmounted by a Crown and the whole being surrounded by rays on an oval plate. Officers also wore the large black cocked hat with a plume.

The pictures showing the 2nd Scots Troop in its later days give the officers lapels of red cloth as the coat, the buttons in pairs and with loops of gold lace on the blue collar and cuffs. Men of the Scots Troop are shown with a red bag and plume to their fur caps, and if a water-colour by Thomas Rowlandson is to be accepted as evidence, the English troop appear to have had a blue bag to their fur cap.

In 1788 when the 1st and 2nd Troops of Horse Guards were converted into the 1st and 2nd Regiment of Life Guards, the two troops of the Horse Grenadier Guards were also absorbed and a picturesque uniform disappeared from the British Army.

HORSE 1760—1799

Another branch of the Army due to disappear was that of Horse. The four remaining regiments had some minor changes in the next few years. In 1764 the 2nd Horse changed the colour of their waistcoats and breeches from full green to white, and the buttonholes were to be made plain without lace. In 1766 the 3rd Horse or Carabineers, were permitted white waistcoats and breeches instead of the yellow ones, and they also discontinued the lace on waistcoat and coat. The 4th Horse also omitted lace from the officers' coats and the tape or braid was left off the men's clothing.

The 1768 Royal Warrant stated that instead of Horse being lapelled all the way down, the lapels were to go to the waist only. It gave the facings as blue for the 1st, full green for the 2nd, white for the 3rd or Carabineers, and black for the 4th Horse. In 1788 Horse were deemed unnecessary and the four regiments became respectively the 4th, 5th, 6th and 7th Regiments of Dragoon Guards.

DRAGOON GUARDS 1760—1799

The first few years of the reign were spent in war, but the peace of 1763 gave an opportunity for high-ranking officers to divert their thoughts to clothing and suchlike. In 1764 it was ordered that all horses (except those of Light Dragoons) should have long tails. In the same year, officers and men of the Dragoon Guards were to discontinue the shoulder-knot and to wear an epaulette instead on the left shoulder.

The waistcoat and breeches of the 1st Dragoon Guards were changed from blue to buff and the buttonholes were to be made plain without lace—although in point of fact the officers continued to wear gold lace. This discontinuance of lace or tape on the buttonholes of waistcoats was a fairly general order. In 1765 the 3rd Regiment of Dragoon Guards was honoured with the title of the Prince of Wales Regiment of Dragoon Guards. In 1766 that awkward practice of having drummers mounted on horseback was discontinued, and Dragoon Guards had trumpeters instead.

In 1767 the linings or the turned-back skirts of the coats of the 1st Dragoon Guards were changed to buff, thus matching the breeches and waistcoats. In the same year it was ordered that Regiments of Dragoon Guards were not to put their numbers on their buttons and the Warrant of 1768 makes it clear that the initial letters of the titles were to be used instead of a number. In the case of the 3rd Dragoon Guards, they were to have the Prince of Wales's feathers. Coats were now to have turn-down collars which could be buttoned up to the necks. The epaulette was now described as being the colour of the facing and with yellow or white tape and worsted fringe. The sleeves were no longer to be split. The epaulettes of sergeants were to have a narrow gold or silver lace around them and a gold or silver fringe. The waist sash was now to be of crimson spun silk with a stripe of the colour of the facing of the regiment. The quartermasters were to have the same distinctions as those of Horse. The three regiments were noted as having blue, buff and white facings respectively, with lace and loops as before.

In 1774, the waistcoats, breeches and linings of the coats and cloaks of the King's Dragoon Guards were changed from buff colour to white. The 2nd Dragoon Guards changed their facings from buff to black in 1783. In November 1787, heavy cavalry were to wear their swords slung over their coats and both the sword belt and the pouch belt were to be made three inches wide; to keep these belts in place, a shoulder-strap was necessary and so in January 1788, a General Order was made for officers and men of Dragoon Guards to wear epaulettes. In 1788 the remaining four regiments of Horse were converted to Dragoon Guards and thus the new regiments numbering from Four to Seven had facings of blue, yellow, white and black respectively. The button was to be white metal for all except the 7th Dragoon Guards, who had yellow metal buttons.

The pouches of cavalry which had been white, were in 1793 changed to black leather, and the next year the gold or silver lace on the edge of the hats was discontinued. In 1795 velvet facings were noted for the Dragoon Guards, but this material had been in use many years earlier. Velvet cloth remains the distinction of certain Dragoon Guards right up to modern times.

In 1796 the coats of heavy cavalry were modified by having shortened skirts which were to clear the seat when on horseback. There was now no space for the pockets on the skirts and so they lapsed. At the same time the epaulettes were discontinued and red wings edged with white cloth were worn instead. The next year it was ordered that in future no lapels were to be worn, but officers when off duty, or in 'Dress' could wear the old long-tailed coat.

The adoption of the general fashion of closing the coat down the front prevented the waistcoat from being seen, but in 1798 the Board of Officers made red waistcoats regulation for regiments of Heavy Dragoons. The shortened coats of the Dragoon Guards were known as jackets and were to have a double row of buttons after the manner of those worn by officers of the Foot Guards, but the closed coat being the new fashion is best dealt with in the next period.

DRAGOONS 1760—1799

During the strenuous campaigns in Europe the Light Dragoons were not the only ones to wear a head-dress that afforded some protection against sword-cuts, for the Dragoons, despite the fact that they wore ordinary hats, had their own form of protection in the shape of skull caps or small iron salets worn inside the normal headgear.

The shoulder-knot placed as it was at the back on the shoulder could be deemed little more than an ornament. So when the warrant of 1764 for an epaulette on the left appeared to be introducing another ornament, it should be noted that the epaulette also served the purpose of retaining a shoulder sash. When waistcoats and breeches were coloured as the facings on the coat, a rich appearance was presented, but such distinctive features presented great problems for cleaning and fading. A common garment seemed more practicable as was to be seen in the Prussian Army, where straw-coloured waistcoats and breeches were the fashion, so the change gradually took place in the British Army. In 1764 the 1st Dragoons had permission to change the colour of their waistcoats and breeches from blue to white, but apparently this regiment was too enthusiastic for a change and the following year they received a reprimand for making the linings of their coats white also.

From estimates we learn that this regiment had, as well as regimental coats, frocks costing only 2s. 6d. each. These frocks were made of white kersey and served for all the regiment, excepting the farriers, to drill in and do rough duties. The frocks had blue facings as might be expected, except for the drummers who had scarlet facings and wings. For their regimental coats the men had worsted epaulettes, the corporals silk and the sergeants gold ones. The hat lace and cords were similarly graded, the privates having gold half lace with scarlet and white tassels, the corporals gold scallop lace and scarlet and yellow silk tassels and the sergeants gold scallop lace and scarlet and gold tassels.

Pictures about 1767 showing the Colonel of the Royal Dragoons, give him a long scarlet coat without lapels, a turned-down collar and small cuffs compared with the 1751 pattern. The next year saw the issue of the regulation which made all cuffs small, so this regiment anticipated the fashion. The regulation coat was to have cuffs, not slit, and the buttons set lengthwise up the arm. The waistcoat and breeches were no longer to be the colour of the facings, except that those having buff facings could have buff breeches and waistcoats; but the others were to have white waistcoats, breeches and linings.

Officers' sashes which had been worn over the left shoulder were now worn around the waist, but the knot stayed on the same side. The hat, instead of being an equally balanced object of three corners, was the subject of experiment in different regiments, and after the various essays had appeared and brought down official comment, sealed patterns were deposited in 1770. The front was now tending to point upwards and the angle of the sidepoints was dissimiliar. The front of the coat, although worn open, had loops on both sides and buttons at the ends, thus making the effect of a double-breast. The row of buttons on the left side was later omitted and the right row moved inwards, thus making a single-breasted coat.

The 2nd Dragoons, the Scots Greys, had not only the usual black hat, but also their distinctive grenadier caps. Although the infantry grenadiers had fur caps authorized by the Warrant of 1768, and provision was made for the Royal Scots Greys, they continued to wear their old cloth caps. By 1777 these items were reported as old and worn. The next year new grenadier caps of bearskin were fitted and each man's name was put in his cap. A plea to have the horse furniture changed from blue to red was granted in 1782. The Scots Greys are noted at a review in 1784, as having two epaulettes like grenadiers although other heavy cavalry had but one.

The turn-back of the skirts was becoming permanently turned back and a small heart-shaped ornament (as seen on a specimen of 1787 in the Zeughaus) served as a place of attachment. The pocket flaps on the back were still laced but the opening was difficult to manage and the actual pocket was forced to take a new position—inside and only to be reached by lifting up the coat tails. The epaulettes, especially for officers, were becoming objects for complicated embroidery. In fact the times of peace were gradually changing uniforms from clumsy and hard-wearing garments of necessity into well-fitting and pretty styles. The Prussian ideas of intensive drilling, tight-fitting clothes and mechanical uniformity were making their mark throughout the civilized world. Even the hair styles followed the victorious German's fashion. Powdered and floured hair also had pigtails and clubs behind. But apart from these refinements the clothing of heavy cavalry changed little basically in the last part of the eighteenth century. Details like the addition of badges to pouches, the changing of the colour of the pouches in 1793 from white to black, and the gradual appearance of plumes in the hats about 1788 made but minor variations in the appearance. Dragoons continued to be the solid core of cavalry, but changes were taking place. They steadily became reduced in numbers as regiments were converted or even disbanded, as in the case of the Fifth Royal Irish at the end of the century.

The uniforms continued in the basic colours. The 8th Dragoons were singled out in the 1768 Warrant as being the only regiment permitted to wear cross-belts instead of one shoulder-belt. The unofficial hat feathers which had been noted at various reviews were tolerated, and regiments took their own fancy. The small skull caps worn under hats were in use again in the campaign of 1793. The hat was now a much different shape from that worn in the middle of the century; it had so altered that the front point had disappeared and a half-moon remained. The lace around the edge of the hat was discontinued in 1794.

Cavalry regulations of 1795 noted that sergeants were to have two stripes of the facing colour on the right arm. These distinctions had been in use earlier but it is difficult to put a date to the innovation. The sword which had been carried in a shoulder-belt since 1787 was changed in 1796 for one with slings, at the same time as the feather hat plumes were recognized officially and regulated for Dragoons. In the same year, the long musket which had been used for so many years was discovered to be 'very inconvenient, useless and cumbersome' and so it was changed for a short carbine. Actually, the change in many cases did not take place for several years.

The coat tails were shortened and thus the buttons, the vestiges of the pockets, disappeared from the back. Epaulettes were also now in abeyance and shoulder-straps of the facing colour and wings of red replaced them. These wings were to be laced and also to be interlined with iron or brass plates of sufficient strength to resist the cut of a sword. The warrant for regulating the clothing of cavalry, 1796, ordered that the coat was to be buttoned down to the waist and looped down the breast, in the same manner as already in use. The cuffs, collar and turn-back of the skirt were to be the colour of the facing.

LIGHT DRAGOONS 1760—1799

The Light Dragoons were becoming the fashion although the end of the Seven Years War saw the disbandment of one: Lord Aberdour's Regiment never achieved full strength and when it disappeared it left the 'Death or Glory Boys' holding the 17th place. Similarly, the old 19th took the new number of 18 with white facings and silver lace. The 15th and 16th Light Dragoons had performed such creditable service in Germany and Portugal that they were made Royal in 1766 and were called the 1st or Kings,' and the 2nd or Queen's Regiment of Light Dragoons, respectively. This brought about a change of facings to the Royal blue, instead of the green and black which had previously been in use. Waistcoats and breeches were to be buff instead of white and officers who had previously been distinguished by wearing red waistcoats and breeches now took to white. In April 1763, when General Elliot's Regiment, the 15th Light Dragoons, returned from Germany and marched over Westminster Bridge, every man had 'a sprig of box in his hat in token of victory, having been in almost every engagement in Germany and always beat the enemy.'

In 1766 according to Hinde, the use of side-drums in light cavalry was discontinued, and brass trumpets were carried instead. Bugle horns were used for field calls. These trumpeters when dismounted, formed a band of music and played on French horns, clarionets, bassoons and fifes. Whereas the drummers had worn helmets like the rest of the regiment, the trumpeters now wore hats and feathers of the colour of the facings, an exception being those of Royal Regiments who had red feathers. They also rode on grey horses and carried swords with scimitar blades. The hanging sleeves worn by the drummers were discontinued. The coats were red faced with blue and laced blue and yellow for the Prince of Wales's, the King's and the Queen's regiments. The 17th and 18th wore white coats faced with red; the former had white lace with a black edge and the latter red and white lace. The Prince of Wales's regiment mentioned above was the old 12th Dragoons, which had been converted to Light Dragoons in 1768. They retained their black facings but the music took on the Royal colours.

The Royal Warrant of 1768 contained many details for the dress of the light dragoons. Epaulettes were to be worn one on each shoulder; officers of light dragoons were to wear helmets; black half-gaiters were to be worn, the coats of the private men were to be lapelled to the waist, the width of the lapel was to be three inches, the sleeves were to be turned up with the colour of the lapel, the breadth of the shoulder-belts was to be two-and-a-half inches. Many other details were of course as for the other cavalry. Buttons were to be numbered with the rank of the regiment and also the initial letters of the title in the case of Royal Regiments. For example the 15th King's Light Dragoons had 'K.L.D.15'.

In 1778 another regiment was converted to Light Dragoons: the 8th. This change made it necessary for them to discontinue the two cross-belts of which they were so proud. An appeal for compensation for this loss resulted in the permission for the Regiment to become Royal. Thus the new King's Royal Irish Light Dragoons took the Royal facings of blue.

In the same year, light troops were again added to certain regiments of heavy cavalry. These troops apparently had a modified uniform with a distinctive head-dress: these were helmets with metal fronts, mounted with the Crown 'GR' and the regimental number; turbans and bearskins also adorned the helmets. But the life of these auxiliaries was very short.

Later in 1778 the light troops were taken away from the regiments of Dragoon Guards and Dragoons to form three new regiments of Light Dragoons. The Light Troops of the 1st and 2nd Dragoon Guards, the 4th and 10th Dragoons made the nucleus of the six troops of the 19th Light Dragoons under Major General Russell Manners. The light troops of the 3rd Dragoon Guards, the 1st, 6th and 11th Dragoons made the basis for the 20th Light Dragoons under Major-General Phillipson and the light troops of the 2nd, 3rd, 7th, 15th and 16th Dragoons made the 21st Light Dragoons under Major-General John Douglas. All these newly formed units wore red coats and silver lace, but the 19th had green facings, the 20th yellow and the 21st had white facings. A contemporary letter tells us that the 21st's uniform was like that of the 75th Foot of the period but without embroidery or lace. The white lapels were shaped as those of the 15th Light Dragoons. An inspection report of 1781 repeats the basic information and mentions that the head-dresses were black leather helmets with bearskin tops.

In January, 1780, the 22nd Light Dragoons were raised by Major J. B. Holroyd, who later became the Earl of Sheffield. The regiment was also called the 22nd Sussex. The new commander had progressive ideas regarding clothing. In America, Tarleton's Legion and others had found the value of dark clothing for field work, and thus the new 22nd Light Dragoons appeared in dark green jackets relieved only by a little white lace. White breeches and short boots were the normal netherwear, but the head-dress was striking, being made with an elaborate crest on top and a turban around the base. Tarleton also had a black helmet with a fur crest, which was known by his name, not only in this country but in France. The wearing of a pelisse made this dress a close resemblance to that of the continental hussar, but the latter term was not yet to be adopted. The armament was a light sword, a short musket suspended from a shoulder-belt and also pistols were carried. The white shabraque had a red and yellow edge and the device of a star was on the fore and hind quarters. All four of these newly raised Light Dragoons were disbanded at the peace of 1783.

Yet another Light Dragoon regiment was raised during the American Revolution, that of the 23rd. Their destination, however, was not to be the West but the East, for they were the first British cavalry regiment to be sent to India. Its officers were drawn from other regiments of Light cavalry and the Colonel was Sir John Burgoyne. He was authorized to clothe them in red uniforms faced with deep green; the white metal buttons were to be set on two and two, the breeches and waistcoats were to be white, and the helmets were to be the same as those worn by the Queen's Light Dragoons. But Sir John Burgoyne was another commander with ideas of his own, and he too adopted a jacket of green for undress and field work. A portrait of this gentleman shows him in such a garment with small white turnbacks on the chest, and silver lace. The black shoulder belt for the sword has an ornament with the regimental number. The head-dress shows yet another variety of the inspiration of the age—it has a turned up front edged with silver, a dark green turban and a loose black fur tail as could be then found in the backwoods of America. Whether the regiment received the general issue of plain green jackets before proceeding to India is not clear, but they did have the red coats available for that country.

The reduction of cavalry in 1783 did not affect this regiment, serving as they were, so usefully in India, but the disappearance of lower numbers permitted their rank to be changed from 23rd to 19th, although this did not take place until 1786.

The year of 1784 saw a great change in the dress of Light Dragoons, and the several experiments in dark colours of coats, the green, etc., were tacitly acknowledged and blue now became the distinguishing colour for Light Dragoons. The uniform was now considered to have changed to a Hussar pattern, but actually it differed in many points from the Hungarian Hussar. The actual dress was a new fashion—a jacket and shell. The first top garment was a flannel waistcoat with sleeves which buttoned onto the waistband of the buckskin breeches. Over this under-waistcoat went a jacket which closed down the front and reached just to the waist. Then finally on went the shell, which was an open jacket without sleeves. As the last two garments were both blue, the sleeves of the under garment looked as though they belonged to the top one and, to make the shoulders more attractive, narrow wings were added to cover the join. The lacing was to be white except in the case of the 11th and 13th Light Dragoons who had buff facings and, following the army practice, had their linings of buff to match the facings. The front of the jackets and shells had an elaborate system of cord loopings; these loops also had tufts or tassels at the ends and were usual for all Light Dragoon Regiments. The officers and quartermasters were to have similar garments, but with sleeves and of course, silver lace in lieu of white cord, the 13th Light Dragoons being an exception with gold lacing. The sergeants had gold or silver chain looping accordingly and the corporals had their minor distinctions in gold or silver cord around the collars and cuffs. The trumpeters, following the pattern of previous musicians, had their jackets and shells the colour of the facing of the regiments with lace instead of looping down the front and the seams.

It took time for old clothing to wear out and for the new to be introduced in an economical fashion. It was not until 1786 that it was deemed necessary to change the colour of the cloaks from the old colour of red to blue. In 1788 the order for epaulettes on both shoulders was to apply to Light Dragoons as well as heavy cavalry, but the practice of wearing unauthorized wings continued, and two years later several regiments were ordered to discontinue them.

Although some Light Dragoon regiments had been disbanded on the cessation of hostilities, their use had been justified and the conversion of Dragoons to a lighter role continued. In 1783 the 7th, 10th and 11th Dragoons were adapted to the new style, the 7th becoming the 7th or Queen's Own Light Dragoons, and the 10th becoming the Prince of Wales's Own Regiment of Light Dragoons.

In 1784 the 12th Light Dragoons changed their facings from black to yellow, although they retained black horse furniture until 1792. The 8th, on the adoption of the new blue dress took scarlet facings, the officers' lace and buttons still remaining silver in colour. The 19th in India on conversion to a blue uniform, lost their green facings. Green with blue was not considered suitable and so very pale yellow was adopted instead. From an actual dress coat which still exists, we know that the buttons were continued in pairs on the lapels and that the loops were of silver. The epaulettes although still with narrow fringe, were beginning to change in pattern and have a 'feathered' ornamentation on the strap. This pattern of coat with turned-back lapels was after the style of the year 1768, and on service gave way to the shorter jacket and shell as authorized in 1784.

In 1788 a critical investigation into the dress of five Light Dragoon regiments brought forward the information that although most of them wore the black fur crested cap with the turban and peak to shade the eyes, the 15th Light Dragoons still clung to their ancient brass helmet. No doubt they felt that the new pattern would not give them sufficient scope to display the trophies and honours of Emsdorf where they had conducted themselves so well. The cap was to be the regulation head-dress with a turban in the regimental facing colour. A feather was to be on the left side, also in the facing colour, except where the facing was white and then it was to be mixed with red. No doubt as white was the colour of the French Army, then a powerful enemy, no Britisher would wish to show the white feather. An attempt was made to preserve regimental badges, and these were to be placed on the right side of the cap. In front, each regiment was to have its number in plated silver, following the established practice of the 11th Light Dragoons. The peak of the cap was also to be bound with silver plating.

The practice of certain officers lining their upper jackets with fur and achieving something of the effect of a Hussar pelisse was frowned upon, and the offending articles ordered to be discontinued. Light Dragoon swords were now noted as being slightly curved and another step towards the dress of the continental hussar was achieved.

A new 20th regiment was raised in 1792 and was called the Jamaica Light Dragoons. On the front of their tinned helmets was worn the device of an alligator and 'XXLD'. Their dress was the blue Light Dragoon jacket with yellow facings and silver lace. The head-dress *circa* 1800, is shown as a shako with a red-and-white plume and cap lines. When the regiment returned to England in 1802, it lost the badge of the alligator.

The trumpeters of Light Dragoons had worn black cocked hats, according to regulation, and even helmets as the other men, but in 1792 a circular order stated that in future all these trumpeters should wear black bearskin caps, designed after the pattern lodged at Messrs Hawkes in Piccadilly. The regimental badge was to be fixed on the front of the caps.

Renewed warfare with France saw a large increase in the Army, and as far as the cavalry was concerned the new units were Light Dragoons. In 1794 four new regiments numbered from the 21st to the 25th were raised. It seems as though the authorities had second thoughts and decided to have dragoons instead of light dragoons. A letter was sent out ordering that the clothing of the 22nd, 24th and 25th regiments was to be in red instead of blue, but it was too late in the case of the 24th which was already made up in blue. All other newly raised regiments of Dragoons were to be red if not already made up. The 21st appear to have had yellow facings and gold lace. The coat of the 22nd may have originally been blue with red facings, but with the change the coat was now entirely red with gold buttonholes, as may be seen from an actual coat.

The 23rd were raised in Ireland and had light yellow turbans, collars and cuffs. The 24th were also raised in Ireland and as noted above were already clothed in blue before the order for red coats appeared. The facings would seem to be light yellow and the turban on the Light Dragoon helmet was leopardskin. A painting of an officer gives a glimpse of the regimental motto on the helmet which was 'Death or Glory'. The 25th were raised by Colonel Francis E. Gwyn and were nicknamed 'Gwyn's Hussars'. They might have worn the red coat for a short length of time, but going on service to South Africa and India they took into wear a grey jacket with scarlet collar and cuffs; they were a unit to adopt an early form of the shako.

In 1795 four more Light Dragoon regiments were formed from drafts of men from three Dragoon Guard regiments, from five Dragoon regiments and seven of the Light Dragoon regiments. The red coats may still have been in the minds of the authorities when green facings were ordered for the 26th Regiment, but by the King's command, the green was changed to blue. These blue facings appear in pictures to be the same hue as the blue jacket, but an undocumented statement says that they were the shade of blue or purple as used by the 56th Foot for their facings. The officers had twenty-five rows of silver lace across the front of their jackets.

The 27th Light Dragoons had white facings from the beginning, and early in 1796 were authorized to have 'grey jackets with white collar and cuffs' when destined for India. The 28th were also known as the Duke of York's own Regiment of Light Dragoons, and had yellow facings. They were soon ordered to the Cape of Good Hope and wore grey jackets with yellow collars and cuffs. The 29th Regiment raised by Francis Lord Heathfield, were given buff facings and went to San Domingo in the West Indies.

Another group, of four Light Dragoon regiments was raised in Ireland in 1794, but it was not until they were placed on the British establishment in 1795 that they gained their numbers, 30 to 33rd. The 30th became the Princess of Wales's Light Dragoons and the 33rd were known as the Ulster Regiment. Very little is known of the dress of these short-lived regiments although the 31st may have worn yellow of buff facings. All four were disbanded in 1796.

Every now and then, the authorities at home were made aware that local conditions were not always suitable for the thick clothing so desirable in the United Kingdom. Usually it was the soldier on the spot who made the alterations, but in 1796 it was decided by the home authorities that Light Dragoons serving in tropical climates should wear a more suitable costume. Thus it was that the old 23rd, now the 19th, which was still serving in India, were to wear grey clothing with yellow collars and cuffs instead of the blue issue. The 25th and the 27th due for the East Indies, and the 28th, due for the Cape of Good Hope, were also to have grey clothing with scarlet, white and yellow facings respectively. The Board of Officers who had to report on this clothing were not very happy that the King had expressed preference for the grey clothing. When they expressed their displeasure in a memorandum, the King reversed his order and allowed that the grey pattern coats were to be replaced by blue ones. However, one Commander, Major-General Burgoyne of the 25th Light Dragoons, had been quickly off the mark and his grey clothing was made up before he received the order. As a concession he was allowed to keep it, but for the year only. However, it must have been realized that someone was making a storm in a teacup, and by the summer the grey clothing was again permitted. Orders were sent to the 8th, 19th, 25th, 27th and 28th Regiments, permitting them all to have the fashionable grey dress.

Leather helmets were found to be 'objectionable in hot climates' and the Board of Officers advised that they should be made of tin and lined with white linen. Prints exist showing the 8th Light Dragoons still wearing the heavy black helmet up to 1800, but they did take the tinned helmet in wear about this period, for an actual example is still preserved. Instead of a bearskin crest, a brass comb is used with a red horsehair mane and the front bears an elaborate badge on the crown over the harp.

The 25th Light Dragoons who liked also to be called the British Hussars, wore a different head-dress with their light blue-grey dress. This was a wide-topped shako, a pattern which was not adopted by British cavalry until several years later.

A new cut of coat came in 1796 when a Warrant said that the several articles of clothing of Light Dragoons were to be made in exact uniformity to the new patterns sent. The uniform of the officers was to be shaped and laced in the same manner as those of the men, but with scale epaulettes and wings. The change of pattern did not involve any alteration in the colour of the collars and cuffs. The new pattern jacket had rows of braid on the chest after the fashion made popular by the Royal Horse Artillery. The helmet continued in use with minor modifications.

FOOT GUARDS 1760—1799

For once the Foot Guards were not in the van of changing fashion, and although it might be expected that they would not be mentioned with common infantry in the details of the 1768 Warrant, in fact they did not take alterations into use until some time later.

The 1st Foot Guards were authorized in 1770 to make alteration in their clothing the following year, and in this case let lapse certain features which had been obsolete in line regiments for some years. The sergeants' coats were now to have a neat round cuff instead of the old slash and frame, the round buttons were replaced by flat gilt buttons and the loops were made diamond- or bastion-shaped, instead of being square. The sergeants' and privates' waistcoats were now to be plain instead of laced scarlet and the breeches also became white instead of blue.

An original Guardsman's coat of this period is preserved in the Royal United Services Museum and shows the red as a poor scarlet and the facings as dark blue. The worsted lace used for ornamentation and strengthening is plain white. The plain buttons are pewter and about an inch across.

The grenadier company's red shoulder wings were changed in colour to blue ones and corporals were now to have a silk epaulette instead of a worsted shoulder-knot. The drummers' coats were to have white linings instead of blue and the drummers' lace, which had been an orange colour, was changed to white silk with tinsel stripes. Plain round cuffs were to be worn instead of the tip.

The Coldstream Guards had changes in their dress in 1773. Most distinctive was the change of the shape of loops which was now scallop-headed in pair instead of pointed. The lace on the pockets and sleeves which had been in the shape of a branch, was now changed to simple loops of the new pattern. The sergeant was to have a gold epaulette on his right shoulder.

The 3rd Guards adopted the white linings and breeches in 1768, but continued to wear the scarlet cloth waistcoats with white lace and buttons in pairs. The narrow blue lapels which reached down to the waist had the buttons and holes in pairs and the uppermost button was connected to the blue turn-down collar. Sergeants had a single epaulette of gold lace on the right shoulder and gold lace around the pockets, buttonholes and other parts. Corporals had the same dress but with the lace on the collar, cuffs, epaulette and shoulder-strap in silver. Grenadier company sergeants and corporals had epaulettes on both shoulders. The grenadier company wore black fur caps with white metal plates

PLATE 66. 7th (the Queen's Own) Hussars, *circa* 1833. Print by Mansion and Eschauzier.

PLATE 67. The 15th Hussars, 1825. From an engraving by William Heath.

PLATE 68. 11th Light Dragoons, *circa* 1833. Print by Mansion and Eschauzier.

PLATE 69. (*Left*) Private 7th Dragoon Guards. Print by E. Hull. (*Right*) Officer 6th Dragoon Guards, 1825. Print by del Vecchio.

PLATE 70. Officer and trumpeter, 4th Light Dragoons, 1822. Oil painting by J. Pardon.

PLATE 71. 42nd Regiment of Infantry. Highlanders, 1828. Print by E. Hull.

PLATE 72. 16th (or the Queen's) Lancers, *circa* 1833. Print by Mansion and Eschauzier.

PLATE 73. 10th (Prince of Wales's Own) Hussars, 1844. Print by H. Daubrawa and J. Harris.

in front. The drummers, according to this order of 1768, wore white coats lined with blue, the collar, cuffs, lapels, and wings being blue and the lace gold as the sergeants. The drummers also were to have very distinctive white fur caps with metal plates. It will be noted that the 3rd Guards continued to have their buttons and holes in pairs until 1774, when the lapels were ordered to be looped three and three, having nine on each lapel. Three loops were placed on each cuff, pocket and back skirt.

When the Foot Guards were due to leave for America in 1774, an historian noted an officer in Hyde Park as wearing a white frock coat trimmed with gold cord, to say nothing of blue satin for the cuffs, waistcoat and breeches.

A group of drawings in the Grand Ducal Library at Darmstadt, gives the dress of the three Foot Guard regiments *circa* 1776. These show the grenadiers of the three different regiments, all appearing similar but differing in detail. All wear the black fur cap but the front plates vary, the 1st being white metal on black, the Coldstream white on red and the 3rd Guards white on white. The loops on the lapels are in ones, twos and threes respectively. With regard to the waistbelts, only the buckle of the Coldstream Guards varies, being distinguished by the letters 'CG'. An officer of the 1st Foot Guards appears with a red coat, blue lapels, collar and cuffs, all laced in gold with the loops of the bastion fashion; he wears a gold epaulette and a gilt gorget; his gaiters, breeches and waistcoat are white and over the latter is a crimson sash tied on the left side.

The American War saw a composite battalion of Foot Guards formed for overseas service in 1776, and to conserve the officers whose position of duty led them into perilous positions, it was permitted for them to wear a simpler uniform. Instead of gold lace, the officers and sergeants wore plain white lace like the men. Officers' spontoons and sergeants' halberds were temporarily laid aside for the service. The long weapons which looked so imposing in slow evolutions of the parade ground were a serious encumbrance in the rough country of America. In fact, officers' spontoons were discontinued in 1786.

The regiments of Foot Guards, individualistic as usual, had no permanent light companies until 1793 when these were added to each regiment and assumed a distinctive dress. The head-dress was in the shape of a tall hat, but with the addition of a black fur crest. Round hats as they were called, were also being used for recruits in training. The coats were cut down and the netherwear was white gaiter-trousers, also worn by recruits over their breeches to preserve them; these particular garments were tight-fitting trousers which buttoned from the knee downward and finished in an overlap over the shoes. In 1796 it was pointed out that the flannel waistcoats and trousers worn by these light companies were originally intended as a temporary measure only, and were to be laid aside at the next clothing, when they were to assume cloth breeches and such other articles as worn by the rest of the Guardsmen.

In 1790 the Adjutant-General approved the hats of Guardsmen, in future to be made without any lace around the brim. A feather was also authorized at the same time. The prints by E. Dayes show these hats as having stays or loopings to keep the large brims in position, and the feathers vary according to the rank. The officers of the 1st and 2nd Guards wear no plumes at all. White plumes were common to the three regiments but there were differences, for the grenadiers of the 1st Foot Guards had red tips to theirs. The battalion sergeants of the 1st and 2nd Foot Guards had black tips to their plumes.

The halberd carried by sergeants was discontinued in 1792 for a spontoon or a kind of spear with a cross bar. In 1796 the white looping worn on the hats of Foot Guards was ordered to be laid aside, except for that around the button. The feathers were ordered to be white and the little tufts in the corners were also to be white. These feathers came to have the same distinctions as for line regiments, white and red for the battalion companies, white for the grenadier and green for the light companies.

INFANTRY 1760—1799

The Seven Years War (1756 to 1763) was but half run when George III came to the throne and, although the necessary modifications enforced by warfare may have been made, no elaborate attempt at glorification was made. Realization that all was not well with the soldiers' uniform—that one uniform would not do in any part of the world at any season —led to an order in 1761 that regiments in hot climates should have a bladder between the hat and its lining. Not a very sweeping change but a step in the right direction.

In 1770 the three-cornered hat was taking on a new shape. The right-hand corner was being worn practically horizontal while the left one rose in the air. The cord and tassels which were worn around the crown of the hat were encouraged to show and then occasionally hang down from the right-hand corner; the front corner became less important and, about 1787, the hat developed into a bicorne although the front peak did not entirely flatten out. By 1790 the back peak had become quite high and the front turn-up needed two laces or stays each side to keep it in place. The lace or tape on the edging of hats of N.C.O.s and men of the Foot Guards was discontinued in March 1790, and the hats were to be ornamented only by loopings and feathers. The black cockade which was kept in place with a button and a loop of gold or silver lace in the case of officers, continued in use, but the material of the cockade changed from silk or material to pressed leather.

Hats for ordinary soldiers had been without feathers, although officers had worn them in the days of Queen Anne. However, the freedom and bravado of the campaigns in North America had brought about the wearing of adornments like feathers and tufts. Light companies, grenadiers and then finally the battalion companies, the solid central fighting mass, all succumbed to the new fashion. Many different colours and fashions were chosen. Officers did not always wear feathers like the men; when they did, black was a popular colour even for General Officers. For men, the cheaper worsted tufts were supplied as mentioned before, in so many different colours, that eventually an order had to be made simplifying the number. In 1796 it was ordered that for the future, infantry of the line were to have plain hats without the lace, which had previously gone around the brim. White feathers were also ordered, but whether this was only an incomplete instruction is not clear, for the next year the feathers were specified as being red and white for battalion officers, white for grenadiers and green for light infantry, which system remained for many years. When the hats were simplified by having the lace restricted to the loop holding the rosette, all infantry officers were to have a crimson and gold cord around their hats with crimson and gold rosettes or tufts brought to the edge of the brims. The men were to have white loops around the button and white tufts mixed with the colour of the facings.

In 1798 five of the regiments which had been permitted to build up with boys, were wearing caps instead of hats. What precise pattern these may have been is not clear, but they were not the shako which came in to use later, as an order of 1799 permitted these youths to wear their old cap which was to be given up for the general pattern then under consideration. In this year the grenadiers were still permitted to wear their fur caps when in full dress, but on all other occasions were permitted the cap approved for infantry and to have a grenade in the centre of the garter on the brass plate.

The coat was a garment that served not only as a necessity to the troops, but as a vehicle for displaying the subtle regimental differences. This, too, was also receiving considerations for foreign service, and regiments raised in 1761 to go to tropical climates were to have linen linings to their coats. Even the 11th Foot serving no further away than Minorca, were ordered to have their clothing lined with brown linen.

In 1767 the number of the rank of the regiment was to be placed on the buttons of officers and men of infantry. This was repeated in the Royal Warrant of 1768, the one which attempted to consolidate and codify the changes in dress since the last Warrant of 1751. Pockets which had been made in a 'slash' fashion were ordered to be 'cross' and the sleeves were to have round cuffs and no slit at all. The new cuffs were to be three-and-a-half inches deep and made to turn up. The large cuff had now gone out of fashion. The flaps on the coat pockets were to be sewn down, in fact to be made into dummies, and the genuine pockets were to be in the lining. All coats were to be lapelled to the waist with cloth of the regimental facing.

The coats of officers were to have buttonholes of gold or silver lace or embroidery, sergeants were to have white braid and the other ranks, loops of worsted lace with their distinctive patterns; four of these loops were to be on each cuff, four on each pocket and two on each side of the split skirts. The grenadiers' coats had at the point of the shoulders round wings of red cloth with six loops of lace or braid. In 1784 it was ordered that the shoulder-straps should be made of cloth of the same colour as the regimental facings, but the practice of one regiment that had adopted an upright collar was de-precated and the usual fall-down pattern was to be worn.

The alterations of 1796 were the first steps in drastic alterations in the appearance of the infantryman. The coat which had been worn open in a gently curving manner, just caught at the top, was now to be closed all the way down to the waist. The waistcoat which had always been visible, now disappeared from sight and only remained as an article of undress, or drill, occasions. The lapels of the colour of the facings were continued in use without any alteration in width and made so that they could 'either button over occasionally or to clasp close with hooks and eyes'. The cape or collar which had lain down according to former regulations was now to stand up. An opening was to be made in the flap outside the pocket to admit the hand into it. The wings on the point of the shoulder of the grenadier coats were to remain in use; and the pocket flaps of light infantry were to be made oblique or sloped.

The closing of the coat front also brought about a shortening of the tails. Officers of the Line when on duty were to wear short coats with epaulettes, made up in the fashion like those approved for N.C.O.s and men, except that they were to be quite plain and without lace. When officers were off duty or in Dress they were to wear their uniform coats, that is with the long tails as already established. The complicated lapels were deemed unnecessary for the infantry men and so late in 1797 an order abolished them, leaving the coat a single-breasted garment with a row of buttons and lace loops.

Although white waistcoats were becoming the general fashion, as late as September 1767 permission was given for red waistcoats to be made out of the old coats for the men. This preference for white gradually spread throughout the infantry. In 1765 the breeches and linings of the 4th King's Own were ordered to be white. In 1766 the 14th Foot had breeches of buff instead of red, thus matching the facings and the waistcoat. The 5th Foot took white breeches instead of green. White waistcoats and breeches instead of red were taken by the officers of the 12th, 20th and 25th Foot, and in the case of the 46th white breeches took the place of the red ones. By 1767 a general suggestion was sent to all Colonels proposing white breeches and so eventually white was chosen for the waistcoats and breeches of all infantry except those who had buff facings, and in their case buff was the colour of their waistcoats and breeches.

Although breeches continued to be the general form of dress, tight-fitting pantaloons were worn in the last decade of the century. Officers had their own knitted version of these in bright blue but other varieties were worn. The loose overall trousers were also being worn by recruits and for fatigue duties.

In 1767 it was ordered that His Majesty's Regiments of Foot were to lay aside their white gaiters and to have black ones in future. These black linen gaiters had small stiffened tops which came up above the knee. At the time of the American Revolution it was found convenient to wear calf-length gaiters in the field and these were adopted by light companies; linen was also found not to be very practical when damp, and worn for long periods; thus woollen ones were worn and made regulation with white metal buttons, in 1784. The tops on the long gaiters were discontinued and they finished just below the pan of the knee.

Equipment also underwent changes of fashion. In 1767 swords were discontinued by the battalion men, but the grenadier companies continued them though they were little more than ornaments. In 1786 the officers' spontoons were discontinued and swords were the weapons of their rank. In 1788 these swords were to be hung from shoulder-belts. The long-shafted halberds which were the sign of rank for sergeants, were at last realized to be cumbersome and awkward. In 1791 a trial issue of pikes was made to certain regiments on home stations. These were considered successful and in 1792 it was ordered that these pikes should gradually replace the halberds. The pike, or spontoon as it was also known, had a simple spear head instead of the combined spike, hook and blade, and as the weapon was still to be of use in actual warfare, a crosspiece was added to prevent it entering a body too far. The Foot Guards appear to have retained the obsolete halberd as long as possible and prints by Dayes *circa* 1792 show it still in use.

The opportunity was also taken to relieve the officers of grenadiers, light infantry and fusiliers from the obligation of carrying fusils; and they were permitted to use their swords on ceremonial occasions. Light infantry sergeants were not so lucky and they had to continue with the fusil.

The Warrant of 1768 specified two epaulettes for officers of grenadiers but only one for those of battalion companies. The epaulettes of officers were ordered in 1791 to have the addition of a grenade in the case of grenadier company officers and a bugle for light company officers. At the same time, Field Officers were permitted to wear two epaulettes like the grenadier officers.

Officers' swords were regularized at the same time, all in future to have guards, pommels and shells of gilt, thus abolishing the silver ones carried by silver-laced regiments. The gorget was now also made of a universal pattern and in all cases to be gilt with ribbons and tufts (or rosettes) at each end in the colour of the regimental facing.

The practice of putting the waistbelt over the right shoulder when on service in America was eventually permitted by an order of 1784, by which date it was also realized that grenadier swords had not been used and they were 'laid aside'.

The actual number of regiments of foot went down in times of peace and up in times of warfare. Numbers appeared for a short while and then disappeared. In many cases even the facings are unknown, let alone the finer parts of the dress. The list as given in the 1768 Warrant gives a good basis, but there does not appear to have been another complete official list until the next century.

FROM THE ROYAL WARRANT DATED 19TH DECEMBER 1768

Regts.	Facings	Lace			Officers' Lace
1st	Blue	White	with	Blue double worm	Gold
2nd	Blue	,,	,,	Blue stripe	Silver
3rd	Buff	,,	,,	Yellow, Red and Black stripe	,,
4th	Blue	,,	,,	Blue stripe	,,
5th	Gosling Green	,,	,,	2 Red stripes	,,
6th	Deep Yellow	,,	,,	Yellow and Red stripes	,,
7th	Blue	,,	,,	Blue stripe	,,
8th	Blue	..	,,	Blue and Yellow stripe	,,
9th	Yellow	,,	,,	2 Black stripes	Silver
10th	Bright Yellow	,,	,,	Blue stripe	,,
11th	Full Green	,,	,,	2 Red, 2 Green stripes	Gold
12th	Yellow	,,	,,	Yellow, Crimson and Black stripes	,,
13th	Philemot Yellow	,,	,,	Yellow stripe	Silver
14th	Buff	,,	,,	Blue, and Red worm, Buff stripe	,,
15th	Yellow	,,	,,	Yellow and Black worm, Red stripe	,,
16th	Yellow	,,	,,	Crimson stripe	,,
17th	Greyish White	,,	,,	2 Blue, 1 Yellow stripe	,,
18th	Blue	,,	,,	Blue stripe	Gold
19th	Deep Green	,,	,,	2 stripes, Red and Green	,,
20th	Pale Yellow	,,	,,	Red and Black stripe	Silver
21st	Blue	,,	,,	Blue stripe	Gold
22nd	Pale Buff	,,	,,	1 Red, 1 Blue stripe	,,
23rd	Blue	,,	,,	Red, Blue and Yellow stripe	,,
24th	Willow Green	,,	,,	1 Red and 1 Green stripe	Silver
25th	Deep Yellow	,,	,,	Blue, Yellow and Red stripe	Gold
26th	Pale Yellow	,,	,,	1 Blue, 2 Yellow stripes	Silver
27th	Buff	,,	,,	1 Blue, 1 Red stripe	Gold
28th	Bright Yellow	,,	,,	1 Yellow, 2 Black stripes	Silver
29th	Yellow	,,	,,	2 Blue, 1 Yellow stripe	,,
30th	Pale Yellow	,,	,,	1 Sky Blue stripe	,,
31st	Buff	,,	,,	Blue and Yellow worm, small Red stripe	,,

Regts.	Facings	Lace		Officers' Lace
32nd	White	White with	Black worm and Black stripe	Gold
33rd	Red	,, ,,	Red stripe in middle	Silver
34th	Bright Yellow	,, ,,	Blue and Yellow worm, Red stripe	,,
35th	Orange	,, ,,	1 Yellow stripe	,,
36th	Green	,, ,,	1 Red, 1 Green stripe	Gold
37th	Yellow	,, ,,	1 Red, 1 Yellow stripe	Silver
38th	Yellow	,, ,,	2 Red, 1 Yellow stripe	,,
39th	Green	,, ,,	Light Green stripe	Gold
40th	Buff	,, ,,	Red and Black stripe	,,
41st	Blue	,, ,,	plain buttonhole	,,
42nd	Blue	,, ,,	1 Red stripe	,,
43rd	White	,, ,,	1 Red, 1 Black stripe	Silver
44th	Yellow	,, ,,	Blue, Yellow and Black stripe	,,
45th	Deep Green	,, ,,	Green stripe	,,
46th	Yellow	,, ,,	Red and Purple worms	,,
47th	White	,, ,,	1 Red, 2 Black stripes	,,
48th	Buff	,, ,,	Black and Red stripe	Gold
49th	Full Green	,, ,,	2 Red and 1 Green stripe	,,
50th	Black	,, ,,	Red stripe	Silver
51st	Deep Green	,, ,,	Green worm stripe	Gold
52nd	Buff	,, ,,	Red worm and 1 Orange stripe	Silver
53rd	Red	,, ,,	Red stripe	Gold
54th	Popinjay Green	,, ,,	Green stripe	Silver
55th	Dark Green	,, ,,	2 Green stripes	Gold
56th	Purple	,, ,,	Pink coloured stripe	Silver
57th	Yellow	,, ,,	Black stripe	Gold
58th	Black	,, ,,	Red stripe	,,
59th	Purple	,, ,,	Red and Yellow stripe	Silver
60th	Blue	,, ,,	2 Blue stripes	,,
61st	Buff	,, ,,	Blue stripe	,,
62nd	Yellowish Buff	,, ,,	2 Blue, 1 Straw coloured stripe	,,
63rd	Very Deep Green	,, ,,	Very small Green stripe	,,
64th	Black	,, ,,	Red and Black stripe	Gold
65th	White	,, ,,	Red and Black worm, Black stripe	Silver
66th	Yellowish Green	,, ,,	1 Crimson and Green, 1 Green stripe	Gold
67th	Pale Yellow	,, ,,	Yellow, Purple and Green stripes	Silver
68th	Deep Green	,, ,,	Yellow and Black stripe	,,
69th	Willow Green	,, ,,	1 Red and 2 Green stripes	Gold
70th	Black	,, ,,	narrow Black worm stripe	,,

LIGHT INFANTRY 1770—1799

In 1770 the previous usefulness of the light companies in America was remembered and estimates were made for adding a tenth Light Infantry company to every Marching Regiment. These were intended to carry out special tasks and, although attached to the eighteen infantry regiments then stationed in North America, they were frequently employed on detached duty. To travel over and through the difficult terrain, their dress and equipment was modified from that of the usual battalion companies. They were given shorter and lighter muskets and carried bayonets and hatchets. The long skirts of the coats were shortened to produce jackets, and new headgear was introduced to stand up to hard wear: the new cap was to be of black leather with three chains around the crown and a piece of plate included in the centre of the crown; this made a good defence against the blows of swords and tomahawks. The small turned-up front was to carry the devices of a Crown, 'GR' and the number of the regiment. A Board deciding on the Light Infantry clothing in 1771, accepted a cap of the pattern as used by the 14th Foot but recommended that the letters 'LI' be left out.

Another distinction for light infantry was the red waistcoat, but the breeches were to continue white or buff as already worn in the regiments. Long black gaiters were not thought suitable for bush warfare, and in 1771 they were to come no higher than the calf of the leg, thus permitting freedom to the legs, yet performing their functions of protecting the flimsy covering of the feet. The damp conditions of the warfare showed linen as the basic material to be unsuitable and soon after the war the gaiters were ordered to be made of black wool.

The accoutrements were to be after the pattern used in the 46th Foot—with a small cartridge box containing nine rounds in one row, to be worn before, on a belt of tanned leather around the waist. The belt was to have two frogs, one for the bayonet and the other to take the hatchet.

Overcoats were not worn and a 'maude' (a grey plaid) was recommended for the Light Infantry in the time of war, to be used instead of a blanket. A man of the 25th Foot wrapped in one of these is shown on sentry duty in a picture in Edinburgh.

Powder horns were also a feature of the light companies, especially in North America, where the soldiers spent much time in carving the horns with a wealth of elaborate detail.

Although the printed references to leather caps were frequently being made on the lines as described above, other evidence shows that many varieties were worn. It was in America that the habit of using feathers and plumes to deck the head-dress came into prominence. Needless to say that at first this custom was unauthorized and thus a variety of colours was used. It will be noted that the Black Watch used a tuft some years before it is mentioned in 1761, and the Light Company of the 46th Foot dyed their plumes red out of bravado so that the enemy should recognize them. The Light Company of the 5th Foot in America had a head-dress with a brass St George and the Dragon in front and a red horsehair crest.

Water-colours made in Minorca by an Italian artist, show what must have been the dress of some early light companies before the dress had become regularized and was still in an experimental stage. The 11th Foot are shown with a shortened version of the grenadier fur cap with a black tuft on the left side and the front ornamented with a Crown 'GR' and 'XI', apparently in brass. The 13th Foot are shown with a black head-dress bearing in front the Crown 'GR' and 'XIII' in white metal while a full yellowish mane sweeps across the top. The 25th Foot had a red head-dress with a black fur edging and on the small red front was the device of the Thistle and the Motto *Nemo Me Impune Lacessit*. A light company officer has the same type of cap with a sprig of green on the left side.

The equipment is still shown as of white leather and with the pouch at the side. The waistcoats in these pictures are still shown as white, and the gaiters long, although the light company men of the 25th Foot in a group painted soon after, wear the short gaiters.

When the Light Dragoons were given a new pattern helmet-cap in 1784, the Light Infantry were also given a new pattern. This may have been the same style, for the so-called Tarleton type was in use at the end of the century when the shako became the general head-dress. The priming horn, bullet-bag and powder horn were to be discontinued at this time but the hammer-hatchet was still to be carried.

The general change to the closed coat in the order of 1797 no longer let the red waistcoats of the light companies be seen, and these were changed to plain white ones, an economical advantage.

GRENADIERS AND FUSILIERS 1760—1799

Although all infantrymen were technically fusiliers, because their weapon was a fusil —the French used the term fusilier to denote the common battalion man—the term was continued in the British Army to denote a more important type of infantryman. Certain regiments, which had been privileged to carry fusils when others had but the matchlock, continued to use their original title and to wear a dress with points of similarity to that of grenadiers. The old 7th, 21st and 23rd Regiments representing England, Scotland and Wales, continued to be 'show' regiments. The 27th Regiment were the Inniskilling Foot and the Royal Irish Fusiliers, not being created till much later.

The cloth caps so long a distinction were superseded by black bearskin ones by the Royal Warrant of 1768, but the Royal Fusiliers clung to their cloth caps until 1770 at least. The black fur caps were also permitted for grenadier companies, but actually had been acquiring popularity in the years previous to the Warrant, and in fact were being worn by several regiments when the Warrant appeared. The 25th Foot applied successfully in 1763 for permission to wear the fur cap. In 1766, the 12th, 20th, 25th and 33rd Regiments of Foot were all permitted the same distinction and the next year the 4th Foot (and possibly others) adopted the new mode. The Warrant of 1768 ordered the caps 'to be of black bearskin. On the front the King's Crest, of silver plated metal, on a black ground with the motto *Nec Aspera Terrent*. A grenade on the back part with the number of the regiment on it. The Royal Regiments and the 6 Old Corps are to have the crest and grenade, and also other particulars as specified. The badge of the Royal Regiments is to be white and set on near the top part of the cap. The height of the cap (without the bearskin which reaches beyond the top) to be twelve inches.' Fusiliers were to have a similar cap but not so high and without the grenade on the back part. No doubt most of the remaining regiments took the new pattern at the next clothing, but we know that the Buffs clung to their embroidered cloth cap with its green dragon for some time at least, for it is shown in an oil-painting produced in Minorca. Many regiments who were not permitted special badges wore plain fur caps without any plates at all, despite the hand-coloured book in the Prince Consort's Library which shows every grenadier in the 1768 dress strictly according to regulations.

As fusilier regiments had the semblance of all being grenadiers there was no reason to have a special grenadier company. But light companies were something different and so we find that in 1771 the Royal Fusiliers had one such company, although it was known in the Regiment as the left flank company. The 7th Royal Fusiliers had Prince Edward, later the Duke of Kent, as their Colonel from 1784 onwards and his period of command saw much dandification of the men's dress. A series of water-colours made soon after he took command show many interesting details of the uniform. The normal officers wear a tall black fur cap, a long white feather on the left, gold cords and tassels across the front and finishing on the right side while the lower front is occupied with the regulation plate. The red coat has a 'stand-up, fall-down' collar, the side-loops of which fasten on to those of the lapels. The gold epaulettes have the regimental device of the white rose inside a crowned Garter.

It is the light company which has the most striking dress. The black helmet-cap has the fur crest running transversely instead of from front to rear. The metal ornaments in front have *Nec Aspera Terrent* on a curved band under which is a Garter Star with yet another band running from ear-boss to ear-boss just above the peak. The officers had gilt ornaments, the men white metal. The open coat shows to perfection the red waist-coat, braided and looped. The musician for the light company is strangely enough a drummer, not a bugler or horn-blower as one might expect for light infantry.

The pioneer is a most imposing person in his tall fur cap with white plume and red fronted plate. From his waist hangs his dark apron tucked in on one side, but ready to let fall down when rough work comes along. His stout axe is held upright in his left arm and his curled mustachios meet his elegantly powdered 'side-chops'.

The mention of the white plumes notes that the habit adopted during the American War was becoming official. In fact white was usually the mark of a grenadier or fusilier. A new pattern bearskin cap was authorized in 1784, presumably regularizing the practices already in being. The sword carried for so many years by the grenadiers was now abolished as being an unnecessary item as was also the match case—that last relic of the use of grenades.

Grenadiers were also distinguished by the manner in which they wore their hair: it was turned up at the back in an elaborate plait and when powdered was as elegant as any lady's coiffure. The hat was also worn by the grenadier although not on full dress parades.

HIGHLANDERS 1760—1799

The Scottish dress in this period changed from the rather rough and ready one based on civilian attire into something quite military and much like that last full dress uniform still to be seen on some occasions. Once again it was the proving ground of the American continent which saw to the abolition of some features and the introduction of others.

Regimental orders of the Black Watch in 1761 when they were on service in America, spoke of the black feathers for the officers and the bearskin tufts for the men being worn in their new bonnets. 'Tomihawks', powder horns and shot bags are mentioned for the light company. The bonnets of this period were beginning to achieve the elements of the diced border. A contemporary picture might show a simpler border of red or one of red and white squares.

The peace of 1763 brought about a general reduction in the armed forces, and all the newly raised Highland regiments disappeared, leaving the 42nd or the Black Watch the sole kilted representative in the British Army. In 1768 the 42nd Regiment came back to Ireland where they were to adjust themselves to the new Warrant. This affected the cut of their coats, for although they remained short, to enable the plaid to be worn, the cuffs and lapels were of the new fashion.

Waistcoats were changed from red to white at which time, according to Stewart of Garth, the old badgerskin purses were replaced by ones of white goatskin and buff leather. The officers who, in America, had dressed simply to make little difference between the men and themselves, now elaborated the narrow edging of gold lace on the coats, and had embroidery. The sergeants of the Black Watch for many years wore silver lace on their coats. The officers who had worn shoulder-knots now changed to epaulettes. The crimson sashes of officers were not worn in normal infantry fashion (around the waist) but over the left shoulder. By doing this the ends of the sash would not become entangled with the broadsword belt. The men at this time carried the sword. In fact, when the American War began and the regiment went to America, they had pistols and swords, but proving inconvenient these were laid aside and never again taken into wear.

The growth of the American War gave the opportunity for new Highland regiments to be raised. Of these, the 71st or Fraser's had white facings, the 73rd or McKenzie's had buff, the 74th or Argyll's yellow, the 76th or McDonald's had dark green and the 78th under the Earl of Seaforth were described as 'oranges', or dark yellow. The 81st or Aberdeen Highlanders, had white facings and the Royal Highland Emigrants had blue facings as might be expected for a Royal regiment. As to the tartans of these various regiments, information is very sparse—normally one expects a basis of Black Watch or Government tartan possibly combined with a regimental overstripe.

Examples of pictures *circa* 1780 show extra black feathers or tufts in the bonnet, but these feathers still remain in a group near the cockade. Most of the newly raised Highland regiments were disbanded in the peace of 1783, but the 73rd and the 78th continued in being although renumbered the 71st and 72nd, now better known as the First Battalions of the Highland Light Infantry and the Seaforth Highlanders. In 1786 the Second Battalion of the Black Watch became numbered the 73rd regiment of Foot. In 1787 fresh regiments were raised for service in India, the new 74th and 75th being Highland regiments with white and yellow facings respectively. These last two continued in being to modern times as the Second Battalion of the Highland Light Infantry and the First Battalion of the Gordon Highlanders.

The rumblings of the French Revolution and the threat of war brought into being many new regiments of infantry, numbering even up to the 135th Foot. Of these the 78th, 79th, 94th, 97th, 98th, 100th and 109th were Scottish. The first two became the Second Battalion of the Seaforth and the Cameron Highlanders, but the others were disbanded or drafted within a couple of years and little information remains. The 78th had buff and the 79th had green facings, both with gold distinctions for the officers. On a reduction of the army in 1798 the 98th and 100th were renumbered the 91st and 92nd respectively. They both had yellow facings and continued in existence to be known as the First Battalion of the Argyll and Sutherland Highlanders and as the Second Battalion of the Gordon Highlanders.

The Highland dress underwent certain alterations during the service conditions in America. So much of their clothing suffered that they appeared rather as a regiment of infantry in short coats but retaining their bonnets. Instead of tartan plaids, the men wore white ticken trousers with short black gaiters.

Once again the Black Watch returned to the United Kingdom, and a report of 1790 comments at length on their head-dress. 'Their bonnets are entirely disfigured. They are so covered with lofty feathers that they appear like grenadier caps of black bearskin and are made by that reason, expensive to the men.' The next year saw a striking change in their equipment and the black belts which they had worn for so long were changed into white ones like the rest of the Line. This brought forth the comment that their 'appearance was improved by now having white accoutrements in lieu of black.' The most cherished feature of the Black Watch dress is the red hackle; these were distributed to the regiment in June 1795 in honour it is said, of their good behaviour at Geldermalsen in the beginning of the year. When the Black Watch had to proceed to warmer climes they temporarily lost their Scottish items of dress.

LIFE GUARDS 1799—1820

The prints that appeared in the *British Military Library* (mentioned in the last section), show the uniforms of the 1st and 2nd Life Guards in September and December 1798 respectively, and as such they are little different from that of the beginning of this period. The uniform shown in Atkinson's print of 1805 of the Lottery Wheel being drawn through London streets, shows the same dress for Life Guards, some mounted and others on foot. The large black cocked hats were worn 'athwart' the head and carried large white and red feather plumes. The dismounted guard carry muskets with fixed bayonets and the long sword and scabbard is hooked up on the left hip.

Dighton also made pictures of officers of this regiment, emphasizing the large white gauntlets, the crimson waist sash and the high jack-boots. The officers wore wide white belts crossing the chest, one to take a sword and the other a pouch. The whole of the equipment was on the large scale and no doubt cumbersome on foot but more manageable when mounted on the large black steeds.

Large epaulettes were worn by officers and men, but in 1812 a print by Charles Hamilton Smith shows an officer of the 2nd Life Guards without epaulettes, wearing instead a gold aiguillette on the right shoulder. The cumbersome dress with a cocked hat and high boots which had been worn on active service in the Peninsular War, was about to give way to a more practical uniform. The Prince Regent ordered that the cocked hats with feathers were to be discontinued and that brass helmets with black horsehair crests were to be substituted. The long red coats trimmed with gold lace across the front, the skirts and the cuffs, were to be replaced by short jackets or coatees, with less gold lace on the collar, cuffs and ends of skirts. The officers were to adopt a gold and scarlet sash, and the men were to wear one woven in blue and yellow. The high jack-boots and leather pantaloons were still continued for state occasions but on others shortboots and blue-grey overalls with scarlet side seams, were to be worn. The stiff gauntlet gloves were still worn with the jack-boots but short leather gloves were for ordinary duties. Even the long muskets and bayonets and horse pistols were placed in the Tower stores, and short carbines and small pistols were issued.

The new helmet was somewhat like a pattern being worn by the Dragoon Guards.

The black skull had a peak and metal scales to fasten under the chin. A metal crest on top held a flowing black horse-hair mane and there was also a small pompon in front. The general effect of this helmet was very like the pattern worn by the French heavy cavalry and this may be the reason why it was discontinued and altered in 1814 to have a high-standing, fore-projecting woollen crest of blue and red. An addition to the new pattern helmet was the cut feather plume of white set in a red base on the left side. This head-dress was the one worn at Waterloo and for two years later. It was deemed sufficiently distinguished to be permitted to be worn at court instead of the cocked hat.

The exact pattern of the new coatee is not clear. Some pictures of 1812—13 show it with two rows of buttons down the front, but by the time of Waterloo it is generally shown as single-breasted. Some examples are shown with lace around the top of the collar, continuing down the front and around the skirts which may be that of the 1st Life Guards. Then there are others with a single row of buttons down the front which might be the 2nd Life Guards, or even represent a more undress version of coatee. The flat collar loops were distinctive for heavy cavalry.

In 1814 there was a review by the Prince Regent at which the King of Prussia and the Emperor of Russia were present; this occasion was notable because after many years of lapsing cuirasses were again taken into wear, this time by a subdivision of the 2nd Life Guards; but the introduction was only a temporary one and their use was again discontinued. This year also saw other alterations in the equipment—sabretaches were added to the sword-belts and instead of the elaborate scarlet horse furniture, sheepskin shabraques and blue horse furniture were taken into use. The blue and yellow sashes of the men were also changed for ones of scarlet and yellow. The full dress sabretaches and pouches with their expensive devices of embroidery and sequins, would not have been seen on service but they did appear on officers during the occupation of Paris after Napoleon's defeat.

Napoleon having been finally defeated and carefully exiled, opportunity could now be made to beautify the soldiers' dress. Thus in 1817, a new helmet was introduced: this was of polished steel with brass ornaments and a high bearskin crest. This pattern also had a rayed plate in front which bore the Royal coat of arms and the battle-honours of Waterloo and Peninsula. New pattern cloth housings of a striking claret-mixture now replaced the old pattern; this might be considered sufficiently elaborate for service and normal duties, but the Prince Regent also had an eye for State occasions and ordered grenadier caps and long clothing for the Life Guards as well. These fur caps were of a much coveted shape and also appeared in the Foot Guards. The shaggy black fur was topped by a white cut feather and gold cords, and tassels went around the middle of the cap. In February 1820 the Court went into mourning. Officers of the Life Guards were to wear black morocco sword slings of the same pattern as worn with the broad sword, and the tassel was to be covered with black crape.

ROYAL HORSE GUARDS 1799—1820

The dress of the Royal Horse Guards in some measure followed that of the Life Guards. The coat was closed down the front before the turn of the century, and had two rows of buttons down the red plastron front. Head-dress, breeches, sword and high boots were similar to those of the senior regiment, but the colour of the belts and breeches was still buff and the distinctive flask-cord was still carried by the Royal Horse Guards. Gold epaulettes were worn in the first years of the new century.

The *British Military Library* print of November 1798 shows the Horse Guards in the usual long blue coat with scarlet facings and linings. The lace for the officers was gold as the text told us, but the uniform of the privates had plain red lapels, unlaced. The privates also wore 'very broad cross buff belts and gloves'. The troopers' horses were black with long tails. The print of the officer shows his horse as dark brown with a black mane and tail. The harness is black with red rosettes at the ears. Shabraques were not worn but black fur flounces cover the pistol holsters.

The Royal Horse Guards saw service abroad in the Peninsular War and no doubt were authorized the common change of dress which took place in 1812, but there may have been a delay in receiving new clothing while on active service, for prints of the battle of Vittoria which took place in July 1813, show the Horse Guards charging in their old uniforms with cocked hats. However, we know that by 1814 they were wearing the new uniform topped by the black helmet with gilt fittings and black and red worsted crest. The customary plume in red and white was worn on the left side. The ear-bosses were designed as lion's heads and the front plate carried the reversed 'GR' cypher. The short jacket had no buttons down the front but closed with a double row of lace which continued around the edges. The service overalls are shown as light blue-grey with red stripes down the sides. The waist sashes of officers were gold with three red lines. The sabretache was now worn, the full dress version being most beautifully embroidered with the device of the Garter Star surrounded by a trophy of arms. The officers' full dress pouch belt of this period appears to have been all gold. The sword belt was also an elaborate affair with a large white metal star on the gold clasp-plate.

New steel helmets came in for the Horse Guards about 1817 and new clothing was approved in 1818, which must have been very much on the lines and cut of the senior regiment.

DRAGOON GUARDS 1799—1820

The dress of Dragoon Guards is shown in the coloured plates of the *British Military Library* for 1799 to 1802. The bicorne or cocked hat is shown in all cases, but just as this cumbersome head-dress had given place to a shako in the infantry, so did it give place to a cylindrical cap in the heavy cavalry. In 1804 the officers and men of the King's Dragoon Guards were to wear caps on all occasions.

But the great changes of dress in 1812 brought a new head-dress—a helmet: this had a black leather skull with a metal comb and fittings. At first a woollen crest was advocated but this was changed for a black pompon and a long flowing tail of black horsehair. This pattern remained in use even after the Napoleonic wars. These helmets had a front plate with the reversed 'GR' cypher and a band with the name of the regiment written on it.

The heavy cavalry coats which had been shortened in 1796 continued in use until 1812, when they gave way to a pattern without loops on the chest, but having broad lace on the collar, down the front and around the skirts. This pattern coatee or jacket was fastened by hooks and eyes and not buttoned. Wings on the shoulders had given place to epaulettes, but the simplified 1812 pattern had straps only, for the men.

The facings of this period according to C. Hamilton Smith, were dark blue for the King's Dragoon Guards and the Fourth Royal Irish Dragoon Guards, differenced by gold lace for the former and silver lace for the latter. Black was chosen for the Queen's and the 7th Princess Royal's, silver and gold lace being the respective differences. White served for the 3rd Prince of Wales's and the 6th Carabiniers, lace gold and silver respectively, while the 5th or Princess Charlotte of Wales's had green facings and gold lace. In 1815 the 3rd Dragoon Guards changed their facings to blue but in 1819 changed them again, this time to yellow.

In 1819 the short jackets were changed for coatees, that is, that the skirts of the coats were lengthened and the red patches removed from the ends of the collar, the lace being carried from the bottom of the garment up to the top of the collar. In the 5th Dragoon Guards the stripe on the men's trousers was made of green cloth the width of the officers' stripes.

DRAGOONS 1799—1820

The commencement of the period with which we are now dealing began with a disaster. The 5th Irish Dragoons which had performed such valiant services from the days of William III had become involved in the troubles of Ireland and were, rightly or wrongly, disbanded in 1799. Not only that but for many years the number five remained vacant, and the Army Lists jumped from the 4th Dragoons to the 6th Dragoons.

The dress of Dragoons followed that of the Dragoon Guards very closely. Hats were worn with the feather in the national colours of white and red but there was another little-known headgear in use: Charles Hamilton Smith in his original sketches of 1800 shows a cylindrical hat or cap in use for Dragoons; these are without peaks, have a badge in front and a bag at the side. These caps appear to have remained as undress caps, for both hats and caps are mentioned in certain cavalry Standing Orders. The Royal Dragoons had an issue of hats as late as 1811 but 1812 saw new helmets authorized. These were very similar to those adopted by the Dragoon Guards.

The Scots Greys had their own head-dress—the grenadier cap which dated back to the days of Marlborough. True, the cap followed the changes of popular fancy, and the one of 1800 was of black bearskin with a brass plate in front over the leather peak. Plaited cords and festoons were worn, white in the case of the men and gold for the officers. A white-over-red plume was worn on the left side. The back had a circular red patch at the top with the White Horse of Hanover on it. After the battle of Waterloo a label with that honour inscribed upon it was added to the cap and placed just above the front plate.

The jackets were very similar in style to those of the Dragoon Guards. The loops down the front which had been equal in length were noted in 1804 as being tapered from the top down to the waist. The cuff of the dragoon was made pointed, as opposed to the square cuff of the dragoon guard, but when the large gauntlet gloves were worn it was difficult to differentiate. The men's jackets were ordered to be made shorter in 1811, and the loops down the front were discontinued for the broad lace already noted as being worn by the Household Cavalry and Dragoon Guards.

The facings of the Dragoons at this period are shown in C. H. Smith's chart of 1812 where the 1st, 2nd and 3rd all have blue collars and cuffs. Only the Scots Greys have silver lace and the other two have gold. The 4th Dragoons have light blue and silver, and the 6th or Inniskilling have yellow and silver lace. In 1818 the 3rd and 4th Dragoons were converted to Light Dragoons leaving only three dragoon regiments, the Royal Dragoons, the Royal Scots Greys, and the Inniskilling Dragoons representing the three Kingdoms in a Union Brigade of Cavalry.

The leather breeches although lasting well from the point of economy, were super-seded in 1811 by breeches of plush: these were thick and unsuitable on active service. Thus the invading overall or trousers was introduced. Web breeches were worn below and the grey overalls on top. The stripes down the sides were varying in colour, usually being red but the Scots Greys had blue. These overalls were frequently made with rows of buttons down the side seams so that they could make a close fit. Fancy leather strapping was also added to increase the life of the garment.

LIGHT DRAGOONS 1799—1820

In 1800 C. Hamilton Smith made a chart of the uniforms of Light Dragoons which numbered up to twenty-nine at that time. A review of these will be of assistance as the last complete official list of the regiments was in the Royal Warrant of 1768. Regiments were supposed to have brief details of their uniforms inserted in the Army Lists but, in point of fact, the regiments raised since 1768 were not described and the Army List in 1799 contains such information that the 15th and 16th Light Dragoons had blue facings and half lapels, the 13th had green facings and such like, although they had changed as long as fifteen years before when the blue uniform was adopted instead of the red.

C. Hamilton Smith gives blue jackets for all, except the 8th and 25th who are shown with the light blue-grey of tropical wear. Red facings are shown for the 8th, 15th, 16th and 25th. White facings are given for the 7th, 17th, 18th and 27th. Yellow is given for the 10th, 19th, 20th, 23rd, 24th, 28th and 29th, while the 12th are given pale yellow. Buff is the distinction of the 9th, 11th, 13th. Two regiments are unique: the 14th in having orange facings, and the 26th with blue. The breeches are white in all cases except those regiments with buff facings and then they follow the usual custom of adopting buff.

The Peace of Amiens saw several Light Dragoon regiments disbanded. The 22nd, 23rd, 24th and 28th disappeared and the remaining regiments, the 25th, 26th, 27th and 29th took new numbers—the 22nd, 23rd, 24th and 25th. Soon after the commence-ment of hostilities again with France, the 7th, 10th, 15th and 18th Light Dragoons were equipped as Hussars and are dealt with separately, although they retained the same numbers. In 1808 the facings were apparently not thought distinctive enough and those of the regiments numbered from twenty to twenty-five were ordered in future to be orange, pink, pink, crimson, light grey and light grey respectively. The further difference was pointed out in the lace which was to be gold or yellow for the 20th, 21st and 24th, while the other three had silver or white lace.

Despite being in the middle of the great series of campaigns with the forces of Napo-leon, it was deemed a proper moment to change the style of many uniforms and the Light

Dragoons were not overlooked. The fur-crested helmet in wear since 1784 was now to be abandoned for a shako. The new shako was made with a bell-top, that is widened out, and in fact was so similar to that worn by certain of the enemy's cavalry, that when they appeared for the first time in the Peninsular War, they were mistaken for the French. The new shako was of black felt or beaver for normal wear, although a white version was produced for tropical climates. The lace around the top was white or yellow, according to whether the officers had silver or gold lace (which they of course wore around their shakos). The plume in front was white over red, which was becoming the national distinction, made in feathers for the officers and in worsted for the men. The cords to keep the shako from being lost were of white or yellow for the men, but the officers' cords were gold and crimson mixed.

The old heavily braided tailless body garment was changed for a much simpler jacket with small tails behind. The dark blue garment had collar, cuffs, plastron, turn-back skirts and seam-pipings all of the colour of the regimental facings. Instead of the shoulder-cords as worn on the previous garment two epaulettes were now in use, being gold or silver for the officers and the usual yellow or white for the men, the metal buttons also following the same rule. The waist girdle was in parallel stripes, gold and crimson for all officers, but for the men blue mixed with the colour of the facings.

The tight white breeches now disappeared from the battlefield and blue-grey trousers took their place. Down the outward seams were coloured stripes, shown red in pictures of 1812 but of the regimental facing colour in later prints.

The new regulation for the facings and distinction on this new dress had slight changes from the previous dress: an order of September 1811 itemized them. Scarlet was for the 8th and 16th, gold and silver being the respective lace. Crimson was the facing colour for the 9th and 23rd, gold and silver in the same fashion making the difference. Buff for the 11th and 13th, silver and gold in this case. Yellow was for the 12th and 19th, silver and gold for the lace. Orange was for the 14th and 20th, silver and gold in that order. White and silver for the 17th alone. Pink for the 21st and 22nd, gold and silver for the lace and finally light grey for the 24th and 25th, gold and silver for the lace.

It may be that the 21st Light Dragoons never adopted the pink facings as that colour was not a popular one. They were serving abroad and may have avoided that unserviceable colour, keeping their old colour until 1814 when they were given permission to wear black facings with silver lace: even this lace was changed to gold in July 1815. Similarly the 22nd do not appear to have liked 'pink' either, for in October 1814, white facings were permitted. It is not clear whether this colour was adopted, for in December of the same year the men were said to be wearing pink on their new jackets and the officers red. Indecision seems to have been the order of the day, for in July 1815 red facings were permitted, but in November another order had come out definitely ordering white.

In 1816 the 9th, 12th, 16th, 19th and 23rd were converted to Lancers, and the following year the 12th Light Dragoons were quick to seize the opportunity to adopt crimson facings with gold lace. The years that followed saw one after another of the high-numbered Light Dragoon regiments being disbanded until the highest number was seventeen. As a slight compensation, in 1818, the 3rd and 4th Dragoons were converted into Light Dragoons. The change of the red coat to blue meant a change of facings also, and the

PLATE 74. Standard bearer, 1st Regiment of Life Guards, 1829. Print by E. Hull.

PLATE 75. Officer of the 5th (or Prince of Wales's) Dragoon Guards, *circa* 1833.
Print by Mansion and Eschauzier.

PLATE 76. Officers, Infantry of the Line, 1864. Print by Messrs. W. Jones & Co.

PLATE 77. Regiments of the Line. (*From left to right*) 41st, 10th and 55th Foot, Rifle Brigade, 29th Foot, 32nd Light Infantry, Piper and Corporal 78th Highlanders. Print by G. H. Thomas, 1869.

3rd took red facings as being most befitting to the King's Own Light Dragoons, and the 4th discontinuing their green for yellow.

HUSSARS 1805—1820

Although the authorities had toyed with the idea of hussars from the middle of the eighteenth century and even trained men to perform similar duties, they could not bring themselves to make a proper regiment of Hussars in dress or name. But the practices of the Light Dragoons and the gradual adoption of certain items of dress could not keep the change at bay for ever. The Prince Regent had given his own regiment many rich portions of dress and so, in 1805, when the 7th, 10th and 15th Light Dragoons were permitted to call themselves Hussars (but only in brackets ofter their name in the Army List), little visible change was necessary besides changing the head-dress to the fur busby. The new type of cavalrymen do not seem to have been fully converted until 1807.

The fur cap as adopted at this time was a tall cylinder or muff, and the cloth bag which sprang from the top was not fixed to fall on the right side as is the modern practice. The bag which commenced at the crown of the head and rose in the well of the fur walls, emerged as a bag free to fall where it wished. The elements of the stocking cap of Queen Anne's day were still to be found. For officers a tall feather was fixed in front, for men a short tuft, but both coloured white over red. The encircling cords went round the cap and hung down the back after which they were attached to the body with the intention of preventing the loss of the head-dress. Another type of Hussar cap was the mirliton or flügelmutze, which was a kind of shako with a long flying wing of cloth: this cap was worn in the 7th Hussars at least up to 1807.

The jackets of the different regiments had their own subtle differences. The 7th had white collars and cuffs as worn previously and the lace was silver for the officers and white for the men. Around the lace on the collar was a blue line. Although the officers had a crimson-and-gold-barrelled sash this was no guide to that worn by the men who, in fact, had one which was white metal and blue: these barrelled sashes were composed of long threads or cords held together by groups of metal loops or barrels; the ends of the sash were long cords which were looped up on the hip, and the tassels on the extreme ends were pushed through the cords around the waist.

The 18th Regiment was converted to Hussars in 1807 and also had white collars and cuffs. The fur on their pelisses was white and the regiment was distiguished by blue bags in the busbies.

It was a distinction of early Hussars to wear moustaches, thus following the continental fashion; and no doubt for the first few months of their new existence they also wore pigtails or queues; but in 1808 orders were issued for the abolition of the same.

Service in the Peninsula was a sore trial for the elaborate Hussar dress and modifications had to appear. The white breeches would not long stand to the wear of hard riding and fighting; thus the overall not only became popular but a necessity. These loose-fitting garments were made of white and used at first for dismounted and stable duties. Lower garments were also made in blue cloth with buttons down the seams and with chains under the soles of the boots.

The fur cap although it was used abroad, was not an entirely suitable headgear in the battlefield where care and attention could not continually be given to it. Thus an undress head-dress—the shako—was used, which took various shapes and colours in different regiments. One account says that it was in 1809 that some regiments left off the fur caps in favour of castor caps. The 10th Hussars had red shakos and the 15th appear to have had scarlet shakos for the officers and black for the men (although later all took the red colour). Pictures show the 7th with a brown shako.

Hussars at this time had no general issue of overcoat or cloak, but made do in the cold weather and rain with the pelisse: this garment in itself was an interesting object. The Hussars were descended from the Hungarian herdsmen who, to preserve their animals, had to kill the marauding wolves. The flayed skins from these animals were worn across the shoulders as a protection from the weather and a cheap coat. Eventually the skins developed into the short fur-lined coats known as pelisses. The fur was still to be seen at the cuffs, the collar, down the front and around the lower edge of the garment. The fur varied in the regiments—the 7th Hussars had light brown fur for the officers whereas the men wore white.

The tight-fitting white pantaloons and Hessian boots were common items for Hussar and Light Dragoon Regiments for full dress. Sabretaches were carried, in the case of the 7th Hussars with a white cloth face and silver lace edge. The Hussars' swords were slightly curved and intended for cutting and slashing. The plain cross bar of the Mameluke hilt had no knuckle bow or protection for the fingers.

The 10th Hussars continued to wear yellow facings on the jacket but had a red busby bag and a red cloth facing to the sabretache. The officers of this regiment had grey fur not only for the pelisse but for the busby. The silver lace on the jacket took the distinctive form of three loops on the cuffs to make an allusion to the Prince of Wales's feather, that gentleman being the Colonel of the Regiment. The men of the 10th Hussars had white fur on the pelisse which carried another distinction, 'the frame': this was a broad border of silver or white braid which encased the looping on the front of the pelisse and was not worn by other regiments.

The 15th Hussars had scarlet collars and cuffs with the same colour for the busby bags and sabretache fronts. The fur for officers was black as it was for the privates, but N.C.O.s were known to have had other fur.

During this period, the fur cap which had been very tall, was reduced in height and had chin scales added. In actual combat the white and red plumes were left off. The colour of the fur seems to have changed from time to time, possibly due to the commander's whim or the furs available at the time. About 1814 the 7th Hussars seem to have had a new jacket or dolman with gold lace and on which the rows of buttons increased from three to five. In 1815 the regiments were given a choice of dark grey or blue-grey overalls to wear with their short ankle boots. Tight-fitting pantaloons were worn by officers in full dress: in the case of the 7th Hussars blue with gold stripes.

In 1819 a chart showed that three of the four Hussar regiments had shakos. The 18th were alone in retaining the fur cap which in their case had blue bags and silver lace. The 7th Hussars now had an unusual light blue shako with gold lace, carrying an upright white over red feather. The 10th had a black shako with a black drooping plume and the 15th a red shako with gold lace and a red and white plume. The 7th and 10th Hussars had gold lace and the 15th and 18th had silver on their jackets. Now all had black fur on their pelisses, except the 18th who had grey.

LANCERS 1816—1820

The glories achieved by the Polish Lancers in the service of Napoleon reflected all around Europe, and most countries tried to capture some of their spirit by equipping or raising their own version of these showy horsemen. It was not until 1816 that Great Britain decided to convert the 9th, 12th, 16th and 23rd Light Dragoons into Lancers. However, the reductions of the first years of peace gave the 23rd Lancers only a year of life before they disappeared. Another lancer regiment took its place, for the 19th Light Dragoons were ordered to convert themselves into the new arm.

There is no doubt that the idea of lancers fired the popular imagination and they were frequently depicted in contemporary illustrations. The dress as worn at that time was much more glorious than the modern lancer dress and was very expensive. The first changes may have been made with a certain amount of economy, for the jacket to be worn when detachments of the first four Lancers' regiments assembled in London in 1816 to learn their exercise, was of the Light Dragoon pattern of 1812. This jacket had lapels of the colour of the facings and was piped down the back seams of the sleeves, thus resembling the Lancer jacket. The trousers to be worn at this assembly were to be of Cossack pattern, cut very full in the thigh, tightening towards the knee and close fitting over a short boot. The lance cap was very high with a square top, made of cane and covered with cloth the colour of the facing of the regiment. A brass plate in front carried devices peculiar to the regiment and a plume issued from the top on the left side. The carbine was no longer to be carried.

From contemporary illustrations we see the 9th Lancers in their new dress—a very tall lance cap with crimson cloth top, adorned with long red and white swan's feather plume, short blue jacket with crimson plastron front with a high collar and pointed cuffs; the back of this jacket had the 'wasserfall', or row of gold bullion fringe which appeared just below the gold and crimson waist girdle. Heavy aiguillettes, tassels, cords and pouch belt adorned the chest while the wearer's shoulders upheld full epaulettes. The loose-fitting Cossack trousers had gold lace stripes down the sides, and were in crimson cloth for full dress but for undress they were blue-grey with crimson stripes.

When the 12th were converted to Lancers they changed their facings from yellow to scarlet; the 16th kept their scarlet facings and the 19th had yellow facings. The 23rd had crimson facings both before and after their conversion.

The dress of the 19th Lancers is shown very well in our illustration. The high lance caps of the officers are covered with yellow cloth and gold decoration, so that only the front peak and the turned-up back peak show the black leather of the foundation. The plumes are red and white and it will be noted that the chin scales are worn fastened up on the cap. The dark blue jackets have light yellow facings and the officers' pouch belts are gold with a silver flap on the pouch. The girdles are gold and red for the officers, but yellow and blue for the trooper. The light blue trousers have double gold stripes for the officers, but only single yellow ones down the side seams of the trooper. The officers wore yellow metal spurs and the trooper steel ones. The trooper's schabraque is the only one shown and this is blue with yellow triangles around the edge. The elaborate embroidery is in yellow with the exception of the cap in the crown, which is red.

FOOT GUARDS AND INFANTRY 1799—1820

A time of fighting and strenuous effort found the weakness of the picturesque dress of the eighteenth century. Constant changes were being made to turn the uniform into a dress of comfort and practicability for the serving soldier. The practice of occasionally buttoning the lapels across the body was now recognized and permitted. To achieve a satisfactory result the cut of the coat had to be altered slightly; the lapels were made broader and shorter to cross over just at the waist. The collar which had been turned down was now entirely standing up with a wide opening in front; this opening was filled in the case of officers, by the black neckcloth and a small white shirt frill.

The head-dress was now changed. The hat which had endured for scores of years with the brim turned up at all angles and in many sizes, was now obsolescent. Officers, however, did keep the hat on service up to 1812 and it had a further lease of life as a court head-dress and for very high officers who rarely had occasion to fight in it. The new head-dress or cap as it was called, was no more than another version of the shako which had been worn for many years past by the Austrian soldiers, and even this item suffered as many changes of fashion as the previous hat. The shako as generally introduced in 1800 was a round cylinder of leather with a flat top and a peak to protect the eyes, a concession in itself. This 'stovepipe' had a brass plate in front to give full play for national and regimental distinctions. The Crown, the Royal Lion, trophies of war and the regimental number were the normal devices, but the regiments which had their own particular badges were permitted to wear them. The feathers or tufts of the colours as previously used on the hat were continued on the shako, but slightly reduced and placed centrally. The japanned leather shako was a very heavy affair and it was discontinued for a slightly lighter pattern which mainly differed by having the cylinder of felt, but all else the same.

The changes of 1812 saw an alteration in the infantry head-dress, and officers were now expected to take into use the new pattern. This head-dress often referred to as the 'Waterloo' shako, is so called because it was still in use at that world-famous combat. It was still of the cylinder shape but the body was shortened and a false front was added to keep up the illusion of height. Once again the inspiration of the Austrian army was followed, for they too had a somewhat similar shako with the false front but without a peak for the eyes. The British version had not only the front peak but plate, cords and tufts or feathers. The gilt or brass front plate was now more oval with a large crown on top. The devices were simplified and the main design was the Royal Cypher and the regimental number. The cords were white for most infantry and gold and crimson for officers. Green was the distinction of light infantry. The plumes followed the same colourings as used with the previous shakos, cut feathers for the officers and worsted tufts for the men. These tufts sprang from a black rosette which had a regimental button in the centre. The cords began from this point, went down to the centre of the peak and then up to the right side where they finished in two small tassels. On active service there was a black oilskin cover to protect the felt body from the weather, a precaution very necessary in the Waterloo campaign.

The final result of defeating the French Army seems to have inspired the military milliners to new fancies, and instead of keeping a pattern made venerable through successive victories, a head-dress was chosen very similar to that worn by the defeated enemy. It was in August 1815 that a bell-topped shako was approved, although it was at the time called a Prussian pattern. There was the usual delay between approval and actual issue, and it was not until the next year that the majority of the infantry received the new shako. The long plume worn in front created an impression of height to the wearer; these plumes followed the differences of colours as in the previous head-dress. Around the tops of the officers' caps were broad bands of either gold or silver lace in a regimental pattern and a similar, though narrower, band went around the base. Chin scales were an artistic addition. Although the central plates varied considerably, the first types seemed to favour a crowned dome with regimental devices; this was connected to the rosette below the plume by means of a double row of scales. A circle of lace around the plate gave the semblance of a target. Cap lines were also worn for a short period of time; at the back was a turned-up peak which fitted closely to the contour of the cap.

The coats of officers having been made double-breasted, could now be worn in a variety of ways. The faced fronts could be worn outside for full dress occasions; the fronts could be buttoned over for active sevice conditions, or the top part of the lapels could be worn turned in two small triangles to show an attractive splash of the facing colour. The faced section of the fronts had buttonholes of lace and normally the plain front had none, although there are examples of units wearing the laces extended across the front or from one row of buttons only. The long-tailed coat was worn for full dress but there was also a short-tailed version, popular for field service, called 'the jacket'. Epaulettes were now made more elaborate and of stiffer material. Officers wore crimson sashes around the waist with the ends knotted on the side. The sword belt went over the shoulder and under the sash which helped to keep it in place. The Foot Guards wore a uniform very similar to the regiments of the Line, but the men had an additional row of white tape or braid around the top of the round cuffs, and officers had gold lace around the edge of the upright collars, etc. The Foot Guards also had their own plates for the shakos which all wore abroad after 1812, although at home the old dress with long white gaiters still kept in use. It might be mentioned here that the cocked hat in its later days, was not worn sideways but with one point in front and the other at the back; the plume and cockade went to the right side.

After Waterloo an opportunity was taken to make the coat more splendid, mainly by adopting a more positive plastron front; this curved in a sweeping fashion and with padding the new coat was a work of art. The collar still retained a 'V'-shaped opening, but about 1820 this was closed 'after the Prussian fashion' as it was said and the little shirt frill disappeared.

The men's coats were still single-breasted and of red cloth instead of the scarlet cloth worn by the officers. The loops of the buttonholes were of white worsted with distinguishing stripes or worms, and set on the coats singly or in pairs. The Foot Guards had their loops in ones, twos and threes according to the Regiment. Normally speaking, there were ten buttons down the front in white metal or pewter for line regiments, although the officers had silver or gilt buttons depending on their lace. The standing collar was to be three inches high and laced. The cuffs were to be three and a half inches deep with four buttons and loops. At the back were pocket flaps and between the hip buttons was placed a diamond of lace. The 1802 regulations noted that sergeants had plain white worsted lace.

The coats which had been long to the waist were later shortened. The officers' long coats had two separate tails, the linings of which folded back, but the short jackets had but a small portion of the skirts turned back—a section on each hip and nothing at all at the back. The shoulder-straps which were of the colour of the facings had edgings of the regimental lace and woollen tufts at the point of the shoulder. Although plain white tufts were common, later patterns combined other colours.

The men's legwear which had been white breeches and knee-length black gaiters, changed to overalls on service. These overalls were originally intended to be worn 'overall', but eventually they became the main netherwear. White was the popular material in the Peninsular War, but by 1812 grey and shades of blue-grey overalls had appeared. The gaiters, instead of being knee-length, were reduced to a type of short spat and, in some cases, took the colour of the overalls. White overalls were popular during the occupation of Paris, but the white breeches were still to be seen for full dress parades, etc.

Undress uniform took many forms, but the main item to be preserved was the coat, and thus the sleeved waistcoats were worn on many rough duties. These were white or buff in colour with collars and cuffs of the facing colour. Shoulder-straps had tufts and wings as worn in the full-dress garment. Undress head-dresses were also popular and of many patterns. There was a pattern which folded quite flat, made in a cheap material often marked with the regimental marking. The flat-topped cap as seen in German service was also popular and it looked much as the modern forage cap, but without a peak and, of course, not stiffened in the brim. The colours of the band round the crown gave a clue to the type of regiment or particular company.

GRENADIERS AND FUSILIERS 1799—1820

The introduction of the shako to the infantry did not entirely replace the time-honoured fur cap of the grenadiers and the fusiliers. This head-dress continued in use but was found to deteriorate rapidly on overseas service, especially in hot climates. Thus it was discouraged abroad and became an article for full dress wear at home. Abroad and on active service the shako was worn, even at Waterloo, despite modern pictures which show the fur cap on the British side. For officers of grenadier companies the hat remained in use up to 1812 during which time it was worn with a white feather and frequently 'fore-and-aft', although old officers kept to the crosswise style.

In 1802 a new pattern fur cap was introduced; this was to be fronted with a brass plate for the men and with a gilt one for the officers. The officers' pattern was worn with a white feather and a grenade 'at Occasional Parades'. The obsolete cap had the device of the King's crest in brass on the plate which was black japanned. The fur was still black bearskin, twelve inches high for grenadiers but the fusilier cap was shorter. The grenadier cap also had the additional device of a grenade which contained the number of the regiment. These caps, although not for the battlefield, were noted as being worn during the occupation of Paris when the French caricaturists did much to place on record the uniform of those days.

A version with an added peak was worn by fusiliers at the time of the Peninsular War, and continued after Waterloo by which time the shape of the cap had altered to a tall slim erection; now it was elegant with cords around the middle and tassels on the left side.

The stove pipe shako was worn by the grenadier companies 'occasionally' to quote the 1802 Clothing Regulation, and the same men were permitted to wear the grenade in the same manner as other soldiers wore their badges. The tufts now in front were all white and a grenade was also worn in the centre of the cockade instead of a button. Fusilier regiments under the same conditions wore a similar shako. When the pattern of the shako changed in 1812, the white plume or tuft was retained, the cords being white for the men and crimson and gold for the officers. Grenadier officers continued to wear a small grenade in the cockade which was now on the left side. The broad-topped shako taken in wear in 1816 continued the use of the white feather or tuft.

For their distinguished service against the Old Guard of Napoleon in the battle of Waterloo, the 1st Foot Guards were honoured by being re-named the Grenadier Guards and took into wear the fur head-dress for all companies.

The remainder of the dress of the grenadier and fusilier units was much as that worn by the battalion companies, but there were slight differences in the coat. The distinctions of the shoulders were the wings, made of red cloth for men and scarlet for sergeants, with six loops of lace of the same sort as on the buttonholes and laced around the base. The wings of the officers had bullion and fringe besides an epaulette on each shoulder. Each skirt of the coat had an embroidered grenade usually with sequins and expensive wire, which cost the officers a tidy sum.

LIGHT INFANTRY 1799—1820

Light infantry were also dressed much as the battalion companies but, of course, with their own peculiar distinctions. The shako was deemed a head-dress most suitable for light companies and replaced the light though elaborate pattern. The hat was not entirely discontinued but continued for officers because it was convenient to carry at levees and suchlike functions, bearing its distinctive green feather. The men continued to bear dark green tufts on their shakos, even with the next change of shako. Some contemporary pictures show the 1812 pattern shako worn with a light infantry plume but this does not seem to be a general practice. There is ample evidence of the use of the old cylindrical shako being worn right up to Waterloo with the feather or tuft placed in front. The all-leather pattern gave way to one with a softer body and it is this which appears to have a taper towards the top. In 1811 it was ordered that the light infantry should carry a badge on the front of their shakos—a bugle horn with the regimental number below. The 71st Highland Light Infantry wore the tapering shako with the blue woollen bonnet shrunk over it, carrying the diced border below and the black ribbons behind.

The Regency shako which came into use just after Waterloo, was of similar pattern as that worn by the battalion companies, but instead of the plate in front, silver bugle and strings were worn as a badge. The cap lines were green as was the long plume.

The coat of light companies also had minor distinctions, as well as having a much shorter version of the jacket for field work. The 1802 Clothing Regulations noted that the pockets of the uniform coats of Light Infantry officers were to slope diagonally. The jackets of light infantry were to be short-skirted with the front skirts turned back and faced with cassimere the colour of the lining. Small buttons were to be worn on the coat and the scarlet wings were to have bullion fringe as well as epaulettes. The skirts were to be ornamented with bugle horns, which ornament was also to appear on the strap of the epaulette. Bugle horns were to be put on the skirts of the men's coats if the Colonel thought fit, and worsted fringe on the wings was also permitted.

In 1803 a new pattern sword for officers of Light Infantry was approved: these had curved blades and they were to continue to be worn in the same sword belts as previously in use. The sergeants had fusils, and whistles were also being used for field calls.

HIGHLANDERS 1799—1820

The Highlander was always a popular fighting man, but for some reason it was difficult to retain the same number of Highland regiments and in 1809 several were converted to line. One of these, the 71st, although losing the kilt and other Highland distinctions, managed to convert its light infantry uniform into something quite distinctive and Scottish. However, by 1809 the following regiments remained dressed in the kilt. The 42nd (Royal Highlanders) blue facings with gold lace, the 78th (Ross-shire Buffs) buff facings with gold, the 79th (Cameron Highlanders) green with gold lace, the 92nd (Gordon Highlanders) yellow with silver lace and the 93rd (Sutherland Highlanders) also yellow with silver lace.

The feather head-dress was the blue hummel bonnet cocked up with feathers on top, fixed in position by means of a wire cage; from the side hung tails of feathers, but the men of the Black Watch, oldest of the regular Highlanders, did not have 'tails', only 'flats' or uncurled feathers. The detachable peak to shade the eyes was worn in the Peninsular War and during the Waterloo Campaign by all kilted corps. Officers had chin-straps as well as hackle feather plumes—in contradistinction to the men who had worsted tufts or plumes; these plumes usually followed the practice of Line Regiments in colour, being white over red for the battalion companies, green for the light companies and white for the grenadier, but as the Royal Highlanders had been granted a red plume some years before, the green and white of the flank companies had a red top. The red, white and green dicing on the lower band was a relic of the old method of tightening the cloth to the head by means of a slotted edge. The colour of the dicing varied with certain regiments, the 93rd for example, having red and white squares only. The two black ribbons hanging down behind were the vestiges of the tightening strip. The cockades were complex and varied; the 42nd having a bugle horn over a Sphinx for the light company; an 'Elephant' and 'Maida' for the 78th, and so on. The usual centre device for the rosette was the regimental button, but grenadier companies carried a grenade and the light companies a bugle horn.

The jacket was the favoured coat and of the same pattern as worn by other infantry, with none of the distinctions we now expect in a Highland doublet. The skirts were kept short at the back and pockets were set on obliquely. The loops on the buttonholes were either set singly or in pairs, usually numbering eight. The sergeants wore their sashes over the left shoulder after the fashion of their officers, although a sketch early in the century shows a Black Watch sergeant with his sash round his waist; in the centre of the crimson sash was a stripe of the colour of the facing. Sergeants of the 42nd wore silver lace on their jackets according to an ancient tradition, although a warrant of 1802 specifies white silk.

The tartan of the kilts was practically as now but the 42nd at least had a tartan with a red stripe up to 1812, said by some to belong to the grenadier company or by others to be the Colonels' tartan. Sporrans were not worn on active service, and when those of the 42nd were destroyed in 1808 they may not have been replaced until the end of the war. The wearing of these purses in other regiments seems to have been just as rare. The approved pattern was goatskin with six black tassels.

The hose worn at this time was of the cloth type known as 'cath-dath', sewn up the back seam. Red and white dicing was the usual pattern but some had a black edging as in the case of the 42nd, 78th, etc. There was also a 'footless' type known as 'moggins' —an interesting form of economy. Hose was held up by garters of red tape. The knots were plain, as the regimental types had not been introduced at that date. The short gaiters were either black or grey, the 92nd favouring the former as did the 79th and 93rd. Sergeants carried the Scottish broadsword as a sidearm.

RIFLE REGIMENTS 1797—1820

The use of green clothing in warfare had been justified in the American Revolution, and the continued popularity of the colour for military use was not so much for camouflage value as for the prestige brought by previous wearers. The German Jägers had green coats and carried rifles. Thus when it was decided in 1797 to have a regular unit on these lines in the army, certain of the emigré troops served as the basis of the new 5th battalion of the 60th, or Royal American Regiment of Foot. Hompesch's Mounted Riflemen and Lowenstein's Chasseurs were foreign mercenaries of this date who brought the green to the British Army. This 5th battalion was so successful that a 6th battalion was raised on the same lines in 1799 in the Isle of Wight, mainly composed of Germans.

Contemporary water-colours show us the distinctive dress of these men: they appear to be among the earliest to assume the cylindrical shako, ornamented with a green plume in front and carrying a white metal bugle horn badge. The jackets were green but the 5th battalion had red facings and the 6th only red pipings. At the point of the shoulder were rolls of green cloth suitable to act as protection from sword cuts, the 5th having their rolls striped with red. The breeches were bright blue with red side stripes for the 5th, and the 6th are shown in white pantaloons. Short black gaiters finished the netherwear.

The officers' full dress, although similar in many ways, was much more distinctive. The head-dress was the helmet cap, popular with light infantry and cavalry. The green plume or feather, were regimental features as was the red cockade for the 5th Battalion. The short green jacket was laced across the front with rows of black braid and the three rows of white metal buttons gave it the appearance of a hussar jacket. The fringed wings on the shoulders served a similar purpose as the rolls of the men, but in this case they were made of interlocking metal rings. A further tendency towards the dress of light cavalry and hussars was the use of the red barrelled sash worn around the waist. The sword with the curved blade was also cavalry in style as were the Hessian boots, elegant footwear which came just below the kneecap with small tassels. Tight-fitting green pantaloons completed an ensemble quite distinctive and unusual for the regular British Army.

The use of the rifleman was deemed so successful that it was decided to form a completely new body. The men were drawn from fifteen different regiments and were known as Colonel Coote Manningham's Experimental Corps of Riflemen. This corps was made permanent and, on being established in August 1800, was known as the 95th Foot; but its later and best-known title is the one as used today—the Rifle Brigade.

The contemporary regulations for the Rifle Brigade give many details of the uniform. For example, they state that 'the officers parade or service dress will consist of regimental jacket, waistcoat and pantaloons of the same cloth; half boots not three-quarter boots, piqued, bound with black cord and a tassel in front; stock black polished leather, the waistcoat to be hooked at the top or the jacket to be so, as Officers may choose, through the frill of the shirt, leaving about six inches exposed. Hussar sash and sword. Regimental helmet. The field Officers and Adjutant will be at all times distinguished by spurs of a uniform make and wear a longer half-boot, their horses will also be caparisoned after a regimental manner—the hair always queued according to the Commander in Chief's order; powder, side hair for two inches below the ear and moustaches to be worn by those who choose on service. The regimental greatcoat of a grey colour, after the plan in the Quarter Master's possession.'

The officers' helmets were of the same pattern as those in the Rifle Battalions of the 60th Foot, but by 1802 this handsome head-dress was recommended to be discontinued and only the shako like the men's pattern to be used. The dress was very similar in the two rifle units but the cuffs and collars of the 60th were red or scarlet, whereas the Rifle Corps had black, velvet for officers. The black pouch belts were worn over the left shoulder and carried chains with whistles, necessary instruments to give orders to riflemen who acted in extended order. The sergeants also carried whistles, at that time a most unusual distinction for N.C.O.s. The unorthodox method of manoeuvring in the field led to another change. It was decided that the roll of the drum would not be heard clearly, and that it was a cumbersome item to be carried by men who were expected to take advantage of every piece of cover; thus the bugler became the company musician and transmitted field calls on that musical instrument.

The sergeants and men had jackets of dark-green cloth, short-skirted and without lapels; the black cloth cuffs and collars were edged with white cloth; three rows of buttons were worn down the front after the fashion of the officers. Corporals at the beginning continued to wear the shoulder-knot to denote rank, in the case of Manningham's Corps of green and black worsted, but these were soon to give way to chevrons. Buglers also wore green jackets, but for the Rifle Corps the black wings on the shoulders were with black and white fringe. The cap or shako worn by the rank and file differed from infantry regiments by having a bugle horn in front instead of the elaborate brassplate. A green cord was also worn around the cap and the green tuft as worn by the rank and file was replaced by a green feather for officers, sergeants and buglers.

The *British Military Library* of February 1801, shows a coloured print of an officer of Manningham's Rifle Corps and comments that the pouch contains a pistol and ammunition. The man's equipment is also noted: the brass-hilted sword could also be used as a bayonet on the rifle. A pouch held the cartridges and a powder horn was suspended from a cord slung over the shoulder.

The other ranks of rifle corps wore short gaiters of black woollen cloth. Sergeants of rifles did not carry spontoons or pikes, because such weapons would not be suitable for field work and so their armament was a rifle and sword bayonet like the men.

A picture of 1804 shows an officer of the Rifle Brigade still wearing the helmet-cap, the green jacket, green pantaloons and boots, but another appendage of the hussars has been added, for he wears a pelisse. The short green body-covering has black fur on the edges and elaborate froggings, and loopings cover the chest. The officer is shown clean-shaven, but it was the habit of riflemen to follow the continental fashion and to wear moustaches, once again in imitation of hussars.

Although the 5th Battalion of the 60th Foot was dressed all in green, the earlier battalions still had red coats. A gradual change was being made and a *View of the clothing in 1802* noted that besides the 6th Battalion, the rifle companies of the first four battalions had green jackets with collars, cuffs and shoulder-straps of the same colour; for distinction the edges were feathered with red cloth. The sleeved waistcoats were white while the green cloth breeches finished in black cloth or woollen gaiters. The red-coated companies did not change to green clothing until 1813 and it was only when the 7th and 8th Battalions were raised, that the change to green clothing became routine. Even then only two companies in each battalion were called riflemen, the others being considered light infantry. The 60th Foot officers also adopted the pelisse and eventually discontinued the blue trousers, so that all wore green. Charles Hamilton Smith's prints of 1812 show grey pantaloons with red edgings in use for the rank and file of the 5th Battalion.

When the shako was changed in Line Regiments in 1812, the cylindrical type continued in use for rifle corps until 1816, when the new bell-topped shako was taken into use in the infantry. The first pattern shako, according to prints, tended to become narrower at the top, in fact reversing the widths of original type, but as the cylinder was eventually made of felt, this material was liable to alterations of shape according to the head and the weather. The officer had a rectangular peak which could be turned up or down.

The tight-fitting green pantaloons of the riflemen were protected at night and on active service by loose trousers. Although those of the men were sometimes shown as plain green matching the jacket, officers favoured more elaborate patterns, often with an inner strapping and boot cuffs of leather. The active service of the Peninsular campaigns and in the Low Countries kept the overalls in constant use and the tight-fitting breeches or pantaloons remained only for court dress. Immediately after Waterloo the fashions of the British Army changed. Being in contact with foreign armies during the Occupation period brought to the uniforms an elaborate appearance quite remote from the drabness of serious warfare. The customs of the continental armies were adopted either consciously or unconsciously. The broad-topped bell shako came from the French. The loose pleated trousers, usually of light blue material were cut after the Cossack fashion for officers, and the various badges and plates took on complications not thought of previously.

CHAPTER VI

HANOVERIANS (PART 3)—GEORGE IV AND WILLIAM IV

1820—1837

HOUSEHOLD CAVALRY 1820—1830

THE Coronation of George IV, lately the Prince Regent, gave that gentleman full opportunity to exercise his military sartorial preferences. The Household Cavalry now took back into wear the cuirasses, which armour they still retain up to modern times. The Life Guards had their armour distinguished by a blue binding and edging and the front of the cuirasses had a brass oval plate engraved. About 1825 these oval plates disappeared.

As to head-dress, the 1822 Dress Regulations describe the fur cap in detail: it was a 'grenadier bearskin about 20 inches deep, a large gilt plate at the bottom, with gilt raised King's Arms and the regimental badge; a gold bullion tassel at the top, from which proceeds a gold plaited cord line passing over the left side of the cap behind, looping at the bottom and continuing across the front of the cap and fastened on the right side with a rich flounder and bullion tassel suspending, gilt engraved scales, a large gold embroidered grenade behind, a small gilt socket at the bottom on the left' and added to all this was a white feather 'about three fourths of a yard long'. Later a helmet was also worn, a crested version with a steel body.

The coatee had blue velvet collar, cuffs and skirt turn-backs and the embroidered oak-leaf patterns were in gold wire. Epaulettes and aiguillettes gilded the lily. The official description of the pouch and sabretache, although lengthy, give a further idea of the magnificence of this period. For undress the coatee was made short, but with all the trimmings of the full dress coatee.

Although white doeskin was used for the pantaloons worn with the long jacked boots, for undress the overalls were of a brown mixed colour; in some places this colour is described as claret. These trousers had two-and-a-half-inch-wide stripes of scarlet cloth for ordinary occasions, but on Sunday parades and special occasions the stripes were of gold.

The fore-mentioned dress is repeated in the 1826 Dress Regulations. According to Cannon's *History*, the sabretaches and sashes were laid aside in 1829. The Royal Horse Guards had for some time worn a red flask-cord on their pouch belt and in 1829 flask-cords were ordered to be adopted for both regiments of Life Guards, the first having red and the second blue. This custom once established continued in being up to 1922.

The Royal Horse Guards—the Blues—were now following the fashions of the Life Guards. The magnificent Coronation of George IV in 1821 saw many fine uniforms in attendance. The entire Household Cavalry was furnished with cuirasses for this occasion and from that time onwards they remained in use for ceremonial occasions. The cuirasses of the Blues had the contrasting colour of red at this time. Another change took place and the buff belts, so long distinguishing features of the Royal Horse Guards, were laid aside and exchanged for those of white, thus conforming to the general practice.

The undress sabretache of this reign was of black leather with gilt metal mounts— the latter being in the shape of an eight-pointed star, two scrolls and a spray of laurel. The helmet is officially described in the Dress Regulations of 1822 as being 'Roman bright plated steel, encircled with richly gilt laurel leaves, rich dead gilt wrought scales and lion's heads, bearskin tops and plated steel pointed peak.' Although the netherwear for 'dress' is described in the Dress Regulations as white doeskin, for undress the overalls were sky-blue with a two-inch scarlet stripe on each outer seam.

DRAGOON GUARDS AND DRAGOONS 1820—1830

The Prince Regent, when he became King, brought about the introduction of printed regulations which give us much information on uniforms. These were the Dress Regulations of the Army issued in 1822 and, although only relating to officers, they do give many valuable details and rules of wear.

The Dragoon Guards and Dragoons are grouped together and superficially had a similar appearance, although varying in small details and regimental facings. A new head-dress is mentioned and is called a Roman helmet: it had a black glazed skull of leather encircled with richly gilt laurel leaves, gilt scales and a fine towering bearskin top. The front plate just above the peak had the device of the Royal Arms embossed, and on a metal band was the name of the Regiment. The old head-dress as worn at Waterloo continued in use for a while longer until the supplies of the new pattern came along. The 6th Dragoon Guards received their new pattern as late as 1823. The Scots Greys of course, continued to wear their fur caps. In 1828 the helmet was again changed in pattern.

The Dress Regulations of 1822 describe the coatee which had, in fact, been introduced a few years earlier. The closed Prussian collar was laced all around and had a loop and button on each side. The single-breasted front had eight loops arranged in pairs for Dragoon Guards and at regular intervals for the Dragoons. The Dragoon Guard coat had four loops on the forearm of each sleeve and the same number on each skirt. The distinction of the Dragoons was to have three loops where the others had four.

In 1822 it was ordered that N.C.O.s and men should have the stripes of their overalls in the colour of the regimental facing and not of the lace (i.e. yellow or white). The stripe on the sides of the blue-grey overalls was to be no more than half-an-inch wide. These coloured stripes may have been liable to fading or change of colour or too expensive, but whatever was the reason, in 1827 they were ordered to be changed back to either yellow or white worsted lace.

The open collars had apparently continued in use, for in 1827 an order repeated that Prussian (or closed) collars were to be substituted. Blue overalls were also advocated and the coloured girdle was to be discontinued. The bars or loops of lace on the chest were also removed about this time.

LIGHT DRAGOONS 1820—1836

The number of Light Dragoon Regiments was further reduced in this reign, when in 1822 the 8th were converted to Hussars, thus leaving only five—the 3rd, 4th, 11th, 13th and 14th. The dress was still very similar to that worn at Waterloo but was more elaborate and expensive. The head-dress was still the bell-shaped 'chaco' with a two-inch lace around the top, either silver or gold being used for decoration. The plume as noted in 1822 and 1826 Dress Regulations was red and white, twenty-three inches long and drooping.

The jackets following the previous style were dark blue with lapels, collars and cuffs of the facing colour. At the end of the reign the facings were scarlet for the 3rd, light yellow (though often appearing as buff) for the 4th, buff for the 11th and 13th and orange for the 14th. The officers' lace was gold for the 3rd and 13th and silver for the other three. Cap lines, being the sign of an officer, were gold as were the girdles, and the latter had two three-eighth-inch stripes of crimson.

The trousers were noted as sky-blue in the 1822 Regulations and as blue-grey in the 1826 ones. The side stripes for officers were in the regimental lace.

The swords were to have a half basket hilt and the sword-knot of officers was gold and crimson for all regiments. The sword belt, pouch belt and slings followed the regimental lace and facing colours. The sabretache had an embroidered cypher on the front and also such regimental honours as might be granted. These sabretaches were quite large, and a show place for regimental distinctions.

The opportunity was still taken to employ men of colour as musicians and the uniform they wore was usually quite distinctive. The red colour used in the head-gear to distinguish music was still in use, and the dress frequently contained white and crimson.

HUSSARS

Very early in the reign the number of Hussar regiments was reduced. The well-known 18th Hussars were disbanded, but the next year another regiment was converted to Hussars and thus the number was kept up. The 18th Hussars retained their fur cap to their last days and when they disappeared, so did the distinctive blue busby bag.

For some reason the fur cap was no longer considered an essential article of Hussar dress and the shako or cap, was the item quoted in the 1822 Dress Regulations; here it said that the Hussar cap should be bell-shaped, of black beaver, ornamented with circles of gold or silver braid. The feather is described as black drooping cocktail, but the greenish tinge of the feathers always encouraged artists to depict it in the brighter colour. In 1828 a lower pattern of shako was introduced for all except the 7th Hussars.

When the Prussian collar was adopted in the Army it was also taken up by the Hussars, for the 1822 Regulations mention the jacket collar as being Prussian in style and full three inches deep, laced all round with russia braid. The front was made single-breasted with five rows of buttons, the centre row being full-ball buttons but the other rows half-ball or domed; between these rows of buttons were lines of lace, dull metal in the main but in between with bright metal braid to increase the effect of richness. The 15th had silver lace and the other two, the 7th and the 10th, had gold.

The pelisse followed the same elaborate pattern as the jacket but had the addition of fur—white in the case of the 10th Hussars, black for the 15th and grey for the other.

For Dress and Full Dress the pantaloons and trousers were to be scarlet with gold or silver for the side rows. The 7th Hussars differed by wearing blue instead of scarlet. For undress occasions the trousers were blue-grey cut in cossack style. Hessian boots were worn in full dress but ankle boots were for the undress.

In 1822 the 8th Light Dragoons were ordered to be converted to Hussars and took this opportunity to change their lace from gold to silver. For a head-dress they had a tall black shako with silver lace and a profusion of green feathers as a plume. The jacket and pelisse were dark blue without facings. The complicated looping and tracery was silver and the fur on the pelisse, grey. The trousers were loose-fitting and dark-grey with red stripes, later changed to silver in the case of the officers. The sabretache had a scarlet face—this colour being their facings prior to conversion.

In 1823 the cavalry in general were to wear blue-grey overalls, but the 15th Hussars were permitted to continue their dark grey overalls. The glorious appearance of the troops of this period had its repercussions, for it meant a great expense to the individual officer. An enquiry in 1829 was made into the relative costs of clothing and it was found that whereas for an infantry officer without lace the cost was £40 for complete uniform, the cost of Light Dragoons and heavy cavalry was £150, the Hussars £300 and in the case of the 10th Hussars, £399 7s. 6d.! Needless to say, economies were the next stage.

It was ordered in 1829 that when Hussars acted as escorts in summer they were to wear the dolman instead of the pelisse which was to be worn on winter escort duty only.

LANCERS 1820—1830

With the general reduction of units in the Cavalry, the 19th Lancers were disbanded in 1821 but the vacancy was remedied in the following year when the 17th Light Dragoons were converted to Lancers, thus keeping four in being—the 9th, 12th, 16th and 17th.

The 1822 Dress Regulations describe the lance cap as having a trencher top, ten inches square, to be covered with cloth the colour of the facings. The detailed description of the lace and cord is long and complicated—it is sufficient to mention that the lace, etc., was gold or silver according to the regiment and the large fluted plate in front had the King's Arms. The chin scales joined the cap with lion-head bosses. The handsome plumes were red and white swan feathers twelve inches long.

The blue jackets had Prussian collars, strap lapels, turn-backs of the skirts and the pointed cuffs were of the facing colour—crimson for the 9th, scarlet for the 12th and the 16th, and white for the 17th Lancers. The back seams of the sleeves and jacket were also welted with the facing material, and in the small of the back were two 'purl bullion' pieces with embroidered heads. Epaulettes and rich aiguillettes were also worn by the officers.

Crimson trousers were a striking adjunct to Lancers' dress of this period, especially when the gold scalloped lace was worn down the sides. More prosaic were the undress trousers of blue-grey which had outer seam stripes of the facing colour. The sword and scabbard were of Mameluke pattern for this new arm. The white grip had no knuckle bow and the wide scabbard was inlaid with velvet. Needless to say the men's swords were more serviceable and much less ornate.

The sabretaches were varied in the pattern of embroidery on the face, and the pouch on the shoulder-belt had a solid silver plate on the flap. Gloves were worn; and the boots were described in the regulations as black Spanish leather. The details of the officers' dress were repeated in the 1826 regulations for the officers.

INFANTRY 1820—1830

Very little special change took place in the dress of the Foot Guards in this reign, although the infantry managed to produce the usual run of changes in the minutiæ of their dress. The shako of the previous reign continued in use but very soon underwent a slight increase in height; this was accompanied by the more or less general adoptiow of a star plate in front and the discontinuance of the peak at the back. The brass chin scales were intended to last four years before replacement. Gold or silver lace, according to the regiment, was worn around the top and bottom of the shako by the officers.

In 1828 the infantry shako was ordered to be altered. The gold and silver lace of the officers and the yellow or white of the men was discontinued, and so was the black cockade which had been worn for many past generations. The gilt plate in front was now large and elaborate, usually bearing the silver star plate worn on the previous shako. Cap lines of gold were worn by the officers on parade and levee occasions. The men had white lines, except in the case of the light companies, which had green. The hackle feather was white and red but, in 1829, a white feather was ordered to be worn by all officers except light infantry. The men, of course, wore their own version in a poorer material.

The short-tailed coat or jacket, was abolished for all except light companies in 1820. In May 1821 a pattern infantry jacket was approved. Officers wore lapels on their coats which were cut in the shape of a plastron and, being made of the regimental facings, made a brave showing on dress occasions. For undress the lapels were buttoned over. The Prussian collar was three inches deep as in other units. In 1826 the coat of other ranks was altered to make the top loops five-and-a-half inches across, the loops gradually being reduced down to two-and-a-half at the bottom. A loop was also added to each side of the collar. The lapels on the officers' coats were discontinued in 1829, but the buttons were left in the old positions of two rows. The collar now took two loops of regimental lace or embroidery, and there were four loops on each pocket flap in the skirts. The old round cuff now had the addition of an upright flap; the flap was the colour of the coat and had four buttons set lengthwise.

White breeches and leggings were still the full dress wear for infantry, but overalls or trousers were popular dress, and eventually in 1823 it was decided to discontinue breeches, leggings and shoes. Blue-grey cloth trousers and half-boots were substituted and white linen trousers were to be worn on dress parades.

The dress of grenadiers and fusiliers followed the normal changes. The white feather in the fur cap was continued and the practice of grenadier companies wearing shakos on certain overseas stations was ordered to be discontinued, and bearskin caps were general wear. However, three years later the use of fur caps was again ordered to be discontinued. In 1829 the brass chin scales on the fur caps were discontinued. As to the other parts of their dress, wings were the distinctions on the coats but a special distinction for field officers was epaulettes only.

PLATE 78. 88th, or Connaught Rangers, *circa* 1840.

PLATE 79. 50th (Queen's Own) Regiment, 1850. Print by H. C. Mornewick and E. Walker.

PLATE 80. Officers of Scots Fusilier Guards, 1855. Print by H. Martens and J. Harris.

PLATE 81. Heavy cavalry, *circa* 1880. Print by Messrs W. Jones & Co.

The light infantry had but minor changes. The light infantry cap had green cap lines and the badge thereon was shaped as a bugle, placed with other regimental distinctions, on the large crown and star plate. The feather was still green. When the short-tailed jackets were discontinued for most officers in 1820, light infantry officers continued to wear them until 1826. The coatee as worn by other officers, was then taken into wear and thus matched the longer tails being worn by the light infantry privates. In 1829 new forage caps for light infantry were to be green with a band of the facings colour. Later in the year it was noted that the privates' green caps had a line interwoven of the colour of the facing, except where the facings were green and then the line was to be red.

HIGHLANDERS 1820—1830

The Highland Regiments, following the general trend, were adopting elaborate and expensive additions to their dress. The Dress Regulations of 1822 give details of the Scottish dress for the first time, but they are by no means full and there is one aspect in which these regulations are misleading. Each regiment, no matter what branch it was, had its own peculiarities. The regulations endeavoured to point out a 'uniform' dress and tended to ignore the differences. Thus the regulations tend to describe the most senior regiments in each group; in the case of the Highland Regiments—the Black Watch; and a statement appeared which caused great confusion: the feather for the cocked bonnet was described as 'red vulture, twelve inches long'. This of course was the privileged colour for the 42nd Highlanders but other Scotsmen seemed ready to take this distinction. A hurried memorandum had to be issued to cover this breach of privilege, and so in August 1822 the statement was made that 'the Red Vulture Feather prescribed by the recent Regulations is intended to be used exclusively by the Forty-Second Regiment.' Thus a storm in a tea-cup was cleared up and the other four regiments continued to wear the white hackle feather.

The feathered bonnet was to be about twelve inches deep and made with a skull of tartan plaid ornamented with six black ostrich feathers—a rather inadequate affair by present standards.

The full dress jacket was scarlet with the usual Prussian collar and straight lapels of the regimental facings. Each cuff was to have four loops and buttons. The turn-backs of the skirts were fastened back with embroidered ornaments of regimental pattern. On the shoulders were epaulettes and/or wings of gold or silver; the epaulettes were worn by field officers on wings and following earlier rules, grenadier and light company officers were distinguished by grenades or bugles. Thistles were worn on the shoulder-straps.

An interesting item mentioned in these first general Dress Regulations is the scarlet waistcoat, to be braided with gold in those regiments authorized to wear lace, otherwise plain. This red garment seems to have been introduced to make an affinity with the old light infantry dress which also had wings much in evidence. However, a memorandum of the following October 'dispensed with' the scarlet waistcoat and permitted the old waistcoats to be continued. Officers of Highland regiments were to adopt white kersey-mere pantaloons as worn by the infantry when the kilt was not worn.

The Dress Regulations shirked the truly Scottish details of the dress—indeed as they continued to do up to modern times. 'Plaid and kilt', 'Hose and Garters' were all to be 'according to Highland costume'—a very vague permission. The setts of the tartans were not mentioned in the Dress Regulations and it would appear that the commanding officer had a very free hand with the special adornments. A further encouragement towards Highland dress was made in 1823 when George IV ordered its resumption for the 71st and 72nd Regiments of Foot but with the more civilized items of dress—the trews instead of the beloved kilt. In 1821 the 91st Foot were again permitted a Scottish title—the Argyllshire, although no concession was made towards the resumption of the national dress.

In 1829 the coatees were altered and the distinctive lapels were abolished. The two rows of buttons were kept, either singly or in pairs. There was to be no alteration in the jackets of officers and men of the Highland regiments excepting in the sleeve which was to be made to correspond with that of infantry generally. The next year the front of the jacket was made to correspond with that of other regiments of infantry, but with ten loops instead of eight for those with plain loops and with nine for those with 'flowered loops'; an exception being for those having pairs in which case eight loops was thought sufficient.

The undress bonnet which was mentioned in the 1822 Dress Regulations as being cocked with a small feather in front, was in 1829 ordered to be abolished and made to correspond with the normal infantry pattern 'with the distinction that the band instead of being of the colour of the facing should be the tartan of the regiment.'

RIFLES 1820—1830

The reductions in the army after the Napoleonic Wars saw the 5th, 6th, 7th and 8th battalions of the 60th Foot disbanded and after complicated changes the First Battalion became a Rifle battalion and the Second a Light Infantry one, the others disappearing in the process. In 1820 the Second Battalion was permitted to be dressed as the First. The Rifle Brigade and the 60th Foot continued to be dressed much alike apart from the facings.

The 1822 Dress Regulations described the dress of an officer as being with a dark green jacket of Hussar style and a green pelisse with black fur and loops; the facings being respectively, of course, red for the 60th and black for the Rifle Brigade. The head-dress was a black bell-shaped cap with a round black ball tuft. The netherwear was also dark green and the equipment black patent leather. Despite all this tendency to green it is unusual to note that the great coat was to be of plain blue.

In 1824 the 60th Foot became the Duke of York's Own. The ball tuft was discontinued for a green cocktail plume, and the greatcoat was changed from blue to green. The mounted field officer was a fine figure on horseback, for the horses of the 60th had scarlet browbands and shabraques with black fur holster covers. The crimson girdle sash worn around the waist and the black pouch belt were also signs of an officer.

The men's jackets had black lace on the collar and cuffs, and on the front were three rows of white metal buttons which perpetuated the dress of the first riflemen.

INFANTRY PRE-1830

	Facings	Lace
1st (or The Royal)	Blue	Gold
2nd (or The Queen's Royal)	Blue	Silver
3rd (or East Kent) or the Buffs	Buff	Gold
4th (or The King's Own)	Blue	Gold
5th (Northumberland)	Gosling Green	Silver
6th (1st Warwickshire)	Yellow	Silver
7th (Royal Fusiliers)	Blue	Gold
8th (or the King's)	Blue	Gold
9th (or East Norfolk)	Yellow	Silver
10th (North Linc.)	Yellow	Silver
11th (North Devon)	Deep Green	Gold
12th (East Suffolk)	Yellow	Gold
13th (1st Somerset) (Light Infantry)	Yellow	Silver
14th (Buckingham)	Buff	Silver
15th (York E. Riding)	Yellow	Silver
16th (Bedfordshire)	Yellow	Silver
17th (Leicestershire)	White	Silver
18th (Royal Irish)	Blue	Gold
19th (1st York North Riding)	Green	Gold
20th (East Devonshire)	Yellow	Silver
21st (Royal North British Fusiliers)	Blue	Gold
22nd (Cheshire)	Buff	Gold
23rd (Royal Welch Fusiliers)	Blue	Gold
24th (Warwickshire)	Green	Silver
25th (The King's Own Borderers)	Blue	Gold
26th (or Cameronian)	Yellow	Silver
27th (or Enniskillen)	Buff	Gold
28th (or N. Gloucester)	Pale Yellow	Silver
29th (Worcestershire)	Yellow	Silver
30th (Cambridge)	Pale Yellow	Silver
31st (Huntingdonshire)	Buff	Silver
32nd (or Cornwall)	White	Gold
33rd (1st Y. W. Riding)	Red	Silver
34th (or Cumberland)	Yellow	Silver
35th (or Sussex)	Orange	Silver
36th (or Herefordshire)	Gosling Green	Gold
37th (North Hampsh.)	Yellow	Silver
38th (1st Staffordshire)	Yellow	Silver
39th (or Dorsetshire)	Pea-green	Gold
40th (2nd Somersetshire)	Buff	Gold
41st	White	Gold
42nd (Royal Highland)	Blue	Gold
43rd (Monmouthshire) (Light Infantry)	White	Silver
44th (or East Essex)	Yellow	Silver
45th (or Nottingham)	Dark Green	Silver
46th (South Devon)	Pale Yellow	Silver
47th (Lancashire)	White	Silver

		Facings	Lace
48th	(Northampton)	Buff	Gold
49th	(or The Princess Charlotte of Wales's, or Hertfordshire)	Green	Gold
50th	(or West Kent)	Black	Silver
51st	(2nd York West Riding) or The King's Own Light Infantry Regt.	Blue	Gold
52nd	(Oxfordshire) (Light Infantry)	Buff	Silver
53rd	(Shropshire)	Red	Gold
54th	(West Norfolk)	Green	Silver
55th	(Westmorland)	Green	Gold
56th	(West Essex)	Purple	Silver
57th	(West Midd.)	Yellow	Gold
58th	(Rutlandshire)	Black	Gold
59th	(2nd Nottingham)	White	Gold
60th	(R. American) 1st Bn. Rifle Corps 2nd Bn. Light Infantry	Regimentals green	
61st	(S. Gloucestershire)	Buff	Silver
62nd	(or Wiltshire)	Buff	Silver
63rd	(West Suffolk)	Deep green	Silver
64th	(2nd Staffordshire)	Black	Gold
65th	(2nd Y. N. Riding)	White	Gold
66th	(Berkshire)	Gosling green	Silver
67th	(S. Hampsh.)	Yellow	Silver
68th	(Durham) (Light Infantry)	Bottle green	Silver
69th	(S. Lincolnshire)	Green	Gold
70th	(or Glasgow Lowland)	Black	Gold
71st	(Highland Light Infantry)	Buff	Silver
72nd		Yellow	Silver
73rd		Dark Green	Gold
74th		White	Gold
75th		Yellow	Silver
76th		Red	Silver
77th	(E. Middlesex)	Yellow	Silver
78th	(Highland) or Rossshire Buffs	Buff	Gold
79th	(or Cameron Highlanders)	Dark Green	Gold
80th	(Stafford Vol.)	Yellow	Gold
81st		Buff	Silver
82nd	(The Prince of Wales's Vol.)	Yellow	Silver
83rd		Yellow	Gold
84th	(York and Lancs.)	Yellow	Silver
85th	(Bucks. Volunteers) or the King's Light Inf. Regt.	Blue	Silver
86th	(or The Royal County Down)	Blue	Gold
87th	(The Prince of Wales's Own Irish)	Green	Gold
88th	(Connaught Rangers)	Yellow	Silver
89th		Buff	Gold
90th	(Perthsh. Vol.) (Light Infantry)	Buff	Gold
91st	(or Argyllshire)	Yellow	Gold

		Facings	*Lace*
92nd (Highland)		Yellow	Silver
93rd		Yellow	Silver
94th		Green	Gold
95th		Yellow	Silver
96th		Yellow	Silver
97th		Sky Blue	Silver
98th		White	Gold
99th		Yellow	Gold

HEAVY CAVALRY 1830—1837

The short reign of William IV saw the issue of two Dress Regulations—1831 and 1834, indicating that the last of the Hanoverian Kings had distinct ideas of the dress of his fighting men, as the fine coloured prints of the period show. The Household Cavalry still retain a rich and antique appearance. The 1831 Regulations quote the Life Guards as well as the Royal Horse Guards as having a Roman helmet with a black bearskin crest: this is the pattern which the Royal Horse Guards had worn before and which the Life Guards took into wear in 1827. In 1833 His Majesty introduced a new Grenadier cap and plume for regular wear similar to the 1821 pattern, but much lighter and with less ornament. The 1834 Dress Regulations note the Life Guards and the Royal Horse Guards as both having a black bearskin cap, fourteen inches deep in front with gold bullion tassels on the right side and a gilt grenade. The Life Guards had a long plume of white swan's feathers which went up the left side of the cap and over the top. The Royal Horse Guards had a similar feather but of red.

The coatee which was single-breasted had a row of buttons down the front. The colour for the Life Guards was scarlet with blue velvet collar, cuffs and turnbacks, the reversed colours being used for the Royal Horse Guards. Each skirt of the Life Guard coatee had an embroidered grenade ornament. Epaulettes were worn on both shoulders and aiguillettes of twisted gold cords were also worn by the officers. A new sash was adopted in 1833. White leather pantaloons and black jacked boots as still worn were part of the dress of those days. Undress trousers were of a distinctive brown mixture cloth, with scarlet stripes down the sides for the Life Guards and dark blue stripes for the Royal Horse Guards. This is according to the 1831 regulations, but by 1833 the Life Guards had also taken the darkblue.

DRAGOON GUARDS AND DRAGOONS 1830—1837

When William IV came to the throne he developed an extraordinary penchant for red; he wished to clothe all his army in red and he even gave red facings to the Navy. The heavy cavalry were not affected by this order for they had worn red from the earliest times. However, the King did change the colour of the overalls from grey to dark blue and, having eliminated silver lace from the regular army, had the side stripes of gold for officers and yellow for the men.

The style of the jacket was slightly altered. The collar instead of having only the fore-part of the facing colour was now to be entirely of the facing colour. The regulations of 1831 give details of the single-breasted coat which was to have nine buttons down the front. There were three gold lace loops on each sleeve and skirt for the Dragoons— the Dragoon Guards were distinguished by having their loops in fours. It will be noted that the Dragoon Guards and Dragoons are dealt with jointly in the Dress Regulations which show how closely they had converged since the days when one had been horse and the other mounted infantry. The epaulettes worn on the shoulders were gold bullion and 'boxed'—that is to say with the bullion fringe fixed so that it was not loose and liable to damage. The men and the officers in undress wore shoulder scales which were a kind of metal epaulette without the fringe. The sword belt round the waist and the pouch belt over the left shoulder were elegant and expensive items of gold lace. The silver distinctions of regular units were discontinued in this reign and the use of silver lace and buttons became the mark of a militia regiment.

The helmets were still the 'Roman' pattern with a bearskin crest, usually distinguished by the name of the regiment on a front band. In 1834 a new pattern helmet came in use, being of brass or gilt instead of the black leather type. The Scots Greys continued their own regimental pattern of a bearskin cap with a long white hackle plume rising from a grenade socket on the left and going across the top of the head-dress; the gilt or brass plate in front was worn up to about 1834.

The uniform had white gauntlets and the horse furniture, although simplified, was elegant and expensive. The last order of the reign referring to a change of detail in cavalry clothing was that discontinuing the button on the end of the skirt.

LIGHT DRAGOONS 1830—1837

King William's desire for red coats was satisfied in the Light Dragoons, for he was able to change their blue coats to scarlet ones in 1831. There was a slight delay in taking the new jackets into wear but when they did come into use, the facing colours had to be changed. Thus in 1832, the 3rd Light Dragoons took blue facings being a Royal Regiment, the 4th took yellow but changed in 1836 to green, the 11th continued with buff and the 13th had buff facings which became almost white, while the last regiment, the 14th, instead of their distinctive orange, took into wear blue facings.

The lapels down to the waist were discontinued but two rows of buttons, eight in each row were continued. The collars, cuffs and turnbacks of the jackets continued in the facing colours. Gold braid went all round the collar and cuffs and at the back the gold bullion fringe continued a peculiar fashion. The girdle round the waist was gold with two coloured stripes.

The broad-topped chaco had gold lace around the upper edge, a large crowned maltese cross with the regimental device and across the front a heavy festoon of gold cord. The officers' plume was of white drooping cocktail feathers according to the Dress Regulations, although some paintings show a red base. Hair plumes were also worn.

The 1834 regulations more or less repeated the foregoing except that the girdle was specified as having crimson stripes. In 1836 the 13th Light Dragoons took green facings instead of buff.

HUSSARS 1830—1837

The Sovereign's desire for red coats did not have an unqualified success in the case of Hussars. They managed to retain their normal hussar dress but changed the colour of their pelisses to scarlet. The 1831 Dress Regulations noted this change and the official pelisse is described as scarlet with five rows of buttons, loops and ornaments the same as on the jacket. The fur around the edges was to be black astrakhan, the other varieties disappearing. The 8th and 15th Hussars who had silver lace were ordered to change to gold in 1830 but the actual replacement took place about a year later.

As to head-dress, the 7th Hussars continued to wear a tall shako or 'chaco' as the spelling was changed to. The 15th Hussars had special permission to wear a scarlet cloth cap. In 1831 overalls of light cavalry were to be changed to dark blue, but this did not affect the 7th Hussars as they had worn this colour previously. Single stripes of yellow were worn down the outward seams, gold in the case of full dress.

When dismounted the officers appeared very similar, the distinctions of the head-dress and the pattern of the lace being the most distinctive parts; but mounted, the fancy leopard skins and pointed shabraques with complicated cyphers and devices, made more obvious differences.

LANCERS 1830—1837

The Lancers were one branch where the change from blue jackets to scarlet as noted in the 1831 Dress Regulations made a notable difference. The double-breasted front had two rows of buttons, nine on each side. The three-inch deep collar had two embroidered buttonholes on each side, five inches long. The cuffs were the colour of the facing and had small scarlet flaps each holding five small buttons. The turnbacks of the skirts were of the facing colour, and made plaited at the back where there were also slashed pocket flaps. The bullion patches in the small of the back are not mentioned now. The girdles were gold with stripes of the facing colour.

The facings of the Lancer regiments were now blue for the 9th, 12th and 16th, while the 17th Lancers continued white as before. The colours of the tops of the lance cap changed to match the new facings. The elaborate rosette or plume holder changed and now bore the new cypher. The plumes were at this time made of black cocktail feathers drooping sixteen inches in front. Trousers were made of blue cloth with gold stripes down the sides for dress wear.

The 1834 Dress Regulations practically repeated the previous edition, but also noted that black horsehair plumes were to be used in India. Short white gloves had been worn, but in 1833 gauntlet gloves were ordered for Lancers. Sabretaches had been worn by all Lancers, but in 1834 they were abolished for privates.

INFANTRY 1830—1837

This short reign gave little opportunity for many changes in dress but one striking change was in the alteration of style of the 2nd and 3rd Regiments of Foot Guards to match the 1st Guards. It will be remembered that this premier regiment had been converted to Grenadiers after Waterloo. In 1831 a submission was made that the other two should be re-named and given an increased prestige; they were to be re-named the Coldstream Fusilier Regiment of Foot Guards and the 3rd Fusilier Regiment of Foot Guards and they were to be dressed as fusiliers. Although the fur cap was adopted by all the men, the titles eventually adopted were The Coldstream Regiment of Foot Guards and The Scots Fusilier Guards. White plumes were to be the original adornment, but the Coldstream Regiment finally took a scarlet cut feather on the right side and the Scots Fusilier Guards took none.

For the line infantry the shako of the previous reign continued in use, but the feather plume in 1835 was changed to a white ball tuft in an elegant pierced gilt-metal holder. The men at the same time took a ball tuft instead of the elongated worsted plume.

As mentioned before, 1830 saw all regular officers given gold lace or embroidery for their uniforms, and silver was in future reserved for Militia. The gorget which had dropped out of favour and needed reminders for its continued use, was finally abolished. The cypher 'GR' which had been worn for so many years on buttons and appointments was changed to 'WR'.

The infantry coat was altered in 1836 and the skirts, instead of being made in one piece with the body, were cut across. In this coat the upper edge of the cuff came level with the centre point of the slashed flap. The lace on the men's coats which had previously been distinguished by various patterns of lace was abolished in 1836 and plain white lace was worn, but applied in the particular fashion as previously worn. The sergeants in 1836 discontinued their coatees which had plain white lace and adopted one without lace, somewhat after the fashion of officers.

The grey cloth trousers of all infantry were to have red stripes down the side in 1833, but the white summer trousers continued in use as before. The old-fashioned opening of trousers was altered in 1836 to a fly front.

Light infantry continued their normal differences from the line dress. In July 1830 it was ordered that the green feather worn by officers of light companies and Light Infantry Regiments was to be changed for a dark green ball tuft. Certain Light Infantry wore green tufts on their wings and light company officers and sergeants made a good show of their whistles, which they carried on their sword-belts just under the breast-plate.

Grenadiers and fusiliers had but few changes in this reign. The cap of grenadier companies was to be twenty-one inches high with a large brass or gilt plate in front and the chin strap was covered in scales. The white hackle feather was carried on the left. An alteration in the pattern bearskin cap for grenadier companies and fusiliers was introduced in 1835: this took away the plate and the peak, but still did not replace the felt cap which was still worn on certain stations. Grenadiers continued to wear white worsted wings and a brass grenade fuse case on the bayonet belt.

This short reign did not give much opportunity for sartorial changes in the Highlanders. In common with other regiments, Highlanders assumed gold lace instead of silver. The 92nd Highlanders had worn for many years silver lace with a black line, and this accounts for the Gordon Highlanders continuing to wear a black line in their gold lace. In 1834 the officers' forage caps were altered and the band on them was to be of regimental bonnet tartan with an embroidered thistle with the regimental number below, or the regimental badge in the case of those regiments which had them.

In 1830 the 60th changed their subsidiary title to the King's Royal Rifle Corps and, once again, the ball tuft came back into favour and was worn on the shortened version of the cap. A large bronze plate was also worn on the front of the cap. In 1833 buttons of black were worn instead of the old white metal pattern, and the jackets were made double-breasted instead of single-breasted. The pattern on the buttons was a bugle horn, with a '60' and 'R.B.' respectively.

In 1834 the large chaco plate and the cap lines were discontinued. Because of the trouble with fading, the rifle green was made a very dark shade. The Rifle Brigade were clothed all in green with the only spot of colour to relieve the sombreness being the crimson waist girdle with the cord loops. The mounted officer wore a black pelisse and had a black sheepskin shabraque and a plain black sabretache.

CHAPTER VII

QUEEN VICTORIA

1837 — 1901

HEAVY CAVALRY 1837 — 1855

THE accession of Queen Victoria did not signal any great change of cavalry dress. In fact the process during her long reign was rather one of simplification and a tendency towards utilitarianism. The glory of war was receding and the frequent outbursts of colonial trouble all brought about a laxity of clothing which would have been unthinkable in the grand wars of the preceding century.

The uniform of the Household Cavalry was now settling down into a traditional dress. True, in previous years the head-dress had undergone many changes. In 1843 an order stated that the officers' bearskin caps were to be worn on all occasions except the evening parades. But this head-dress was obsolescent and a new helmet of Germanic pattern had been approved: this was called the Albert helmet and was a pattern that was adopted a few years later by the heavy cavalry; the white-metal body was crowned by a spike or holder which held a flowing plume—white for the Life Guards and red for the Royal Horse Guards; the front had an elaborate plate, and much ornamentation and foliage was on the peak and the other parts of the central body. This helmet was a more elaborate version of the helmet as worn today. The coatee was still being worn and, in the main, it was these long coat-tails that made the difference from the modern aspect.

The Dragoon Guards and Dragoons, however, were due for several changes in their dress, especially in headgear. The old head-dress with the fur crest or the lion head finial for undress, was changed for a new pattern about 1843: the new pattern was all gilt or brass and had a long flowing crest and mane of black horsehair. The life of this helmet, somewhat reminiscent of a fancy coal-scuttle, was short. A new helmet was ordered in 1847 and introduced a while later; this had a smaller body, of the Germanic type as already adopted by the Household Cavalry and had a falling horsehair plume from a central socket; this was elaborately decorated on the peak and elsewhere, otherwise it was much as the last pattern full dress helmet used by the heavy cavalry.

In 1843 the white duck trousers which had been worn on some dismounted occasions, were abolished. At the same time the white feather of the Scots Greys fur cap was ordered to be discontinued; this order was only temporary, for two years later an official letter said that there was no objection to the resumption of the feather, provided that no charge was made against the men. The first Dress Regulations of Queen Victoria's reign were made in 1846, and this time the bearskin of the 2nd Dragoons is mentioned and described as having a white hackle feather nine inches long.

In 1847 the dress was altered by having the skirts of the coatees shortened and squared. The officers were to be dressed precisely like the men as to pattern and the coatee was 'to be entirely divested of padding and stuffing'.

In 1851 it was decided to convert the 6th Dragoon Guards into a regiment of light cavalry. They were permitted to wear the heavy cavalry helmet but were to change the rest of the dress gradually, so as not to be too great an expense to the Colonel or the general public. The first practical change was when they took on the blue jacket of light cavalry. It may be mentioned here that one of the Victorian changes was to lessen the number of red coats introduced by William IV.

Although the processes had begun for simplification, the greatest influence for change was the Crimean War. However, the full dress was being worn on active service and with only minor adjustments during the first months of this arduous campaign. But the dress was found too constricting and inadequate for serious fighting and thus a change had to be made. The undress overalls of dark blue with scarlet cloth stripes were considered useful for fighting.

LIGHT DRAGOONS 1837—1855

Light Dragoons who had been introduced in the previous century with such acclaim were in the process of losing popularity. Reduced to the number of five, they lost yet another regiment in 1840. In this year Prince Albert came to England to marry Queen Victoria, and the 11th Light Dragoons who acted as his escort were later honoured by being converted into Hussars and renamed the 11th or Prince Albert's Own Hussars.

The red clothing of the previous reign continued in being for a short time, but in 1840 the blue jackets were reintroduced. This meant that the facings were again changed, this time to scarlet for the 3rd, 4th and 14th with buff for the 13th Light Dragoons.

The first Dress Regulations to describe the new uniforms were those of 1846—an indication that the Queen was not so concerned to issue these regulations as frequently as the previous monarchs had been. The jacket was double-breasted with two rows of buttons, eight in each row, the collar, cuffs and turnbacks were of the facing colour as ordered in the 1834 regulations. The gold bullion pieces at the back of the waist were still worn and the small skirts were closely plaited. The epaulettes continued in the same fashion.

The dark blue trousers had two stripes of gold lace for the dress patterns and two stripes of scarlet for the undress. The 13th Light Dragoons differed by having their stripes of buff cloth. The 'chaco' as it was now called was described in the regulations and it was a new pattern, practically a cylinder instead of the bell-topped variety. It was of black beaver, bound around the top by gold lace and on the front had a plate of a cross pattern with the regimental devices below a crown. The large drooping plume was of white swan's feathers in the case of the officers, but in India one of the same dimensions in horsehair was used. On service and in wet weather, oilskin covers were used for the chacos. There was also a special foul-weather chaco for officers, which looked like the normal cap under a cover, but which was, in fact, a light cane affair covered with oilcloth. The horse furniture consisted of round-ended shabraques ornamented with crowns, devices and the regimental title suitably abbreviated; valise covers also with the initials of the regiment, and a black sheepskin over the saddle. Striped girdles were still worn around the waist and the pouches and belts contained stripes also.

HUSSARS 1837—1855

Hussars also underwent the same process of simplification; and they may well have done, considering the great expense to which they were put before. With the lessening costs it was possible to think of converting other units to this arm, and after the 11th Light Dragoons had escorted Prince Albert in February 1840 from Dover to London, they were privileged to become the Prince Albert's Own Hussars—in point of fact the first body to become Hussars outright. The others, although Hussars for so many years, were considered Light Dragoons and only carried Hussars in brackets after their name in the Army Lists. The new 11th Hussars now achieved a great change in dress: the chaco, scarlet Light Dragoon jacket and blue overalls gave way to a fur cap, a blue jacket, a pelisse and overalls of crimson; these crimson overalls and pantaloons had been worn by officers, but this innovation applied to all ranks.

It will be remembered that Hussar regiments had given up fur caps for chacos, but the fact that the new 11th Hussars were to have fur caps seems to have brought a reversion to the original fashion and, in 1841, fur caps were again ordered for Hussar regiments. In 1842 fur busbies were issued to the 10th Hussars instead of chacos. The 7th Hussars are shown wearing fur busbies in Canada even before they returned home in 1842. The busbies were brown fur, all had red bags on the right side and the plumes were white with short red bases. The 11th Hussars differed by having a crimson base. Cap lines of gold for officers and yellow for men encircled the body of the cap and joined under the bag before finishing in long cords and attaching to the body.

The 10th Hussars saw fit to give up their fur caps on undress occasions and in 1846 were permitted a light chaco: this they wore in India and also in the Crimean War. The 15th Hussars kept their scarlet chacos in wear until 1856, but the 8th and 11th wore their fur caps on active service as Fenton's photographs show us.

The blue cloth trousers normally had single stripes of lace down the seams; two stripes were permitted in the case of the 10th and 11th Hussars and, of course, the latter continued to wear their crimson trousers. The gold and crimson barrelled sash was still worn and the shabraques were of the pointed Hussar type, blue cloth for the 7th and 8th, scarlet for the 10th and 15th and crimson for the 11th Hussars.

LANCERS 1837—1855

Early in Queen Victoria's reign the scarlet of the Lancers' jackets was discontinued, with the exception of the 16th Lancers who continued to wear the scarlet with blue facings, a distinction which they kept up to modern times. With the change of colour of the jacket so the colour of the facings had to change in most cases. In 1840 the 9th Lancers went from blue to scarlet as did the 12th Lancers; the 16th kept their old facings as did the 17th Lancers. The double-breasted jacket still had the bullion back-pieces and the cuffs were made pointed. The 16th keeping their old pattern had a slashed flap on the sleeve and instead of the bullion piece at the back had two buttons. The cloth cover to the lance cap was the colour of the facings, and the gold bullion rosette to hold the plume had the 'VR' cypher embroidered on velvet. The gilt rayed plate in front had the Queen's Arms and the gilt chin chain was fastened at the side by a lion's head. The 9th Lancers had permission to wear a cap of regimental design, mainly plain black with gilt ornaments. The elaborate cap lines which finished on the chest with complicated flounders and tassels, were simplified about 1846 and from then onwards had small acorns as finials.

The blue trousers had double stripes down the sides, gold lace for full dress and for undress scarlet for all, except the 17th who had white as may be expected. For dismounted duties white trousers were worn in summer, but these were discontinued by the time the Crimean War had broken out, light grey trousers being taken in use by the men. In the actual Crimean campaign officers had the dark blue trousers strapped and cuffed with black leather.

The shabraques were made with rounded ends and embroidered with a crown, the Royal Cypher, crossed lances and regimental devices. Undress shabraques of black lambskin were also worn. Gauntlet gloves were worn and the prints of the period show that the bands were managing to maintain a striking dress despite the fact that the reversed facings and white tunics were forbidden. The use of drum banners helped make a fine show. The 17th Lancers took the opportunity to display the skull and cross bones on black banners.

INFANTRY 1837—1855

The dress of the Guards was beginning to assume a traditional aspect and much as the present day, but the long coat tails still gave the contemporary look. The new pattern cap of 1835 was the simple one still in use, with the distinction in plumes as before mentioned. The coatee had heavy fringed epaulettes of white for the men but in gold for the sergeants; this was the dress in which they left for active service in the Crimea, although as the months went by modifications came in: the fur cap was worn in the first battles but gave way to the undress cap; the officers' full dress was replaced by the blue frock coat and forage cap; to say nothing of local improvisation and warm fur clothing. The men also fought in the long grey overcoats and approached in some measure the appearance of the enemy.

For the infantry of the line a new pattern cap was adopted in 1839. This was still bell-topped, had a leather chin strap instead of the scales and had a fall behind; the fall was abolished a short while after at which time the chin strap was changed to a brass chain. The other ranks' cap plate was a round cast brass plate under a crown; in the centre was the regimental number. The officers' cap is described in the Horse Guards' circular of May 1842: side supporting straps were still continued in use and the height was increased by half an inch. The gilt chain was attached to the sides of the cap or chaco by means of ornaments shaped as lions' heads. A memorandum of 1843 noted that the ball tuft was to be red and white.

In 1844 a new chaco was issued to the infantry. This was known as the 'Albert' pattern, which although reminiscent of the earlier 'Peninsular' shako with a back peak, was similar to the contemporary Austrian and French head-dresses. It was barely seven inches high, but having a top six-and-a-half inches wide appeared taller than the previous pattern. For the officers the metal chin chain had rose pattern side-fastenings. The men had plain leather chin-straps. This was the head-dress worn in the Crimean war. The large worsted ball tuft was two-thirds white and one-third red at the base.

The imitation pocket flap on the tails of the officers' coats was removed in 1848 and minor alterations were made in various proportions. In 1845 the sergeants' sashes which had for many years past had coloured stripes, were now made in plain crimson, which fashion still remains to the present day. In 1846 the white trousers worn in summer were deemed by the Medical Department to have occasioned colds and rheumatism; grey woollen ones were recommended. The white ones were discontinued at home, but saw active service abroad and in foreign war stations. The new summer trousers were made of a lavender-coloured mixture but the colour faded, and in 1850 this shade was discontinued for a pure indigo blue.

Men of the grenadier companies still wore the bearskin cap at home stations, but these were given up in 1842 for the chaco with a white ball tuft. The 5th Fusiliers were permitted a special ball tuft which was half red and half white. On the new pattern 'Albert' chaco of 1844 the Fusiliers wore a large grenade-shaped badge instead of the star-plate. The ball-tuft on the new head-dress continued to be white for grenadier companies and fusiliers.

The 1846 Dress Regulations tell us that the coats of this branch were as that of officers of infantry of the Line, but with grenade skirt ornaments. Field officers wore epaulettes in Fusilier regiments but the wings of the other officers were as the grenadier officers of the Line. The officers of the 23rd or Royal Welch Fusiliers were permitted to wear the flash, that bunch of black ribbons at the back of the collar.

The cap of light infantry officers was as other infantry officers but with special plate and green ball. The coatee was to be as other officers of infantry but with the ornaments on the skirts in the shape of bugle-horns. Field officers of light infantry regiments also wore epaulettes and the others wings with three rows of chains. The 51st and 85th Regiments had special permission to wear embroidered wings. The ordinary officer's sash was not worn, but a crimson net sash around the waist with cords and tassels. The light infantry forage cap was made of light green with an embroidered bugle in front.

The officers of Highland regiments had double-breasted coats or jackets with ten buttons in each row. Epaulettes or wings were worn with the distinction of a thistle on the strap. The remainder of the dress was much as that of the previous reign for the kilted regiments. The 74th Foot in 1845, were again called Highland and altered portions of their uniform to a Scottish style. Instead of a black chaco, a plaid cap was worn, the plaid scarf as worn by the 71st Foot was adopted and, instead of the Oxford mixture trousers, tartan trews were adopted. The 71st, 72nd and 74th Foot were to wear trews on all occasions. About the same time the pipers of the 93rd Highlanders were wearing the kilt and hose of Rob Roy tartan.

In common with other infantry the bell-topped chaco in the rifle regiments gave way to the 'Albert' pattern of 1844: the new pattern had a black cockade, a bugle-horn badge and a chin strap, but for the officers a bronze chin chain was worn fastening at the sides with rose-pattern ornaments.

The dress jacket was made single-breasted in hussar style in rifle green cloth with three rows of buttons down the front. The black russia braid loops and ornamental trimming were continued for officers. The shell-jacket and pelisse were of the same colour, laced according to regimental fashion. For the N.C.O.s of the 60th Foot, chevrons of black on red were worn. In the Rifle Brigade black gloves were worn even for the men, and black velvet was a distinction of the officers' facings. Brass-hilted straight sword-bayonets were carried by the men.

HOUSEHOLD CAVALRY 1855—1901

The Household Cavalry did not have any active service in the Crimean War but they were influenced by the changing fashions. The change to the tunic by other troops in 1856, also brought the new garment to the Life Guards and the Royal Horse Guards. In the eighteen-seventies, the helmet was simplified to its present pattern and the dress was practically as worn in modern times. There were, of course, the two bodies the 1st and the 2nd Life Guards, who apart from the difference in the colour of the flask-cords, had minor differences in the buttons and helmet. A more obvious distinction was in the undress trousers: the 1st had two stripes of scarlet with a narrow scarlet welt in the centre, whereas the 2nd had but a single stripe with a blue cord down the centre. The officers' sword-knot strap was white for the 1st and crimson and gold for the 2nd.

HEAVY CAVALRY 1855—1901

During the Crimean War the inadequacies of the current uniform were made apparent to the powers at home, although they had long been known by the actual wearers. One of the first places to be protected was the body, for it was now realized that there was insufficient protection for the middle and loins of the soldier. Thus the old coatee with its cutaway front and fancy tails at the rear was discontinued and the tunic with its wide skirts came into use. The continental forces, especially the French, had been wearing a most loose and ample garment. Simplicity was to be the keynote and the profusion of expensive lace disappeared. Field officers were distinguished by gold lace around the collar and so on. Epaulettes were discontinued and the distinguishing devices of rank were worn on the collar: a star indicated a cornet or a major, a crown was worn by a lieutenant or a lieutenant-colonel and the combined devices of a star and a crown were reserved for captains and colonels, the difference between the two grades being in the extra lace for the Field officers as mentioned before. The badges of rank were not moved back to the shoulder cords until after the Cardwell reforms.

The heavy cavalry tunic was scarlet with collar, cuffs and edging down the front the same colour as the regimental facings. These facings were to be velvet for officers of Dragoon Guards and of cloth for others. The eight buttons down the front were of the regimental pattern and in a single row. The cuffs were ornamented with knots of gold lace. Instead of the exquisite and expensive epaulettes the shoulders were now adorned with shoulder cords of gold fastened with a small regimental button at the collar end.

The 6th Dragoon Guards did not take into wear the scarlet tunic but continued to wear blue, after the Light Dragoon fashion. Although their tunic had white collar and cuffs, the front was looped with five rows of cords, and a pouch belt of light cavalry pattern was worn. The clothing was simplified in 1864 when all the yellow worsted lace on the front was removed, but it was retained for the cuff knot and shoulder cords. Apparently the change to Light Dragoons was being tacitly overlooked, for the Light Dragoon sword belt was returned to store and the Heavy Dragoon sword belt was taken into use.

The brass helmet continued in use for the seven Dragoon Guards' regiments as did the white metal pattern for the 1st or Royal Dragoons and the 6th or Inniskilling Dragoons. The 2nd or Royal North British Dragoons continued, of course, to wear their black bearskin caps with a nine-inch white hackle feather. For the other cavalry the three colours of red, black and white were chosen. Red was used by the King's Dragoon Guards, white for the 4th Dragoon Guards and the 6th Dragoons, black for the 2nd and 6th Dragoon Guards and Royal Dragoons. Black and red were used by the 3rd Dragoon Guards, red and white by the 5th Dragoon Guards and black and white by the 7th Dragoon Guards. Although certain plumes were the same for different regiments the dress was sufficiently different. The first Germanic type helmet was rather heavy with floral ornamentation, but in 1873 the decoration on the peak and elsewhere was removed, leaving the body lighter and simpler; this pattern remained in use to modern times. The 6th Dragoon Guards took advantage of the change to the new pattern to adopt a white plume.

The officers' trousers were dark blue with gold lace stripes for dress, and in undress they were later noted as strapped with black patent leather or sealskin, as also worn by the men. The leather booting around the ankle and up the inside of the leg remained a popular though bulky feature of cavalry dress until 1871, when the introduction of knee boots and breeches brought a neater appearance. In the eighteen-nineties, the single stripes on the pantaloons were ordered to be yellow, but the 6th Dragoon Guards having partially taken the Light Dragoon dress had two white stripes on the sides of their trousers.

Undress sabretaches were re-introduced for mounted duties about 1870; these were made of plain black patent leather with a regimental device in the centre. The shabraques were made with a pointed end, edged with lace and with an embroidered crown and regimental devices. The exception was the 6th Dragoon Guards, who carried rounded ends to their shabraques following the Light Dragoon pattern, but with the devices of the Crown, cross carbines—because of their other name 'The Carabiniers'—and '6 D.G.'. The foreparts carried the Royal Cypher also crowned.

LIGHT DRAGOONS 1855—1861

The Crimean War showed up the defect of the clothing and among the imagined improvements which followed this terrible campaign was the adoption of a new chaco for the Light Dragoons; this pattern was 'under consideration' in 1855 Dress Regulations and the details of the 1857 issue show how like a French *képi* it was. The narrow top tilted forward and the body carried a crowned cross pattern plate somewhat similar to the last pattern. The plumes, however, were now different for the various regiments—black and white for the 3rd, scarlet for the 4th, white for the 13th and red and white for the 14th Light Dragoons, in all cases being of hair.

By kind permission of the R.A.C. Journal

PLATE 82. 2nd Dragoon Guards, *circa* 1844.

PLATE 83. 23rd or Royal Welsh Fusiliers, 1855. Print by H. Martens and J. Harris.

PLATE 84. 10th Prince of Wales's Own Royal Hussars, 1891. Original watercolour by R. Simkin.

PLATE 85. No. 1 Dress
King's Own Scottish
Borderers.

(*Top left*) Serjeant
(*Top right*) Piper
(*Bottom left*) Other Rank
(*Bottom right*) Officer

PLATE 86. Officers, 6th Dragoon Guards, 1888. Plate by R. Simkin.

PLATE 87. The 7th (the Princess Royal's) Dragoon Guards, 1867. Original watercolour by Orlando Norie.

PLATE 88. (*From left to right*) 6th Dragoons, 6th Dragoon Guards, 2nd Dragoons, 11th Hussars, 17th Lancers and 7th Hussars, 1869. Print by G. H. Thomas.

PLATE 89. (*Left*) 2nd Dragoons, 1855. (*Right*) Officer, 3rd Light Dragoons. Prints by Gambert.

The body was now covered by a tunic, although still called a jacket in the Dress Regulations. This was—in the case of the Light Dragoons—dark blue with collar and cuffs of regimental facings, that is to say either scarlet or buff; the front was ornamented with five rows of cord loopings after the fashion of Hussars. The trousers were dark blue and later officially strapped with black patent leather. The stripes were yellow except in the case of the 13th Light Dragoons who still retained the buff stripes.

In 1861 the four remaining regiments of Light Dragoons were converted into Hussars, although in some cases the new hussar clothing was not taken into wear until the next year.

HUSSARS 1855—1901

Although the Crimean War took place in hard weather and under difficult conditions, little adaptation from the normal full dress took place at the beginning. True, the full dress shabraques and sabretaches were left behind and busby plumes were not worn, but the gold laced jackets of officers were still worn in charges, as were the crimson overalls of the 11th Hussars. Pelisses, so often thought of as gaudy appendages, were items of necessity, for these were the 'overcoats' of Hussars and had to be worn in the winter. Unlucky were the men of the 8th Hussars, for the transport carrying their pelisses was sunk in harbour and thus lost for the coming winter.

Photographs show officers wearing laced-round caps and long dark blue frock coats which indicate that either the full dress clothing was wearing out or that economy was beginning to prevail. Undress trousers were frequently worn, frequently tucked into locally purchased boots. Later in the war the habit popular with the French of having trousers with leather cuffs was adopted. By the end of the war the Hussars were in the same state of dilapidation as the rest of the army and wore all kinds of unauthorized clothing like fur coats and fleece-lined garments. Full dress headgear gave place to undress caps and even faces changed, for in deference to the cold weather beards became the order of the day.

The end of the Crimean War gave an opportunity for attention to be given to sartorial details and one aspect, that of plumes, was seriously tackled: the majority had been white with a scarlet base. The 1857 Dress Regulations note different types for each Hussar regiment—the 7th had all white, the 8th the old white and scarlet, the 10th white with a black base, the 11th their white and crimson and the 15th all scarlet.

In 1858 the idea of limiting the regiments of Line Cavalry was altered and a new 18th Hussars was raised at Leeds. It was permitted to take the honours of the old 18th Hussars but the colour scheme was changed. The blue uniform had no facings as in keeping with the current custom, but the busby instead of having the scarlet bag had one of Lincoln green which colour was also used for the busby plume. Scarlet was the colour for the sabretache, pouch and belts.

An aftermath of the Indian Mutiny was the absorption of the Honourable East India Cavalry into the British Army. Thus in 1861 there appeared the 19th, 20th and 21st Regiments of Light Dragoons, soon to be turned into Hussars. The Bengal European Light Cavalry formed the new 19th regiment which took the distinctions of the old 19th Lancers. The 2nd Bengal European Light Cavalry became first the 20th Light Dragoons and then in 1862 the 20th Hussars. The Officers of the disbanded Bengal, Bombay and Madras Native Cavalry produced the nucleus which made the 21st Hussars.

The 19th Hussars having had a precedent set, did not have red busby bags as had been the usual fashion but took white bags and plumes. The 20th Hussars took crimson busby bags and plumes, while the 21st Hussars chose french grey for their busby bags thus keeping in use a colour popular in the old Indian Army, but they adopted white plumes.

The ranks of the Hussars, being further swollen by the conversion of the remaining Light Dragoon regiments, brought the necessity of making differences between so many regiments. The facings of the 3rd, 4th, 13th and 14th Light Dragoons had been respectively scarlet, scarlet, buff and scarlet. Normally on conversion to Hussars these distinctions would have been lost, but the 3rd and 13th were permitted to retain collars of the colour of their old facings. The new fashion of taking coloured busby bags of other than the traditional red was continued: the 3rd took Garter blue, the 4th yellow, the 13th buff (white) and the 14th yellow. The new plumes were all white but to make a difference between the 4th and the 14th who had yellow bags, the 4th had plumes of scarlet, thus continuing their old facing colour.

The 19th Hussars were permitted in 1874 to have the old 19th Light Dragoon badges and devices such as the Elephant, Assaye and Niagara. The 18th Hussars in 1878 took into use a blue busby bag and a scarlet and white plume, instead of the Lincoln green items, thus drawing closer to the old head-dress of the Waterloo period. The 20th Hussars in 1894 changed their plume from one of crimson to one of yellow. In 1897 the 21st Hussars were converted into Lancers.

Officers carried full dress sabretaches up to the end of the reign and the full shabraque and leopard-skins also continued in use, despite the great expense.

LANCERS 1855—1901

The clothing reforms of the Crimean campaign also applied to the Lancer regiments. The lance cap was made smaller and less elaborate; although the cloth top was to be in the colour of the facings, the 1855 regulations had made reference to a special pattern for the 9th Lancers which in the 1857 Dress Regulations is amplified; although the waist was of blue cloth the actual top was of black patent leather. The plume which had been of simple black horsehair for all Lancer regiments was in the 1857 regulations noted as different for each regiment. The 9th Lancers had black and white cocktail feathers, the 12th had scarlet, the 16th scarlet and white and the 17th all white.

The most striking difference was the replacement of the jacket by the tunic: this was still double-breasted but the broad plastron front soon gave way to turn-down lapels of the facing colour, giving the appearance of a large butterfly on the chest; these lapels could also be worn buttoned up. The piping was worn up the back seams. The 16th wore a scarlet tunic with blue facings and welts and remained the only light cavalry in red. The two rows of buttons down the front had seven in each but the lowest buttons were made flat to go under the girdle; the girdle continued to be worn in the now established colours of gold and crimson for officers, and yellow and red for the men.

The trousers of blue cloth had two gold lace stripes for the dress uniform of the officers, but for undress stripes of scarlet were worn and the trousers were strapped. The colour of the undress stripes soon changed to yellow with the exception of the 17th Lancers who continued their regimental colour of white. The white leather gauntlet gloves continued in use.

In 1897 it was decided to convert the 21st Hussars into Lancers by the Army Order 162 of 1898; they were called the 21st (Empress of India's) Lancers and had facings of french grey. The top of the lance cap was french grey as were the plastron of the tunic, the cuffs, the collar and the pipings.

Cap lines continued too long and complex in their mode of fastening; and the knee boots of 1873 came to stay.

INFANTRY 1855—1901

Early in 1855 great changes were authorized in the infantry uniform. The head-dress was once again changed, this time with a bias towards the French pattern; the body tapered towards the top and the back sloped forward quite sharply; the body was of black velvet but the narrow chin strap was of black leather. The various coloured balls used to indicate the different kinds of companies continued in use up to 1860 when the flank companies were abolished, leaving the white ball with the red base as the common issue. In time of war this head-dress was no better than the previous pattern. When the fighting troops arrived in the Crimea there was so much damage and loss of these semi-hard head-dresses that the undress caps were worn even in the hottest of actions.

Of all the parts of the soldier's dress which received the most changes in Queen Victoria's reign, the head-dress was the most popular: the 1855 pattern remained in use until 1861 when a cloth type was approved; this new type was not so tall, being only four inches in front; the cork body was covered with blue cloth stitched in sloping lines. The chin strap was of black leather and the ball tuft of white and red was continued in use but made slightly smaller.

In 1869 the last version of the shako was authorized. It was not stitched like the previous pattern and had rows of narrow braid around the top and down the sides, gold in the case of the officers and red and black braid in the case of the men. The chin strap was now made of small interlinking rings worn either hooked on the right side, and under the chin, or when worn up, fastening to a hook at the back of the shako.

In 1876 a new head-dress was being tried by a few regiments, and then finding satisfaction, it was ordered in 1878 to be a general issue: this was the cloth-covered helmet, inspired no doubt by the German nation who were then pre-eminent in military affairs on the Continent. The depot companies kept the shako until 1881 after which time it disappeared from the infantry except in the case of certain Scottish regiments. The helmets had spikes on top and for a short time carried regimental numbers in front on the star plate; but following the Cardwell reforms in 1881 the old regimental numbers disappeared and in future, regiments were known usually by names with territorial connexions.

Another sweeping change was the abolition of the coatee or tail-coat for the tunic. This garment had been in use for several years on the Continent, and familiarity with its protection in the rigours of the Crimean campaigns led to its adoption even in the middle of a major war. The old coatee afforded very little protection around the middle of a man but the tunic, especially the first pattern, had long skirts all the way round.

The first pattern was double-breasted with two rows of nine buttons down the front. The lapels were the colour of the regimental facings and could be worn closed or with the tops turned down. The collar was not so high as previously. White piping went around the collar, cuffs, slashes and shoulder-straps. The double-breasted tunic was ordered to be changed to a single-breasted type in 1856, with only nine buttons down the front.

Epaulettes which had evolved into gorgeous and expensive adornments were abolished: as they had carried the badges of rank, a place still had to be found for these devices and they were placed on the fore part of the collar. The distinctions were as mentioned before—Field officers had gold lace all around their collars, colonels had a crown and star, lieutenant-colonels a crown and a major a star. Other officers had lace only on the top and front of their collars and were distinguished by a crown and star for captains, a crown for lieutenant and a star for a sub-lieutenant. The shoulders now being left free, the opportunity was taken to move the crimson sash from the waist to a position crossing the left shoulder where it was kept in place by a narrow crimson cord.

The shoulder-belt which the officers had worn for years to suspend the sword was now discontinued for a waistbelt, and thus another elegant item of equipment disappeared —the crossbelt plate. The new waistbelt was now enamelled leather with slings and closed with a round clasp, usually having the number of the rank of the regiment or special badge.

Short leather leggings were introduced in 1859; these were to be worn in wet or muddy weather and served the purpose that gaiters had earlier in the century. In 1865 the blue trousers of infantry gave way to 'Oxford mixture tartan' which merely meant a very dark tone.

The slash flaps and buttons on the skirts of the tunic were abolished in 1868, at which time the shape of the cuff was altered to a pointed one ornamented with regimental lace and tracing braid. In 1871 the cuffs of the men's tunics were ornamented with a trefoil. In 1873 the men's tunics had shoulder-straps changed from the regimental facing colour to scarlet ones with brass numerals, instead of embroidered ones.

A single universal button with the Royal Arms was introduced in 1876 with the idea of replacing the many varying patterns of the different regiments. Unfortunately collar badges were then introduced to make regimental differences, and there is no doubt that the change was all the more expensive and troublesome.

In 1880 it was decided to alter the position of the officers' badges of rank back to the shoulders and they were placed on gold twisted cords. When the regiments were amalgamated in 1881, an attempt was made to simplify the facing colours. Royal regiments were to have the Royal blue; white was used to indicate the English and Welsh regiments, yellow for the Scottish and green for the Irish. The cuffs of the men's tunics were altered from pointed to round cuffs, nicknamed the 'jampot' cuff.

The authorized national colours may have been a good economical move but did not satisfy ancient regiments who had their own facings honoured for scores of years. Attempts were made to have them restored, and one by one the old facings were fought for and regained by certain regiments. The 'jam-pot' cuff was replaced by one with a crows-foot or knot on the tunic of sergeants, but it was not until the end of the reign that the point cuff came back for all the rank and file.

LIGHT INFANTRY 1855—1901

With the introduction of new head-dresses, the light companies continued to have their distinguishing colour of green in front, but with the abolition of these companies only the Light Infantry regiments remained to carry on the tradition. The shako of the 1861—1869 pattern for Light Infantry, differenced by having a dark green horse hair plume. In the last pattern shako the Light Infantry were distinguished by having the body of the cap made of dark green cloth with a dark green drooping plume. In 1874 the hair plume was changed for a very dark blue green ball tuft. When the helmets were introduced, those of Light Infantry were distinguished by being covered with dark green cloth.

The rest of the uniform was more or less assimilated with that of the rest of the infantry, with, of course, the regimental exceptions. A light infantry feature still retained was the whistle on the pouch belt carried by sergeants.

FUSILIERS AND GRENADIERS 1855—1901

Grenadier companies suffered the same demise as the light companies, but to the end carried the white head-dress ornament in front and the grenade as a distinguishing sign. The cap plate was made in the shape of a grenade with the badge of the regiment on the ball. The ball tuft of 1855 gave way, a couple of years later, to a drooping plume of white horsehair. The Northumberland Fusiliers were an exception and wore a red-over-white ball tuft which changed later to a plume of red and white horsehair. The white horsehair plume was continued in the 1861 pattern shako.

In 1866 the fusiliers were permitted a fur cap or busby made of sealskin, which was gradually taken into wear. In 1871 a racoon skin cap was issued to the Royal Fusiliers according to their regimental history, and by 1874 all fusiliers had them. The white plume did not continue with this new head-dress and, in fact, the only regiment permitted to wear a hackle plume, was the Northumberland Fusiliers who wore their long-permitted combination of red over white on the left side. Other regiments did eventually get hackles, but much later. By 1900 the Royal Irish Fusiliers were wearing green hackles and the Lancashire Fusiliers had primrose yellow hackles about the same time.

The changes of tunic followed the normal infantry of the line, but one feature Fusilier regiments seemed to delight in more than others, was the employment of pioneers in striking dress. The long white aprons and the long beards at the front of a regimental parade made an effect quite imposing, especially in the case of the Royal Welch Fusiliers who displayed their regimental goat in the same prominent position. Officers of Fusilier regiments wore a much taller head-dress than their men, in fact one almost of Guards dimensions.

RIFLE REGIMENTS 1855—1901

The Rifle regiments took the new chaco as worn by other infantry, and in the 1859 Regulations it is noted as being black felt with bronzed metal fittings and gorgons' heads at the back for ventilators. The new tunic was rifle-green with collar and cuffs of the facings, five loops of square cord with netted caps and drops at each end and fastened in the middle with worked olivets. The old epaulettes and wings had disappeared. The garment was double-breasted at first with plain red or black collars and cuffs, shoulder-straps, slash and piping down the front but the single-breasted pattern was soon adopted. The great-coat was of grey cloth instead of green.

In 1861 a smaller and new version of the chaco was introduced—this time being of cloth stitched instead of the previous beaver or silk types. In 1873 the chaco was out of fashion with rifle regiments and they adopted busbies; for the officers these were of black lambskin and for the men they were of sealskin, the plumes being made short with black over red. Gaiters also came in about this time.

By 1878 a new head-dress was on the way in—the helmet made of black with bronze fittings. The reforms of 1881 saw the removal of numbers from the clothing and the use of badges and titles. Two of the newly organized regiments were the Cameronian or Scottish Rifles and the Royal Irish Rifles, later known as the Royal Ulster Rifles. The two regiments had dark green facings as befitting rifle regiments, to their green uniforms. The horse furniture of the King's Royal Rifle Corps included a black sheepskin with a red scalloped edge, and a black and red throat-plume. The cuff of the men's tunic had a simple loop of red braid.

In 1890 the busby was restored and officers of the King's Royal Rifle Corps had a black egret plume over scarlet vulture feathers which was changed later to a scarlet plume with a black base. The men, however, continued to wear a black plume over red. The green dye as used in the tunic had not been very effective and was liable to fade and change colour; and thus a tendency arose to adopt a colour which was almost black. In fact, the sealed pattern of 1896 showing cloth of rifle green No. 2 was pure black, but by 1900 the new green dye was more effective and the colour became more definite and pleasing.

HIGHLANDERS 1855—1901

The introduction of the tunic brought a change to the Scottish dress also, but instead of the simple all-round lower line of the skirts, the new Scottish doublet took four separate flaps, two in front and two at the back. The first pattern 'jacket' (as it was still called) was double-breasted with collar, cuffs and lapels of the facing colour: the lapels could be either fastened over or turned back from the fifth buttonhole. The collar was made with a rounded front and the cuffs had a slashed flap with three buttons and loops on each. The double Inverness flaps or skirts also had three buttons and loops on each, the loops in the case of the officers being of gold braid. The double-breasted version soon gave place to a single-breasted one with eight buttons down the front. Later in the reign the gauntlet cuff was adopted.

In 1861 the 42nd, 92nd and 93rd Highland regiments assumed the additional titles of Black Watch, Gordon Highlanders and Sutherland Highlanders respectively. In 1862 the 75th Foot which had once been Highlanders were called 'Stirlingshire' but this did not regain them their Scottish dress, although the next year they were permitted to wear a Kilmarnock forage cap with a diced border. About this time the 91st Foot was permitted to become the Argyllshire Highlanders and took on a Scottish dress, but with the fashionable limitation to trews of Campbell tartan instead of the kilt. The usual Highland jacket or doublet was adopted. The chaco instead of being plain black was made with a blue cloth cover and a diced border. Officers were to wear 'plaids and claymores'. The normal white waistcoat issued to Highland regiments was not to be worn by the 91st Foot.

When a detachment of the 93rd Foot acted as a guard of honour to Queen Victoria at Ballater in 1870, the Queen noted that the men's knees were much scratched; this was due to the wind and rain which acted on the hard tartan of the kilts which cut and damaged the men's legs. As a charitable thought Her Majesty was pleased to direct that in future soft, instead of hard, tartan should be supplied to the Highland regiments.

In 1871 the 91st Foot provided the guard of honour at the marriage of Princess Louise to the Marquess of Lorne. In honour of this occasion the regiment became 'Princess Louise Argyllshire Highlanders' and were permitted to take the crest and motto of the Argyll family as their badge, thus bringing the famous boar's head into use. A suggestion that the kilt be restored was vetoed.

The 79th Regiment was, in 1873, directed to be called the 'Queen's Own Cameron Highlanders' and, being made Royal, the facings were changed from green to the Royal blue.

The 109 different regiments that comprised the infantry were deemed an unwieldy organization and the idea of 'linked' battalions was put forward. This scheme actually took place in 1881 but before that time certain regiments were temporarily linked—in a fashion that seems unusual to modern thought. The 26th and 74th were linked as the Cameronian Highlanders, the 42nd and the 79th as the Queen's Own Royal Highlanders, the 71st and 78th as the Highland Light Infantry, the 72nd and 91st as the Argyllshire Highlanders, the 73rd and 90th as the Royal Lanarkshire Light Infantry and the 92nd and 93rd as the Gordon and Sutherland Highlanders. But these combinations were changed and the Highlander regiments were the 42nd and 73rd as the Black Watch (Royal Highlanders), the 71st and 74th as the Highland Light Infantry, the 72nd and 78th as the Seaforth Highlanders, the 75th and 92nd as the Gordon Highlanders, the 79th on their own as the Queen's Own Cameron Highlanders and the 91st and 93rd as the Argyll and Sutherland Highlanders.

In 1881 the reforms in the infantry did at least bring the kilt back to several regiments. The 72nd took the kilt instead of trews. The 73rd and 74th at least had the tartan, the latter taking the same sett as the 71st. The 75th who were now linked with the Gordon Highlanders again received the kilt. The 79th have been mentioned as the only regiment with one battalion, but in 1897 they were at last given a second battalion.

The new reforms also applied to uniform. All the Highland regiments were to have facings of yellow as being the field of the Scottish Royal Arms. The many patterns of regimental lace were to be reduced to one with thistle pattern in gold. Royal regiments, of course, were still permitted blue facings.

The changes as now brought about saw the Highland dress at a stage which remained until the advent of khaki or service dress. The tall feathered bonnet with hanging tails of black ostrich feathers had diced borders of red, white and blue for Royal regiments, red, white and green for others and for the Argyll and Sutherland Highlanders, their distinctive red and white squares. The hackles were white in all cases with the exception of the Black Watch who had red.

The doublets were scarlet with facings of blue for the Black Watch and the Cameron Highlanders, yellow for the Gordons and the Argyll and Sutherland Highlanders. Buff was eventually restored to the Highland Light Infantry and the Seaforth Highlanders. The officers' shoulder-belts still retained the rectangular cross belt plate of ancient days, still with regimental devices; and the Scottish broad sword in the case of officers, hung from white leather slings. The waist or dirk belt of officers was of gold lace, holding an elaborate dirk of regimental fashion in black bogwood with cairngorms and complicated scabbard carefully chased and decorated.

The kilts were made with regimental differences of pleating and fastening. The actual tartans are described as Black Watch for that regiment, MacKenzie for the Highland Light Infantry and the Seaforths, Gordon for the regiment of that name, Cameron of Erracht for the Cameron Highlanders, and Sutherland for the Argyll and Sutherland Highlanders.

The officers' full dress sporrans or 'hairy purses' were made with beautifully cast and engraved gilt tops and with golden tassels. The officers' sporrans for ordinary occasions were not so expensive but just as complex. The Argyll and Sutherland Highlanders had a badger's head instead of the metal top, with six short white tassels on a dark ground. The other ranks' sporrans were somewhat similar, but with a brass rim instead of the badger head at the top.

Pipers of course had their distinctive dress—green doublets with wings cut in regimental fashions but without regimental facings. The tartans were Dress Stewart for the Black Watch but others had the tartan of the regiment at this period. The head-dress of the pipers was the glengarry—a simple little head-covering with black ribbons behind; no dicing was worn but feather tufts made them outstanding. The hose of pipers was, and is, of sombre hue like the black and red of the Rob Roy pattern. The garter ends are often made into elaborate knots of regimental designing.

LOWLAND REGIMENTS

The Cardwell reforms of 1881 did much to make the Lowland regiments as distinctive as the Highland. Previously Highlanders and Scottish units were loosely defined, but now the Lowland were given Scottish trimmings, whereas previously they had often been considered no different than any other Line regiment. The Lowland regiments were not given the kilt but the next best thing: the trews. Thus the Royal Scots, the Royal Scots Fusiliers, the King's Own Scottish Borderers and the Scottish Rifles all adopted tartan trousers.

The Royal Scots had Sutherland tartan, the Royal Scots Fusiliers the government or Black Watch tartan, as did the King's Own Scottish Borderers up to 1897 when they took the Leslie, and the Scottish Rifles had the Douglas tartan. The pipers had the same tartans as their regiments with the exception of the 2nd battalion of the Royal Scots who had the Hunting Stewart after 1892, and the pipers of the King's Own Scottish Borderers who had the Dress Stewart as became a Royal regiment.

Lowland regiments did not have the feathered bonnet like the Highlanders. The Royal Scots and the King's Own Scottish Borderers had the helmet as worn by the line regiments in blue or white cloth. The Royal Scots Fusiliers had the normal fusilier fur cap. The Scottish Rifles had chacos of dark green with black braid and the large regimental badge of the Douglas mullet or star.

The Scottish doublet was worn, scarlet with blue facings, for all except the Scottish Rifles, in which case it was dark green with facings of dark green. The Scottish broadsword was worn by officers, and thus the broad sword belt had the cross belt, except in the case of the Scottish Rifles, who wore rifle appointments. The officers' crimson sash was worn over the shoulder in Highland fashion instead of the normal fashion, the Scottish Rifles, of course, having the pouch belt instead.

LINE BATTALIONS

Old Numbering	*Before 1881* Facings	*After 1881* Abbreviated Territorial Title	Facings
1st Foot	Blue	Royal Scots	Blue
2nd Foot	Blue	Queen's Royal West Surrey Regt.	Blue
3rd Foot	Buff	Buffs, East Kent Regt.	White
4th Foot	Blue	King's Own Royal Lancaster Regt.	Blue
5th Foot	Bt. Green	Northumberland Fusiliers	White
6th Foot	Blue	Royal Warwickshire Regt.	Blue
7th Foot	Blue	Royal Fusiliers	Blue
8th Foot	Blue	King's Liverpool Regt.	Blue
9th Foot	Yellow	Norfolk Regt.	White
10th Foot	Yellow	Lincolnshire Regt.	White
11th Foot	Lincoln Green	Devonshire Regt.	White
12th Foot	Yellow	Suffolk Regt.	White
13th Foot	Blue	Somersetshire L.I.	Blue
14th Foot	Buff	West Yorkshire Regt.	White
15th Foot	Yellow	East Yorkshire Regt.	White
16th Foot	Yellow	Bedfordshire Regt.	White
17th Foot	White	Leicestershire Regt.	White
18th Foot	Blue	Royal Irish Regt.	Blue
19th Foot	Grass Green	Yorkshire Regt.	White
20th Foot	Yellow	Lancashire Fusiliers	White
21st Foot	Blue	Royal Scots Fusiliers	Blue
22nd Foot	Buff	Cheshire Regt.	White
23rd Foot	Blue	Royal Welch Fusiliers	Blue
24th Foot	Grass Green	South Wales Borderers	White
25th Foot	Blue	K. Own Scottish Borderers	Blue
26th Foot	Yellow	1st Bn. Scottish Rifles	Dark Green
27th Foot	Buff	1st Bn. Royal Inniskilling Fus.	Blue
28th Foot	Yellow	1st Bn. Gloucester Regt.	White
29th Foot	Yellow	1st Bn. Worcester Regt.	White
30th Foot	Yellow	1st Bn. E. Lancashire Regt.	White
31st Foot	Buff	1st Bn. E. Surrey Regt.	White
32nd Foot	White	1st Bn. D. of Cornwall L.I.	White
33rd Foot	Scarlet	1st Bn. West Riding Regt.	White
34th Foot	Yellow	1st Bn. Border Regt.	White
35th Foot	Blue	1st Bn. R. Sussex Regt.	Blue

Before 1881		After 1881	
Old Numbering	*Facings*	*Abbreviated Territorial Title*	*Facings*
36th Foot	Grass Green	2nd Bn. Worcester Regt.	White
37th Foot	Yellow	1st Bn. Hampshire Regt.	White
38th Foot	Yellow	1st Bn. S. Stafford. Regt.	White
39th Foot	Grass Green	1st Bn. Dorset Regt.	White
40th Foot	Buff	1st Bn. S. Lancashire Regt.	White
41st Foot	White	1st Bn. Welsh Regt.	White
42nd Foot	Blue	1st Bn. Royal Highlanders	Blue
43rd Foot	White	1st Bn. Oxford L.I.	White
44th Foot	Yellow	1st Bn. Essex Regt.	White
45th Foot	Lincoln Green	1st Bn. Derby Regt.	White
46th Foot	Yellow	2nd Bn. D. of Cornwall L.I.	White
47th Foot	White	1st Bn. N. Lancashire Regt.	White
48th Foot	Buff	1st Bn. Northampton Regt.	White
49th Foot	Lincoln Green	1st Bn. Royal Berkshire Regt.	White
50th Foot	Blue	1st Bn. R. W. Kent Regt.	White
51st Foot	Blue	1st Bn. Yorkshire L.I.	White
52nd Foot	Buff	2nd Bn. Oxford L.I.	White
53rd Foot	Scarlet	1st Bn. Shropshire L.I.	Blue
54th Foot	Grass Green	2nd Bn. Dorset Regt.	White
55th Foot	Lincoln Green	2nd Bn. Border Regt.	White
56th Foot	Purple	2nd Bn. Essex Regt.	White
57th Foot	Yellow	1st Bn. Middlesex Regt.	White
58th Foot	Black	2nd Bn. Northamptonshire Regt.	White
59th Foot	White	2nd Bn. E. Lancashire Regt.	White
60th Foot	Scarlet	K.R. Rifle Corps	Scarlet
61st Foot	Buff	2nd Bn. Gloucestershire Regt.	White
62nd Foot	Buff	1st Bn. Wiltshire Regt.	White
63rd Foot	Lincoln Green	1st Bn. Manchester Regt.	White
64th Foot	Black	1st Bn. N. Stafford. Regt.	White
65th Foot	White	1st Bn. York. & Lancs. Regt.	White
66th Foot	Grass Green	2nd Bn. Royal Berkshire R.	White
67th Foot	Yellow	2nd Bn. Hampshire Regt.	White
68th Foot	Dark Green	1st Bn. Durham L.I.	White
69th Foot	Lincoln Green	2nd Bn. Welsh Regt.	White
70th Foot	Black	2nd Bn. E. Surrey Regt.	White
71st Foot	Buff	1st Bn. Highland L.I.	Yellow
72nd Foot	Yellow	1st Bn. Seaforth Highlanders	Yellow
73rd Foot	Dark Green	2nd Bn. Royal Highlanders	Blue
74th Foot	White	2nd Bn. Highland L.I.	Yellow
75th Foot	Yellow	1st Bn. Gordon Highlanders	Yellow
76th Foot	Scarlet	2nd Bn. W. Riding Regt.	White
77th Foot	Yellow	2nd Bn. Middlesex Regt.	White
78th Foot	Buff	2nd Bn. Seaforth Highlanders	Yellow
79th Foot	Blue	The Cameron Highlanders	Blue
80th Foot	Yellow	2nd Bn. S. Stafford. Regt.	White
81st Foot	Buff	2nd Bn. N. Lancashire Regt.	White
82nd Foot	Yellow	2nd Bn. S. Lancashire Regt.	White

Old Numbering	Facings (Before 1881)	Abbreviated Territorial Title (After 1881)	Facings
83rd Foot	Yellow	1st Bn. Royal Irish Rifles	Dark Green
84th Foot	Yellow	2nd Bn. Yk. & Lanc. Regt.	White
85th Foot	Blue	2nd Bn. Shropshire L.I.	Blue
86th Foot	Blue	2nd Bn. Royal Irish Rifles	Dark Green
87th Foot	Blue	1st Bn. Royal Irish Fusiliers	Blue
88th Foot	Yellow	1st Bn. Connaught Rangers	Green
89th Foot	Black	2nd Bn. Royal Irish Fusiliers	Blue
90th Foot	Buff	2nd Bn. Scottish Rifles	Dark Green
91st Foot	Yellow	1st Bn. Argyll & Suth. Highrs.	Yellow
92nd Foot	Yellow	2nd Bn. Gordon Highlanders	Yellow
93rd Foot	Yellow	2nd Bn. Argyll & Suth. Highrs.	Yellow
94th Foot	Lincoln Green	2nd Bn. Connaught Rangers	Green
95th Foot	Yellow	2nd Bn. Derbyshire Regt.	White
96th Foot	Yellow	2nd Bn. Manchester Regt.	White
97th Foot	Sky Blue	2nd Bn. R.W. Kent Regt.	White
98th Foot	White	2nd Bn. N. Staff. Regt.	White
99th Foot	Yellow	2nd Bn. Wiltshire Regt.	White
100th Foot	Blue	1st Bn. Leinster Regt.	Blue
101st Foot	Blue	1st Bn. R. Munster Fusiliers	Blue
102nd Foot	Blue	1st Bn. R. Dublin Fusiliers	Blue
103rd Foot	Blue	2nd Bn. R. Dublin Fusiliers	Blue
104th Foot	Dark Blue	2nd Bn. R. Muns. Fusiliers	Blue
105th Foot	Buff	2nd Bn. Yorkshire L.I.	White
106th Foot	White	2nd Bn. Durham L.I.	White
107th Foot	White	2nd Bn. R. Sussex Regt.	Blue
108th Foot	Pale Yellow	2nd Bn. R. Innis. Fusiliers	Blue
109th Foot	White	2nd Bn. Leinster Regt.	Blue
Rifle Brigade	Black	Rifle Brigade	Black

CHAPTER VIII

FROM 1901 TO MODERN TIMES

THE TWILIGHT OF THE FULL DRESS

THE growth of khaki and service dress was taking its toll of the full dress. The actual development of service dress is dealt with later but its slow and inexorable advance gradually pushed the glorious full dress further into the background, away from the battlefield, from overseas stations, from off-duty periods, from parades; reducing its use to officers and bands; and even now the struggle goes on to retain it in the bands on informal occasions. Overseas the struggle has been more successful, but at home one feels that economy and lost causes are the only outlook.

However, to the history of the uniform. The South African war brought the service dress into strongest prominence, but the Household Cavalry managed to keep it at bay for a long period. The manoeuvres of 1913 saw the Life Guards in khaki and with cap badges approved, something not necessary before for them. The outbreak of the First World War pushed the traditional dress of the Household Cavalry into store for a time and the re-issue of full dress was delayed until 1920. Then two years later in the general reduction of the Army the 1st and 2nd Life Guards were amalgamated into one unit— The Life Guards. Articles from the dress of both units were selected. At first A and B Squadrons had the crimson flask-cord and C and D Squadrons had the blue cord but, when in 1927 the squadrons were reduced to three, red was chosen as the colour to be worn by all ranks. Minor changes occurred, due to the drastic salvage made in the last war, but at least representative squadrons of both the Life Guards and the Royal Horse Guards can appear at public functions, though how it may be possible to replace worn-out equipment presents an ever-growing problem.

As to the other heavy cavalry, the main change in the uniform from Victorian to Edwardian times was the change of the crown from the type with the depressed arches to the Imperial, or Tudor, version with the fully rounded top. The use of service dress for manoeuvres was deemed so successful that its use was extended. The Yeomanry lost their full dress for khaki with coloured trimmings and this might have spread to the other cavalry, but the need of full dress for ceremonial and state occasions brought a respite up to the outbreak of the First World War. Unfortunately, when the war was finished full dress was not generally restored; the Household Cavalry eventually received it, but otherwise only officers used it for levees and bands took it into wear, presumably permitted for recruiting reasons and for appearing at public engagements.

But the dress had to be regulated for the officers and although amalgamations took place in 1922 there were no printed dress regulations until 1934. The provisional regulations of 1928 were very uninspiring. Thus the regulations of 1911 were sufficient to

150

cover the period up to 1922. The King's Dragoon Guards, the Bays, the Royal Dragoons and the Royal Scots Greys suffered no alteration, but the remaining heavy cavalry were combined in name and dress. The 3rd and 6th Dragoon Guards became the 3rd Carabiniers, the 4th and 7th Dragoon Guards became the 4/7th Dragoon Guards and the 5th Dragoon Guards and the 6th Dragoons became first the 5/6th Dragoons and then the 5th Irish Dragoon Guards.

The helmets were now gilt for all except the Royal Dragoons and 5th Irish Dragoon Guards, who had silver with gilt fittings. The new plumes for the combined regiments were black and red for the 3rd Carabiniers, white for the 4/7th and red and white for the 5th Irish Dragoon Guards. The tunics were now all scarlet including the Carabiniers', who lost their blue tunics and the new regiment had yellow velvet facings. The 4/7th had Royal blue facings. The 5th Irish Dragoon Guards had primrose cloth facings but on being made Royal in 1937 took velvet facings of Royal blue.

Overalls and pantaloons were of blue cloth for all, except the 5th Irish Dragoon Guards who officially took into wear dark green netherwear. Down the side seams were single yellow cloth stripes, exceptions being the Bays who had white, the 3rd Carabiniers who had two white stripes and the 5th Irish Dragoon Guards who had their primrose cloth stripes. Gold lace shoulder-belts were worn with gilt ornaments. In the case of the 5th Irish Dragoon Guards the ornaments were of silver, and the 3rd Carabiniers continued to wear the silver chains and pickers of the Light Dragoon period.

The regiments of Hussars managed to retain their entity until the reductions of 1922, then amalgamations and reductions disturbed an establishment centuries old. The 3rd, 4th, 7th, 8th, 10th and 11th Hussars remained untouched but the 13th was combined with the 18th, the 14th with the 20th, and the 15th with the 19th Hussars. The 18th, 19th and 20th had been raised in 1860–1, so they were the ones due to go if any were to suffer.

The amalgamated regiments combined distinctions of each regiments. The busby bags of the 13/18th, the 14/20th and 15/19th were made respectively buff, yellow and scarlet while the plumes of the first two were white and the last, scarlet. The buff of the 13/18th was practically white and was also worn as a facing colour for the collar of the tunics and on the stripes of the overalls and pantaloons. The other uniforms continued as before.

The reduction of the army did not leave the Lancers untouched. The 9th and 12th Lancers remained complete but the 16th was combined with the 5th and the 17th with the 21st. The 5th and the 21st were the last Lancers to be raised and thus the first to go. The 16/5th had scarlet tunics with blue facings and welts, while the 17/21st had blue tunics with white distinctions. The tops of the 16/5th Lancers' caps were blue and those of the 17/21st white, the plumes being black and white respectively. Occasions were found when the men could appear in full dress, though this was not an issue but old clothing carefully preserved by the regiment.

When King George V died and Edward VIII came to the throne, appointments incorporating the Royal Cypher should have changed, but generally speaking the reign of the latter was so short that no substantial change was made. The introduction of a special Coronation dress for King George VI only helped the old full dress gradually to disappear. The rising cost of materials prohibited the production of new items. The gradual change in the methods of manufacturing and the gradual loss of the old craftsmen and women who specialized in the military arts now place the old full dress, head-dresses and uniforms in a bygone and lost age, practically all museum pieces.

INFANTRY

The full dress uniform of the Irish Guards (formed in 1900) and the Welsh Guards (created in 1915), is distinguished by the buttons which are in fours and fives respectively. The fur caps are distinguished by a plume of St Patrick's blue on the right for the Irish Guards, and of white and green on the left for the Welsh.

The Highland Light Infantry although originally clad in kilts did not receive their kilts again until modern times—after World War II in fact. Thus in their last full dress period they wore a combination of English and Scottish dress. The full dress head-dress was the blue cloth chaco which gradually disappeared from man to man until its last stronghold was in the drums. Colonels and lieutenant-colonels were distinguished by having two rows of gold thistle lace around the top, majors had but one and those less than Field rank had none. The Dress Regulations specified a green tuft to signify the Light Infantry connexion. The scarlet doublet was worn and trews also. The bandsmen of the Highland Light Infantry managed to retain other Scottish items like the feathered bonnet with red hackles and shoulder plaids of tartan, which the privates did not have.

Early in King Edward VII's reign the Lowland regiments took on other striking items of dress. In 1903 a new head-dress appeared when the Royal Scots took into wear the Kilmarnock bonnet: this version was a wide topped, dark blue bonnet with a diced border and a red toorie on top. The badge on the left side was placed on a black rosette above which black cock feathers were placed. The King's Own Scottish Borderers had a similar dress, the main difference being in the badges on the collar and head-dress and, of course, in the tartan. Early in the same reign the distinction of rank by means of lace on the officers' full dress doublets was discontinued. In 1913 the shoulder straps of the men were altered from the red of the doublet to the blue of the facings.

The idea of Irish regiments being distinguished by green facings after the reforms of 1881 was almost a fiasco, because so many of the Irish regiments were Royal and so wore blue facings, and the only one remaining to take the national green was the Connaught Rangers, the second battalion of which had worn Lincoln green previously. The Royal Irish Rifles had dark green facings, not because of being Irish but by virtue of being Rifles. The dress of the Irish regiments was either that of Line, Fusiliers or Rifles without an especial national distinction except in the badges and afore-mentioned exception of national colour. The breakaway of Ireland in 1922 saw the disbandment of many of these ancient and honourable regiments—the Royal Irish Regiment, the Connaught Rangers, the Royal Munster Fusiliers, the Royal Dublin Fusiliers and the Leinster Regiment, passing into history.

The regiments remaining were now given certain extras which helped create an Irish flavour: one special addition was the dress of the Irish piper. The Irish Guards are well known in London for their striking dress and of course the London Irish, a volunteer body, also maintain the tradition. The dark blue bonnet, also known as a 'caubeen', usually carries for the piper an imposing badge and feather plumes. The doublet cut in a style proclaimed as Irish, has black lace for the pipers of the Irish Guards and silver lace for the Pipe Major of the same regiment. The Irish pipe, or the 'War Pipe', differs from the Scottish by having one less tenor drone. The kilt was called 'saffron', but was actually a shade of brown, darker and not so pure as the traditionalists desired, for they seek a definite yellow. Pipe banners although not generally adopted, are used by some Irish regiments, usually in dark green and silver.

Since the end of World War II blue bonnets have been worn by other ranks of the Irish regiments, usually with feather plumes of distinguishing colours, light grey for the Royal Inniskilling Fusiliers and green for the Royal Irish Fusiliers. The Royal Ulster Rifles, originally the Royal Irish Rifles, wear green bonnets as riflemen and have white metal or silver badges.

KHAKI

As mentioned in previous chapters, the colour of a soldier's coat served originally to indicate his employer. Later it became the proud distinction to be seen wearing it in the most noble parts of the battlefield. However, the 'unfair' methods of fighting employed by the backwoodsmen in America brought about a realization that there was something to be said for concealment and that the red coat was not the ideal coat for all occasions. If a uniform was necessary, then the rangers and the locally employed colonial troops preferred their own colour, usually of green. The fact that the green faded was a sin in the eyes of the authorities, but to the fighting men it was an added attraction, for they pointed out that this was as an example of artificiality following the processes of nature. The leaves faded and changed colour as the year went by; if the coats did likewise it was all for the best. Brown coats and buff garments were also chosen in these overseas conflicts, but when the battles returned to the continent of Europe the old idea of concealment was abandoned and the long rows of serried ranks came back into their own.

The growth of the British Empire saw various trial uniforms being worn, but it was in India that the idea took firm root and germinated. In 1846 Sir Harry Lumsden, then a humble lieutenant, raised a corps of Guides at Peshawar. These he clothed in loosefitting garments specially made. According to one account the original white cotton was dyed locally with majari made from a dwarf palm; according to another, merely dyed with the river mud. Whatever the method the result produced garments of the shade that blended with the dull countryside.

The first European troops to follow this example seem to have been the 74th Foot who, when fighting during the Kaffir War in South Africa, 1851 to 1853, wore drab-coloured smocks with their tartan trews. White trousers and other utility garments were common for summer wear in the Army, and so when the Mutiny came to India it was not a revolutionary idea to stain or dye the uniforms. The 52nd and 61st Foot dyed their garments a drab colour in 1857 and soon after, the 32nd Foot dyed their white uniforms an earth colour. Most of the regiments raised in the Punjab at this time wore the new shade called 'khaki' based on a Persian or Urdu word meaning 'dust'.

The British infantry which advanced into Magdala in 1868 during the Abyssinian Campaign were ordered to appear in khaki. In the Second Afghan War, both khaki and red clothing were in use. The khaki was once again created by having the white clothing stained with tea leaves or river mud. However, by 1880 most of the Indian Army had properly-dyed khaki clothing.

The Egyptian War which began in 1881, being a British rather than an Indian affair, saw the red coats still in action. However, white helmets were made khaki by extemporary treatments like the tobacco juice of the 19th Hussars. Khaki did become common in the compaign but the cavalry retained their red coats, although taking into use khaki breeches.

All these experiments were made overseas but attention was being turned to the home troops. Many of the volunteer rifles who had been raised about 1860 wore grey and tweed uniforms. The regulars were now given an opportunity to wear a more informal dress, and in 1881 the 39th Foot were issued with a trial grey tweed uniform. Grey serge frocks and trousers were sealed as patterns for the Egyptian Campaign of 1882 and saw action beside the khaki-clad Indian troops.

The home authorities were not pleased with the fugitiveness of the khaki dye, but a patented dyestuff in 1884 produced a fast khaki cloth. The grey serge was replaced by khaki in 1886 for active service. In 1898 an experimental issue of khaki drab frocks and trousers was made to all troops serving outside the United Kingdom with the exception of Canada; this was the dress worn at the outbreak of the Boer War. This drill was found too thin and in 1900 drab, or khaki serge, replaced it. The value of a nondescript colour was now apparent to the authorities and in January 1902 an Army Order introduced a universal service dress for wear on most occasions, but excluding full dress ones.

Gaiters were now replaced by puttees of khaki. Although the white helmet was worn overseas with a khaki cover, at home a wide-brimmed felt hat was tried; this gave way to the short-lived 'Broderick' cap, a peakless round cap, at no time popular with the troops. By 1905 a peaked cap of khaki was being worn by other ranks. The cut of the tunic was very loose with a low turned-down collar; there were two patch pockets on the chest. Officers wore a service dress jacket with a collar and tie; the turned-down collar and revers provided a place for bronze regimental badges. The 'Sam Browne' belt, a product from India, was a feature of the officers' service dress.

The outbreak of the First World War brought the usual crop of service alterations and infringements of dress rules: some were logical and necessary. The cap which had a stout wire ring in the crown to make it smart was also found to make it a fine flat surface capable of reflecting the sun; the increased use of aircraft for spotting made this feature a dangerous one. The removal of this wire in the battle area produced a soft top capable of assuming a variety of weird shapes. The brown leather chin-strap, although rarely used, did come to a practical use when dispatches were carried by motor-cycle; the riders did begin by placing the strap under the chin, but eventually most internal combustion drivers assumed a contempt for the orthodox fashion and wore the strap over the top of the cap.

A feature of World War I was the widespread adoption of formation signs both on vehicles and clothing. The sleeves of the old soldiers became covered with a variety of coloured patches, chevrons and woven devices. The advent of peace brought a simplification of this heraldry and the printed title of the unit became the most common mark on the point of the shoulder.

The birth of the Tank Corps saw a new head-dress appear in the British Army—the beret. This small close-fitting black cap was similar to the Basque head-dress and eminently suitable for the confined spaces of the armoured fighting vehicle.

PLATE 90. Officer, Royal Horse Guards, 1888. Plate by R. Simkin.

PLATE 91. The Rifles, 1846. Print by M. A. Hayes.

PLATE 92. (*Left*) 68th Light Infantry, *circa* 1870.
(*Below*) Captain, 14th Hussars *circa* 1867.

From original photographs

From original photograph

PLATE 93. Officer, Coldstream Guards, *circa* 1860.

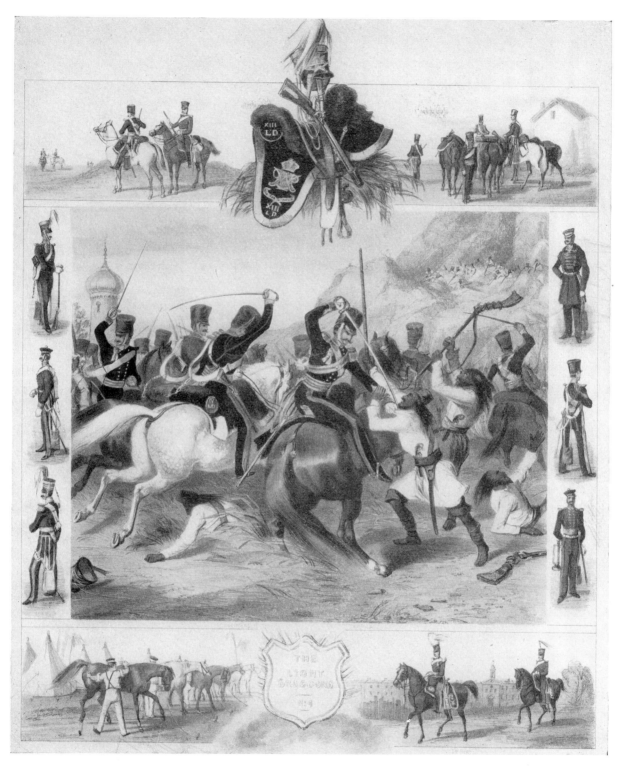

PLATE 94. The Light Dragoons, 1846. Print by M. A. Hayes and Walker.

PLATE 95. (*Above*) Band of the 17th Light Dragoons (Lancers). (*Below*) 12th (or the Prince of Wales's Own) Royal Lancers, *circa* 1840-4. Prints by M. A. Hayes and J. Lynch.

PLATE 96. Officer, 9th Lancers, 1889. Print after R. Simkin.

Drummer:
Review Order.

Private:
Undress.

Field Officer:
Review Order.

Irish Guards 1902
After print by R. Simkin.

Officers:
Undress. Guard Order.

Colour-Serjeant:
Guard Order

PLATE 97

PLATE 98. The Duke of Cambridge's Own (Middlesex Regiment), 1895. Coloured print after R. Simkin.

PLATE 99. Northumberland Fusiliers, 1891. Coloured print after R. Simkin.

PLATE 100. The Cameronians, Scottish Rifles. Coloured print after R. Simkin.

PLATE 101. The King's Royal Rifle Corps, 1895. Coloured print after R. Simkin.

PLATE 102. (*Above*) The outlying picket, Indian Mutiny, 1857. (*Below*) Repulse of a sortie, Indian Mutiny, 1857.

From contemporary prints

PLATE 103. 17th (The Duke of Cambridge's Own) Lancers, South Africa.
After original watercolour by R. Simkin.

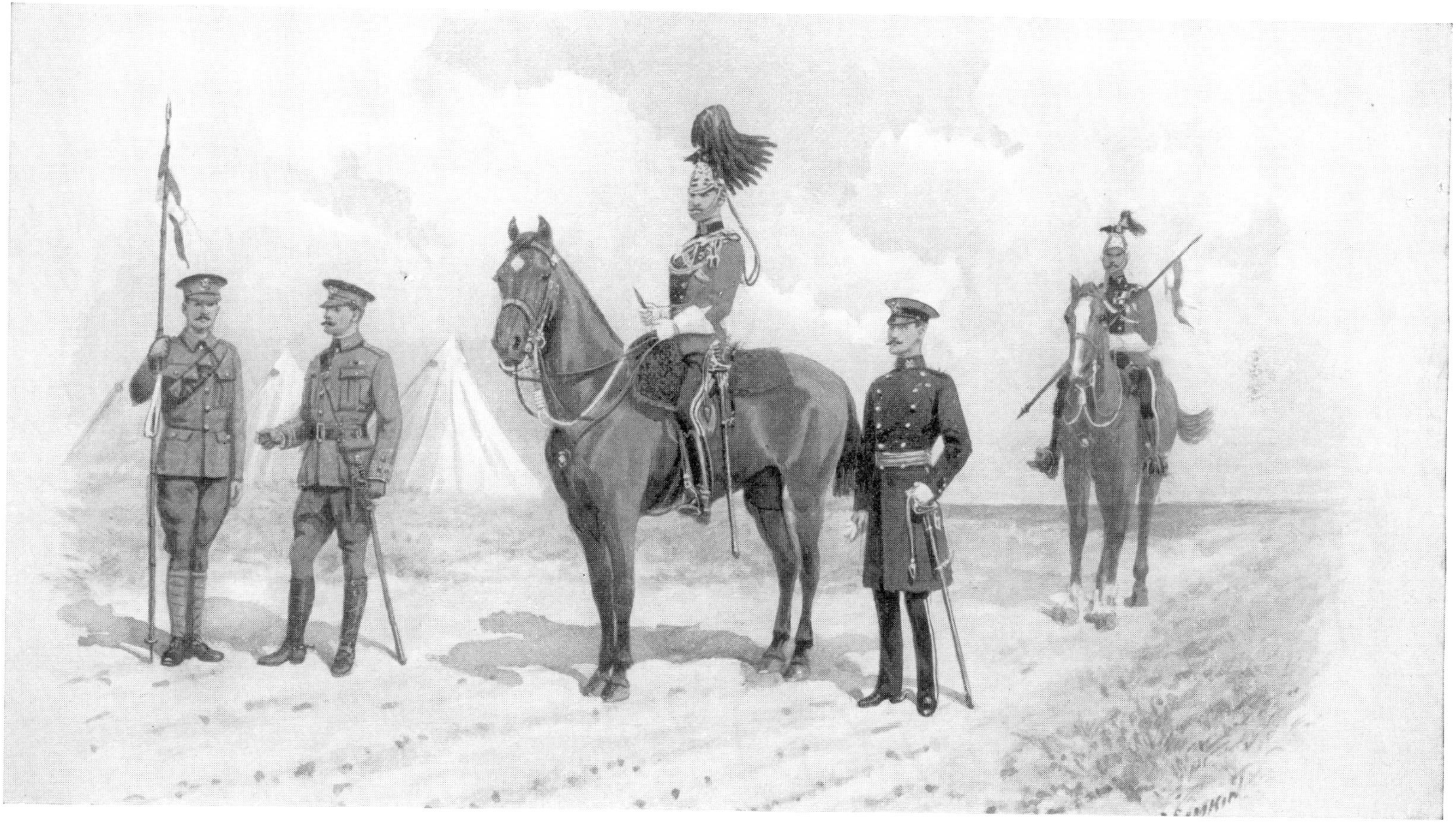

By courtesy of the Parker Gallery

PLATE 104. 16th (Queen's) Lancers, 1912. Original watercolour by R. Simkin

PLATE 105. 6th Royal Warwickshire Regiment. Infantry on the march. Original watercolour by R. Simkin.

By courtesy of the Parker Gallery

PLATE 106.

Guardsman:	Field Officer:	Subaltern:	Serjeant:
Service Dress	Service Dress	Service dress	Service dress
Fighting Order	Drill Order	Marching Order	Drill Order

The First or Grenadier Regiment of Foot Guards, 1925.

Royal Fusiliers

Photographs by courtesy of the War Office

8th Hussars

No. 1 Dress.

Royal Dragoons

PLATE 107. E. Surrey Regiment

PLATE 108. (*Left*) Battle dress worn for guard mounting. (*Centre*) Pipers of Royal Ulster Rifles, present day. (*Right*) Gloucestershire Regiment, walking-out order.

Photographs by courtesy of the War Office

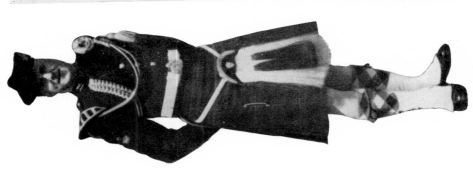

Photographs by courtesy of the War Office

PLATE 109. (*Left*) Drummer. (*Centre*) Officers. (*Right*) Piper. Gordon Highlanders in No. 1 Dress.

The in-between war period saw the khaki dress still in use but suffering from the usual process of tightening and tidying. The collar of the tunic became closer in fitting and the trousers were cut in a better fashion and folded over the puttees. The 'over-hang' of the trousers was frequently checked for width by a packet of ten cigarettes.

There was an experimental issue of clothing in 1933. The trial head-dress, a deer-stalker hat, was soft and capable of being folded and rolled without damage. The tunic had a turn-down collar capable of being opened as revers, four large pockets and buttoned cuffs. The khaki flannel shirt was made with a collar but no tie. Leg wear was of two patterns, shorts worn over puttees and long trousers with gaiters. Having been tried out at manoeuvres, the costume was placed in abeyance, although many of the portions did come back again into use at later periods.

In 1938 the 'battle-dress' consisting of 'cap.f.s.', blouse, trousers and anklets was approved by the War Office. The cap was the old field service cap as worn earlier in the century, still with the hooked-up flaps but made in khaki. The body garment was no longer a tunic—the lesson of the Crimea was forgotten—but a waist-length blouse inspired by the ski-ing suit. The cuffs buttoned at the wrist. There were two patch pockets on the chest, with an inner pocket. The front was closed by a fly front which concealed the buttons: economy which prevailed at a later date discontinued this fly and permitted the buttons to be exposed.

With the outbreak of war, formations' signs gradually came back into use but were not so complicated as previously. One sign for the higher formation was frequently sufficient. Arm of service strips, narrow lines of colour, were introduced after the war had begun and indicated the different branches like the artillery, the infantry, the armoured corps and so on. Although there were examples of regimental or battalion signs being worn, their use was by no means widespread.

The battle-dress trousers not only had side pockets but a hip pocket, one in front for the field dressing and a large awkward one on the left thigh. Flaps made to button at the bottom of the trousers helped to keep the legs closely fitted. Short puttees were worn over the lower part of the trousers but gaiters capable of being blancoed or scrubbed were the new idea.

An item known as the 'cap.g.s.', was approved in 1943. This general service cap was a khaki cloth cap somewhat on the lines of a gaberdine beret or bonnet; it was not a popu-lard head-dress with the men on account of the tight-fitting headband, lack of ventilation and unsmart shape. No protection was afforded for the eyes in the strong sun of the Middle East, nor was it proof against the rains of the United Kingdom. Certain units and all officers adopted a khaki beret of better material and more stylish cut.

In 1945 the battle-dress blouse was allowed to be worn open to show a collar and tie. The first collars were sewn on to the khaki shirts and the material was found in the tails of the actual shirt, which produced an uncomfortable result. The first ties available in the Middle East were also made from khaki material as used in shirts but later were better made. The revers of the blouse were permitted to be faced—a habit which had developed unofficially—including Rifle regiments who used coloured cloth. Attempts to smarten (unofficially) the battle-dress included sewn creases to the trousers, and pressed box pleats in the back of the blouse. These practices were frowned upon but the present day battle-dress suit is well cut and tailored, much the same as the first issue but with minor alteration like the removal of the trouser loops for walking out. The new beret generally introduced after the war was a properly shrunken and designed article.

CORONATION AND NO. I DRESS

After World War I officers were allowed to wear the full dress uniform, which meant that the 'red coat' was to be seen at levees and such special occasions. As these garments were found at the officers' own expense the Government had little reason to complain. Household troops were permitted to regain their full dress but the majority of line cavalry, line infantry and corps were without full dress.

The occasion which brought this deficiency into prominence was the Coronation of King George VI; for the troops to appear on this memorable occasion in khaki was unthinkable. Great Britain had been one of the strongholds of tradition and pageantry and so a half-way step was made. Men had been permitted to purchase and wear an all-blue walking-out patrol dress consisting of tunic, trousers and peaked cap. In November 1936 it was announced that this dress would be adopted and improved into a 'Coronation' uniform. Various trial wearings were made in April 1937 and a representative contingent went to Buckingham Palace for the King's approval — an officer and man from the Royal Scots Greys, the Royal Artillery, the West Yorkshire Regiment, the Royal Scots Fusiliers, the Seaforth Highlanders and the Rifle Brigade. The officers wore their usual blue undress uniform with certain alterations. The Scotsmen wore glengarries instead of the peaked caps and the Highlanders wore their traditional kilts. Already the 'Coronation blues' were beginning to assume their regimental differences.

The basic dress did attempt uniformity and system of distinctions. The peaked cap was made in dark blue with a black patent leather peak and chin strap. Royal regiments of infantry had a wide red band around the waist of the cap, as did the Royal Artillery. Light infantry, however, had a green cap. Most of the infantry had red welts around the crown of their blue caps. Cavalry in the main had a blue cap with bands of regimental colour and patterns; exceptions were the 3rd Hussars, 10th Hussars, 12th Lancers and 15th/19th Hussars who had all red caps. The 11th Hussars had a crimson cap and the 'Vth' Dragoon Guards (as their cap badge proclaimed them) had a dark green cap with primrose band and pipings or welts. The 16th/5th Lancers had a red cap with a blue band and all Lancers had quarter weltings to continue the tradition of the four-square lance cap.

The new jacket was made of blue serge, with a smarter cut than the normal walking-out dress. No coloured facings were worn but regimental distinctions were preserved in the collar badges. For Rifle regiments dark green jackets were the distinction.

The lower wear were trousers for dismounted men and overalls for mounted men. These latter garments were cut closer to the leg and made with straps below the instep. Two striking exceptions to the normal blue were the cherry-hued ones of the 11th Hussars and the dark green worn by the 5th Dragoon Guards. Wellington boots and spurs were worn by mounted men. An interesting point was that although the Royal Engineers did not wear spurs, the Royal Signals, an offshoot of that body did wear spurs though they mounted nothing more fiery than motor-cycles, and horses were discontinued for their work before they were created as a Corps. The infantry generally wore red pipings or welts down the side seams and the cavalry had two yellow stripes, but there were other varieties like the wide red stripes of the Royal Horse Artillery, the Royal Engineers and the Royal Corps of Signals. Cavalry regiments also had exceptions as in the case of the white stripes being worn by the Bays, Carabiniers, etc.

The Highland units managed to preserve much of their traditional dress, the glengarries, kilts, sporrans, hose and weapons being continued in wear. Even the coat was cut away in front to give a Scottish trend. Thus the main change of appearance was in the replacement of the red coats with blue ones, the reason or value of which has been constantly debated and argued about ever since.

The Lowland regiments retained their trews and also had a cutaway coat, while the Scottish Rifles had theirs in a dark green hue.

The officers wore brown leather equipment in the infantry, but the cavalry had full dress pouch belts as did the Rifle regiments. Men wore white leather waistbelts in the cavalry and web-belts in the infantry. Highland sergeants appeared alone in retaining the red sash worn over the right shoulder. This dress was provided for the troops lining the route but those mounted units taking part in the actual procession wore full dress.

When the 1939—45 War was over, many troops continued to furnish garrisons in overseas stations. Thus khaki remained in use and the demand for a ceremonial dress was small. Gradually, however, the wearing of a blue undress or patrol was adopted mainly by officers to wear at dinners or dances. A few very rich sergeants might have been able to afford these blue jackets and trousers, but generally speaking the lower ranks were neglected until 1946. A pre-war idea of an open-necked bracken-hued suit was considered and dropped, as was the re-introduction of the shako—this incidentally was a long and hard-fought battle behind the scenes.

However, in June 1946 ideas were advanced sufficiently for three officers and a hundred men dressed in the new walking-out dress to proceed to Buckingham Palace and have their dress approved by the King. The tunic was to be blue for most regiments but Highland regiments were to have theirs made of 'piper green', and rifle regiments were to have their distinctive colour. The tunic had a high 'patrol' collar, closed for both officers and men; incidentally, many of the 'old sweats' wrote to the press at the time expressing a preference for an open neck, a collar and tie. Collar badges were worn and a startling innovation was the white collar strip which went inside the main collar; this item was detachable and fixed as a lining on five buttons; although making a smart effect its use was not extended to the rank and file. The tunic had two breast pockets with box pleats and buttons, side pockets without buttons and a cloth belt with a brass buckle. At last an effort was made to restore some part of the regimental facings and the new idea was to pipe the edges of the shoulder-straps with coloured materials: actually this was an idea that the German Army had used for many years before and continued even in the time of war. Where regiments had white, yellow and buff facings there was little difficulty, but where regiments had blue facings it was obvious that there would be no contrast and so red was chosen. On the first trial outing even officers wore these straps, and on each cuff they had two small buttons at the back.

The trousers were cut on civilian lines, loose round the waist and even with braces. For the first time in this century shoes were to be general issue, and socks were made of blue lightweight wool.

This dress was experimental and had many small changes and additions in the ensuing months and years. Another fact that soon emerged was that although the new ceremonial blue serge dress had been approved by the King and the Army Council, battledress would have to be worn for the next three or four years because blue cloth was not available.

A Special Army Order in 1947 gave further details of the new uniform to be introduced, and this time it was called the No. 1 Dress for ceremonial occasions; this was substantially the walking-out dress previously approved to be worn with coloured berets. The wearing of the sword was to be held in abeyance and the opportunity was taken to state that mess dress would be unnecessary. It was also pointed out in the Special Army Order that the patrol collar had been adopted as smarter and more appropriate for formal occasions than a jacket with lapels and separate collar and tie.

Although this order allowed officers to purchase the new dress at their own expense, equivalent clothing for other ranks was not yet available and thus the officers' dress was not permitted on parades. Attention was now turned to the head-dress and in late 1948 it was stated that the blue beret had been finally adopted as the head-dress of most Army units. The blue beret was to be seen at a Hyde Park Review of the Territorial Army which took place in October 1948. Some regiments wore coloured patches behind their badges and the Scottish units wore their own version of headgear which approximated to a 'tam-o'-shanter'; these were mainly dark blue with a red toorie and regimental dicing, but the Cameronians wore one of dark green with a black toorie. The complete change from the crudely made khaki cap to the well knitted beret was a slow process, for large stocks had to be used up.

The beret, although it retained its popularity for walking-out—possibly because the soldier can still roll it up and place it under the shoulder-strap — is not the ceremonial headgear. The forage-cap, coloured, with its protective peak made a come-back and a new idea for ceremonial use was the web girdle to be worn in lieu of a waistbelt. The first occasion when these items were officially worn, seems to have been when the East Surrey Regiment formed the Guard of Honour to the French President when he visited England in May 1950.

The occasion of the Coronation of Queen Elizabeth II was the great opportunity for most members of the public to see the No. 1 Dress in use. Some 22,000 uniforms were ordered and worn. The occasion being over, the regular troops were permitted to retain these fine garments but the Territorials had to return their garments to Ordnance when their brief moment of glory was over.

The process of adding to No. 1 Dress such embellishments (the official word) as lanyards, wings for bandsmen, distinctive embroidered devices and so on, does not slow down, and it may be that in complexity the No 1 Dress will have as many variations and 'uniform' distinctions as the old full dress. As mentioned before the great difference is the loss of the red coat, a point which the traditionalists rightly say has lost us our national uniform. The 'powers-that-be' point out the great expense of the old scarlet cloth dyed in the grain with cochineal dye and by antique processes. Others assert that modern synthetic dyes are every bit as good, fadeless and infinitely cheaper. However, the red coat still remains in abeyance despite the occasional outbursts in the newspapers and questions in Parliament. The traditionalist must wait and hope for the day when the centuries-old red coat receives its reprieve from the unknown dictator of fashion.

But it is strange to think that even the members of the Guards Brigade have their non-ceremonial No. 1 Dress and walk out in blues. The Household Cavalry wear white buff leather shoulder belts with the black pouch. The Royal Horse Guards wear white lanyards. On their trousers the Life Guards wear what looks like two scarlet stripes with a central welt. The Royal Horse Guards have a two-and-a-half inch scarlet stripe.

The cavalry of the line have a great variety of forage caps—blue with a blue band for the King's Dragoon Guards, with a white band for the Bays, with a yellow band for the 3rd Dragoon Guards, Royal blue for the 4/7th Dragoon Guards and a dark green cap with a primrose yellow band for the 5th Dragoon Guards. The Royal Dragoons have a blue cap with a scarlet band, the Royal Scots Greys a vandyked white band, while the Hussars have a scarlet cap with a scarlet band for the 3rd and 15/19th Hussars, with red bands for the 4th, 7th, 8th, 10th and 14/20th Hussars, while the 13/18th Hussars have a white top. For the Lancers all have quarter-welts. The 9th Lancers have a blue cap with a scarlet band, the 12th a scarlet cap with blue welts, the 16/5th a scarlet cap with a blue band and the 17/21st have a blue with a white band. The 8th Hussars also have a special head-dress known as the 'tent side-hat' which the Duke of Edinburgh wears on occasions.

The cavalry jackets are distinguished by steel shoulder-chains. The officers of the 3rd Hussars have red collars and the 9th Lancers also have red collar-patches. The men of the 13/18th Hussars have white gorget patches as do the 17/21st Lancers. The officers, although permitted a white patent leather pouch-belt to be worn over the right shoulder, the 'wrong' shoulder, have shown a preference for the old full dress belt and pouch worn over the left shoulder.

At first 'trousers' were all that were deemed necessary but units that were previously mounted are now permitted trousers which fit more closely and look like the old cavalry overalls. Heavy cavalry had a broad yellow stripe, exceptions being the Bays with a white stripe and the 3rd Dragoon Guards with two white stripes. The 11th Hussars wear crimson trousers and the 5th Dragoon Guards their dark green version with primrose stripes.

The Royal Tank Regiment wear their traditional black beret and they do not wear shoulder chains nor piping on the shoulder straps of their plain blue jackets. The trousers have black stripes.

The officers of the Royal Horse Artillery wear gold lines around the neck and hooked on the breast, while the men have yellow lines. The Royal Artillery wear a blue cap with a scarlet band and a blue jacket with scarlet piping on the shoulder-straps as well as blue trousers with a one-and-three-quarter-inch scarlet stripe on each side. Girdles should be worn with No. 1 Dress, the pattern consisting of a yellow central stripe edged blue and and the outer edges being red. Certain Royal Artillery bandsmen are permitted a Roman type brass-hilted band sword.

The Royal Engineers have a dark blue cap with scarlet welts, jacket and trousers, like Royal Artillery but with a wider stripe on the trousers. The Royal Signals have a blue cap with jacket and trousers like the Royal Engineers.

The Foot Guards' officers do not wear the white strip collar but have jackets with the buttons arranged in regimental fashion, which practice the other ranks also carry out. The infantry have for Royal regiments a blue cap with scarlet bands, for non-Royal regiments—English and Welsh—a scarlet welt around the crown. Light Infantry have green caps as do the Rifle regiments, although in a different shade. Scottish units have the diced bonnet mentioned previously but the Royal Scots Fusiliers are permitted to wear the glengarry. Irish rifles wear the green bonnet but the other Irish regiments, being Royal, wear blue bonnets.

CAVALRY NO. I DRESS UNIFORM

Regiment	Uniform	Facing	
The Life Guards	Blue	Blue	
The Royal Horse Guards	,,	Scarlet	
1st King's Dragoon Guards	,,	Blue	
The Queen's Bays	,,	White	
The 3rd Carabiniers	,,	Yellow	
The 4/7th Royal Dragoon Guards	,,	Blue	
The 5th Royal Inniskilling D.G.	,,	,,	Dark green trousers
1st The Royal Dragoons	,,	,,	
The Royal Scots Greys	,,	,,	
3rd The King's Own Hussars	,,	Garter blue	
The 4th Queen's Own Hussars	,,	Yellow	
The 7th Queen's Own Hussars	,,	Scarlet	
The 8th King's Royal Irish Hussars	,,	,,	
The 9th Queen's Royal Lancers	,,	,,	
The 10th Royal Hussars	,,	,,	
The 11th Hussars	,,	Crimson	Crimson trousers
The 12th Royal Lancers	,,	Scarlet	
The 13/18th Royal Hussars	,,	Buff	
The 14/20th King's Hussars	,,	Yellow	
The 15/19th The King's Royal Hussars	,,	Scarlet	
The 16/5th Lancers	,,	Blue	
The 17/21st Lancers	,,	White	
The Royal Tank Regiment	,,	Black	

NO. I DRESS OF INFANTRY

Regiment	Uniform		Facing	Piping
The Royal Scots	Blue doublet		Blue	No. 8 (Hunting Stewart) Trews Tartan
The Queen's Royal Regt.	Blue uniform		Scarlet	Blue
The Buffs	,,	,,	Buff	Buff
The King's Own Royal Regt.	,,	,,	Scarlet	Blue
The Royal Northumberland Fus.	,,	,,	Gosling green	Gosling green
The Royal Warwickshire Regt.	,,	,,	Blue	Scarlet
The Royal Fusiliers	,,	,,	,,	,,
The King's Regiment	,,	,,	,,	Blue

Regiment	Uniform	Facing	Piping
The Royal Norfolk Regt.	Blue uniform	Yellow	Yellow
The Royal Lincolnshire Regt.	,, ,,	Blue	Scarlet
The Devonshire Regt.	,, ,,	Lincoln green	Lincoln green
The Suffolk Regt.	,, ,,	Yellow	Yellow
The Somerset Lt. Infantry	Dark green Jacket blue trousers	White	Blue
The West Yorkshire Regt.	Blue uniform	Buff	Buff
The East Yorkshire Regt.	,, ,,	White	White
The Beds. & Herts. Regt.	,, ,,	,,	,,
The Royal Leicestershire Regt.	,, ,,	Pearl grey	Pearl grey
The Green Howards	,, ,,	Grass green	Grass green
The Lancashire Fusiliers	,, ,,	White	White
The Royal Scots Fusiliers	Blue doublet	Blue	Trews Hunting Erskine
The Cheshire Regt.	,, uniform	Buff	Buff
The Royal Welch Fusiliers	,, ,,	Blue	Scarlet
The South Wales Borderers	,, ,,	Grass green	Grass green
The King's Own Scottish Bdrs.	,, doublet	Blue	Trews No. 7 Leslie
The Cameronians	Rifle green	Dark green	Trews No. 6 Douglas
The Royal Inniskilling Fus.	Blue uniform	Blue	Blue
The Gloucestershire Regt.	,, ,,	Primrose yellow	Primrose yellow
The Worcestershire Regt.	Blue uniform	Emerald green	Emerald green
The East Lancashire Regt.	,, ,,	White	White
The East Surrey Regt.	,, ,,	,,	,,
The Duke of Cornwall's Light Infantry	Dark green jacket, blue trousers	,,	,,
The Duke of Wellington's Regt.	Blue uniform	Scarlet	Scarlet
The Border Regt.	,, ,,	Yellow	Yellow
The Royal Sussex Regt.	,, ,,	Blue	Scarlet
The Royal Hampshire Regt.	,, ,,	Yellow	Yellow
The South Staffordshire Regt.	,, ,,	,,	,,
The Dorset Regt.	,, ,,	Grass green	Grass green
The South Lancashire Regt.	,, ,,	Buff	Buff
The Welch Regt.	,, ,,	White	White
The Black Watch	Piper green doublet	Blue	Black Watch kilt
The Oxford & Bucks. Light Infantry	Dark green jacket, blue trousers	White	White
The Essex Regt.	Blue uniform	Purple	Purple
The Sherwood Foresters	,, ,,	Lincoln green	Lincoln green
The Loyal Regt.	,, ,,	White	White
The Northamptonshire Regt.	,, ,,	Buff	Buff

Regiment	Uniform	Facing	Piping
The Royal Berkshire Regt.	Blue uniform	Blue	Scarlet
The Queen's Own Royal West Kent Regt.	,, ,,	,,	,,
The King's Own Yorkshire Light Infantry	Dark green jacket, blue trousers	,,	White
The King's Shropshire Light Infantry	Dark green jacket, blue trousers	,,	,,
The Middlesex Regt.	Blue uniform	Lemon yellow	Lemon yellow
The King's Royal Rifle Cps.	Rifle green uniform	Scarlet	Scarlet
The Wiltshire Regt.	Blue uniform	Buff	Buff
The Manchester Regt.	,, ,,	Deep green	Deep green
The North Staffordshire Regt.	,, ,,	Black	Black
The York & Lancaster Regt.	,, ,,	White	White
The Durham Light Infantry	Dark green jacket, blue trousers	Dark green	,,
The Highland Light Infantry	Piper green doublet	Buff	Mackenzie kilt 5
The Seaforth Highlanders	Piper green doublet	,,	,, ,, 2
The Gordon Highlanders	Piper green doublet	Yellow	Gordon ,, 3
The Queen's Own Cameron Highlanders	Piper green doublet	Blue	Cameron ,, 4
The Royal Ulster Rifles	Dark green jacket, black trousers	Dark green	Dark green
The Royal Irish Fusiliers	Blue uniform	Blue	Scarlet
The Argyll & Sutherland Highlanders	Piper green	Yellow	Black Watch kilt 1
The Glider Pilot Regt.	Blue uniform	Cambridge blue	Cambridge blue
The Parachute Regt.	,, ,,	Maroon	Maroon
The Rifle Brigade	Green uniform	Black	Black

Many regiments have a fuller title than that given here, but limitations of space do not permit full use.

INDEX

REGIMENTAL INDEX